WELLSPRINGS
OF THE
AMERICAN SPIRIT

RELIGION AND CIVILIZATION SERIES

RELIGION AND THE WORLD ORDER
WORLD ORDER: ITS INTELLECTUAL AND CULTURAL FOUNDATIONS
FOUNDATIONS OF DEMOCRACY
WELLSPRINGS OF THE AMERICAN SPIRIT
F. Ernest Johnson, *Editor*

GROUP RELATIONS AND GROUP ANTAGONISMS
CIVILIZATION AND GROUP RELATIONSHIPS
UNITY AND DIFFERENCE IN AMERICAN LIFE
R. M. MacIver, *Editor*

LABOR'S RELATION TO CHURCH AND COMMUNITY
Liston Pope, *Editor*

FORTHCOMING VOLUME

PROBLEMS OF THE COMMUNICATION OF IDEAS
Lyman Bryson, *Editor*

GENERAL EDITORIAL BOARD

Louis Finkelstein
F. Ernest Johnson   R. M. MacIver
George N. Shuster

RELIGION AND CIVILIZATION SERIES

WELLSPRINGS OF THE AMERICAN SPIRIT

A series of addresses

EDITED BY

F. Ernest Johnson

*Professor of Education, Teachers College
Columbia University*

Published by
INSTITUTE for RELIGIOUS and SOCIAL STUDIES

Distributed by
HARPER & BROTHERS
NEW YORK AND LONDON

COPYRIGHT, 1948
BY INSTITUTE FOR RELIGIOUS AND SOCIAL STUDIES

*All rights reserved including the right
of reproduction in whole or in part
in any form.*

PRINTED IN THE UNITED STATES OF AMERICA
BY THE VAIL-BALLOU PRESS, INC., BINGHAMTON, N. Y.

DEDICATED TO

THE MEN AND WOMEN WHO,

IN HIGH OR HUMBLE STATION,

HAVE PARTICIPATED IN

CREATING, PRESERVING AND REFINING

THE

American Spirit

The authors contributing to this volume were invited to address the Institute for Religious and Social Studies because of the special contribution each could make to knowledge of the subject. Each chapter represents solely the individual opinion of the author. Neither the Institute nor the editor assumes responsibility for the views expressed.

FOREWORD

The Institute for Religious and Social Studies was established at the Jewish Theological Seminary of America in 1938. Its purpose is to enable ministers of all faiths to study under the guidance of scholars in various fields, representing different religious groups.

The present volume is in some sense a sequel to the one next preceding in the series, *Foundations of Democracy*. There an attempt was made to clarify the meaning of democracy in the light of its remoter and more proximate sources and in relation to some of the major problems of human society. Here the writers examine, each in his own way, the various forms of expression in which the American people have undertaken in characteristic ways to make explicit the values of the democratic tradition. The addresses contain interpretation, evaluation and criticism. They are pitched in different keys and their diverse character shows how far from monolithic the American spirit is. Yet it is the editor's belief that from these varied sketches the authentic spirit of America can be distilled.

In such a series, in which the participants are invited to speak their own thoughts with entire freedom, it is to be expected that points of inconsistency will appear. This fact in itself, however, serves to illustrate the varied and spontaneous forms which expression of the American spirit has taken.

It is a matter of regret that the manuscripts of two of the lectures delivered in the series are not available for publication. One was entitled "The Spirit of American Law" and the other presented a Catholic view of the topic, "The Ideal of Religious Liberty."

THE EDITOR

July, 1947

TABLE OF CONTENTS

	Foreword		vii
I.	The Puritan Tradition	Herbert W. Schneider	1
II.	The Dissenting Tradition	John T. McNeill	15
III.	The Enlightenment Tradition	Ralph Henry Gabriel	39
IV.	The Religion of the Founding Fathers	Robert C. Hartnett, S.J.	49
V.	The Ideal of Religious Liberty— A Protestant View	O. Frederick Nolde	69
VI.	The Ideal of Religious Liberty— A Jewish View	Louis Finkelstein	87
VII.	The Spirit of the Frontier	Harold Rugg	97
VIII.	The Spirit of American Philosophy	John Herman Randall, Jr.	117
IX.	The Spirit of American Literature	Odell Shepard	135
X.	The Spirit of American Education	James Marshall	145
XI.	The Spirit of American Art	William G. Constable	155
XII.	Technology and Freedom	Lyman Bryson	167
XIII.	Woman's Battle for Status	Elinore M. Herrick	179
XIV.	The Struggle for Cultural Unity	Channing H. Tobias	189
XV.	Labor's Coming of Age	Mark Starr	203
XVI.	The Spiritual Role of America	F. Ernest Johnson	225
	Index		235

WELLSPRINGS OF THE AMERICAN SPIRIT

I

THE PURITAN TRADITION

BY

HERBERT W. SCHNEIDER, Ph.D.

*Professor of Religion and Professor of Philosophy,
Columbia University*

There is much talk and writing today on the subject of the Protestant ethic. Our modern sociologists, following halfheartedly the revelation of Marx, according to which religion is a social opiate, or of Freud, according to which religion is a private illusion, have applied this preaching specifically and especially to Protestantism. The Enlightenment had concentrated its fire on the absolutism of papacy and the superstitions of priestcraft; today the fire of the enlightened is concentrated on the profit motive among Protestants and on those individualists to whom self-reliance is sacred. There is no doubt that the ethic of Protestantism and the ethic of capitalism are historically associated. Not all capitalists are Protestants and not all Protestants are capitalists. Nevertheless, there are enough persons who are both to make it worth while investigating in what ways and to what extent they fortify each other both as social institutions and as driving powers in individual persons. The simplest way to make such an investigation is to make it wholesale and if possible *a priori*. If plausible reasons can be found why capitalism and Protestantism *must* go together, if both can be deduced logically from individualism, much inductive labor is spared. It is no accident, therefore, that philosophically trained sociologists have made the greatest contributions to the solution of this problem.

I am tempted myself to take the high road of philosophy, since I am professionally habituated to that road, and to describe the

Puritan ethic in sweeping generalities with the help of a few principles borrowed from the fruitful sciences of culture analysis and of *Wissensociologie*. But I shall attempt the less rewarding, perhaps even narrow-minded task of discriminating among Protestants, discriminating among Calvinists, and even discriminating among Puritans.

Most of the generalizations of Max Weber and his followers were based on an analysis of Calvinism as it existed in Geneva and among the Huguenots and the Scotch Presbyterians, and the early English dissenters. Within these social contexts it was not very difficult to exhibit Calvinism as a middle-class ideology. To extend this interpretation to Lutheran feudal princes, to the Anglicans, and later to the numerous pietistic sects of Protestants proved increasingly dubious "science." A revision was, therefore, constructed hurriedly: the Anabaptists, Quakers, Wesleyans, and kindred groups were now said to exhibit "the religion of the disinherited." These social and moral complexities are evident even among the Puritans, who themselves represented a relatively unified movement within Protestantism. The Quakers were the left wing of the Puritan movement—democratic, individualistic, apocalyptic, revolutionary. They were quite different from the right-wing Presbyterians—theocratic, nationalistic, rationalistic, conservative. Yet even among the Quakers significant differences soon appeared: the majority of English Quakers (it has now been proved) were not "disinherited," but fairly comfortable, lower-middle class. In Pennsylvania the Quakers soon became a wealthy commercial aristocracy, looking down upon their German peasant, Anabaptist neighbors, who were their former allies. Not even the Quakers, therefore, can be studied as a single, homogeneous group, though they all had a common theology—at least, until the radical Hicksite Quakers destroyed even the unity of their faith.

Coming now to Puritanism in America, we note that the term "Puritan" is applied loosely. It sometimes includes the Quakers, as in Professor Ralph Barton Perry's recent work, *Puritanism and Democracy;* and for this use of the term there is certainly some justification, though the New England Puritans would have been shocked at the idea and might have exterminated even more Quakers than they did, had they anticipated it. "Puritan" sometimes includes Emerson, as in Santayana's *The Last Puritan*. In his mind a Puritan is any overly conscientious person, who feels the burden of cosmic responsibility weighing on his shoulders as an individual, but who is in the habit of casting this burden theoretically onto the "omnificence" of God. The "ultimate" Puritan, therefore, would be one like his hero, Oliver, who conceives it to be his duty to repudiate the theory of duty, and who therefore makes a somber mess of everything. "Puritan" popularly means anything puritanical, and these days, which a real Puritan would certainly regard as a "degenerate and apostatizing age," almost anything that is conventional, conservative, or even sober is apt to be condemned by some so-called writer or other as a puritan prejudice. At the other extreme are the conscientious historians, like Professor Perry Miller of Harvard, who, when they write and think of Puritans are apt to mean New England Puritans, and are apt to mean by New England Puritans Massachusetts Bay Puritans, excluding the Separatists of Plymouth and other towns as not representative, and regarding Scotch Presbyterians as the worst enemy with which the Puritans had to contend.

For the purpose of our present discussion I shall take as definite a meaning of "Puritan tradition" as I can, without making the term too technical. If I restricted it to the New England Congregationalists, I would be obliged to describe it largely in theological and philosophical terms in order to distinguish it from its cultural neighbors, and I would not be able to say much about "the Puritan ethic" except in very technical language, and I would be merely repeating the admirable exposition of Professor Miller and his associates. If I followed Professor Perry's example, on the other hand, and included the Quakers and the New Light Presbyterians, I would be obliged to note considerable moral diversity within the tradition. For purposes of describing a distinctive morality, I think it will be wise to fix our attention on the English Puritans of New England, including those Separatists or Independents who made common cause in New England with the so-called "standing order" or town establishments, but excluding the Separatists who were excommunicated—the followers of Quakerism, of Anne Hutchinson, and of Roger Williams—and excluding also the Scotch-Irish Presbyterians, the Baptists, Methodists, and other newcomers in New England. The Puritan tradition obviously must go back to the seventeenth century, if not to the Mayflower. But how far forward shall it be said to go? That is a difficult question, on which I shall try to give a discriminating and judicious, though obviously not a definitive answer. Our most serious problem here will be the relation between Jonathan Edwards and Puritanism, between the ethics of revivalism and the ethics of the covenant. I shall try to explain why Edwards represents only a passing phase of Puritanism; I shall also try to distinguish the genuine Puritan ethic from the "genteel tradition."

When the Puritans first landed and for several decades thereafter, they were faced with an embarrassing liberty. They had preached theocratic doctrines in England in the spirit of protest and reform against powerful worldly interests and a hostile ecclesiastical hierarchy; they were now obliged to regard them as principles of construction, as the legal foundation for their own new cities of God. The "elect" were no longer a struggling minority, but a ruling class. In their eagerness to carry out their beliefs to the full, they made the most of their freedom. They organized themselves literally as a new Israel. They had their covenant relation with God, Who had led them into their inheritance; they regarded the Torah as literally their law (except in so far as the New Testament had abrogated the law of sacrifice.) Their moral and legal code was that of the Mosaic legislation. They tried to forget the common law of England and to enact a genuine "Bible commonwealth." The Old Testament was now studied by them in a new spirit, not as an old and antiquated covenant, but as their law book and their constitution. In short, the ethics of the first New England Puritans were the ethics of Moses; and there never was a closer approach to an Anglo-Israel than among this covenanted, chosen people of God sent into a heathen wilderness in order to build there the true kingdom of God. They were communal enterprises, literally commonwealths.

The unity and simplicity of this ethic was soon shattered. For though the Puritans were organized as a collective economy and not as individual merchant adventurers, they were obligated to the adventurers or capitalists in England. They were supposed to make collective profits and to make these profits for the benefit of the stockholders. They thus had a dual allegiance. They had come, as the founders of Sandwich, Massachusetts, frankly stated, in order to "worship God and make money." They no doubt wanted to make money for God and for His kingdom in the new world, but they were morally and legally bound to make money for the old, corrupt world. Moreover, these saints of the Lord were soon surrounded by unregenerate adventurers who were engaged in private business and who expected to be unmolested in what they regarded as their own affairs. Even so prominent a pilgrim as Captain Miles Standish never joined the congregation; he was frankly a soldier, not a saint. Such men of the world were unable to appreciate the privilege of being governed by the Law of Moses; they appealed to their rights as Englishmen. The Puritans ignored their worldly ties as much as they dared: they sent a minimum of money to England, using as much as possible of what they earned to build their own holy commonwealths. And they treated the "strangers" to their congregational societies as rudely as they dared. Often they needed additional resources and population and therefore welcomed in business those whom they refused to admit as citizens. After a generation of pioneering and of utter dependence on the homeland, the colonists were able to defy their creditors abroad. But the New England societies at the same time lost their spiritual solidarity; private enterprise and secular English law had to be recognized and after the second generation so many children of saints failed to receive grace that the members in full communion were a decided minority. The churches became theocratic oligarchies.

More significant for our present inquiry, however, was the effect of these circumstances on the personalities of the elect themselves. Each Puritan belonged passionately to two worlds—the world of complete dependence on divine grace, and the world of independent, competitive commerce. These two had nothing in common. A picturesque illustration of this dualism in the Puritan conscience comes down to us in the sermons of Samuel Willard, Vice-President of Harvard College, who in 1724 preached to his congregation in Old

South Church, Boston, a series of 250 *Expository Lectures on the Assembly's Shorter Catechism*. They began with the first question: "What is the chief end of man?" Answer:

Man's chief end is to glorify God, and enjoy Him forever. . . . It is man's duty to seek his own best good, which consists in enjoying of God. . . . Man cannot be his own felicity. He is a dependent creature. . . . This it is that hath made the whole world a company of seekers asking for Good. . . . The whole creation affords no such object, the fruition whereof can make a man happy. . . . Man is a creature made for perpetuity, and if his object be not stable, and durable, it will sooner or later leave him under horrible disappointment, and so will these things. They are broken cisterns. They are certain in nothing but uncertainty. . . . How can they make a man happy? . . . God and He only is such an object, in the enjoyment of whom, there is perfect satisfaction and blessedness. . . . Every action in a man's life that doth not serve this great end is a vain action. . . . The greatest number of the children of men live in vain.

Unless you are exceptionally unresponsive, this answer to the first question of human existence must have stirred your faith and emotions. "The world looks bulky, but it is empty, void and waste." You turn, therefore, to the glory of God for your everlasting happiness and in Him alone do you find an adequate home. But now the sermon is over and you leave the meetinghouse. You are plunged into the heart of Boston, the metropolis of New England, growing, enterprising, exciting, absorbing. It is *not* empty, void, or waste. God Himself has elected it and must find Himself at home in Boston!

Some such intellectual and moral somersault every Puritan performed every week. On Sunday he as wholeheartedly lost himself in God as on Monday he devoted himself to business. The holy commonwealth had become a busy market place, which on every seventh day paused to wear its Sunday halo. This is the basic pattern of the Puritan conscience. It was not hypocritical, or, at least need not have been so. There is no literal inconsistency in asserting from time to time your ultimate good while you usually pursue your proximate affairs. There is no difficulty in keeping both Sundays and weekdays, provided you keep them apart. To have a unified pursuit of happiness is, of course, more simple intellectually, and there is certainly an element of comedy and of tragedy in the predicament of an animal that cannot keep soul and body together, whose daily striving does not promote his ultimate destiny. But there is nothing impossible or inconsistent in separating soul and body; it can be done and, in fact, is very generally done.

The Puritan, in other words, was also a Yankee (after he gave up being a neo-Israelite). He lived in two worlds and had two separate systems of ethics. Yankee ethics was quite secular, utilitarian, prudential; there was little or no attempt made by the Puritan to bring his Yankee concerns into the orbit of his Calvinistic theology. Why should he? Each ethic was complete in itself and adequate for its own ends. It is, therefore, a superficial sociology that confuses the two, and takes it for granted that Puritan theology was primarily an attempt to justify Yankee virtues (or vices). Puritanism had its own ethic of Platonic love and eternal happiness; the Yankees had their own secular reasons for their temporal interests. Or, to use Puritan terms, the "economy of redemption" was independent of the economy of trade. The two realms seldom interfered with each other, and there was no more difficulty in being both a Puritan and a Yankee than in being both a musician and a scientist. It is important to keep the two types of ethics distinct in theory today, as they kept them distinct in practice, since there were many Yankees who were not Puritans, and some Puritans who were not Yankees.

In this last class belonged Jonathan Edwards, and he illustrates perfectly one of the occasional crises which the Puritan tradition suffered when the heavenly and the earthly interests happened to conflict. Edwards was from childhood on passionately devoted to God; both his philosophical speculation and his emotional tension were directed toward "General Being" and were interpreted theologically. His whole being was "swallowed up," as he loved to say, in the sovereign glory of God, and he seems to have had no serious concern except for "holy things." He was personally and literally dependent entirely on God. There was nothing of the Yankee in him. When he was put in charge of the congregation at Northampton, he attempted to make his people likewise a community dedicated to the care of their souls. During the great revival, of which he was a leader, he reported that for a short period everyone in the town neglected his temporal affairs and made holiness

> not only to be his business at certain seasons, the business of Sabbath days, or certain extraordinary times, or the business of a month, or a year, or of seven years, or his business under certain circumstances; but the *business of his life*. . . . Our young people when they met, were wont to spend the time in talking of the excellency and dying love of Jesus Christ, the glory of salvation, the wonderful, free, and sovereign grace of God. . . . And even at weddings, which formerly were mere occasions of mirth and jollity, there was now no discourse of anything but religion, and no appearance of any but spiritual mirth. . . . Although people did not ordinarily neglect their worldly business; yet Religion was with all sorts the great concern, and the world was a thing only by the bye.

Such forgetfulness of earth could obviously not last very long. When the reaction set in, the New England Puritans were considerably sobered. They discounted "raised affections" and after making religion for a brief interval "the business of life" they gladly returned to the life of business. The revivals took their course westward and southward. Such "outpourings of the Holy Spirit" were not native to the Puritan tradition, and even Jonathan Edwards and his immediate disciples turned from their attempt to establish the divine sovereignty in each soul by a general "great awakening" to the more sober business of expounding their theology in abstruse treatises. The Puritan ethic of regeneration was usually applied and administered as a regular institution; regeneration meant initiation into the church, and God shed His grace in due season, observing the proprieties. The covenant of grace was quite different in theory and in practice from pietistic conversion.

If Edwards was a Puritan without being a Yankee, Benjamin Franklin was a Yankee without being a Puritan. He repudiated the religious ethic early and thoroughly and preached the discipline of Yankee commercial virtues in a purely secular, practical manner. It is, therefore, misleading to represent Franklin as the exponent of Puritan ethics; he was only half a Puritan and hence no Puritan at all. He had no agonized conscience, and could devote himself wholeheartedly and prudently to becoming healthy, wealthy, and wise in the wisdom of this world.

Neither Edwards nor Franklin seriously upset the Puritan tradition; between them they supplemented each other and *the two taken together* may well be regarded as the classic formulation of Puritan philosophy and morals. The trouble came when the secular ethic began to be heard in the pulpits; politics and humanitarianism, war and peace were gradually insinuated into the gospel. And conversely, the Kingdom of God descended into the market place. A social gospel arose, which made religion more "liberal" and business more sacred. The rigors of Calvinism were discarded and a humane theology took shape. Channing, Parker, Emerson and Company created a new, anti-Puritan tradition. But these transcendental rebels were a minority. The majority of New England became genteel, freely mixing Puritan, Yankee, Jacobin, Transcendental doctrines without taking any of them seriously or clearly. Puritanism, by the time of the Civil War, was merely a tradition. What had killed it? Three causes seem to me worth singling out as basic factors in the undermining of Puritanism:

(1) Prosperity. As Yankee thrift and sobriety made New England prosperous, it created self-reliance, security, complacency. In such an atmosphere the agonized conscience of Calvinism and the covenant of grace become hypocritical gestures and the keeping up of the forms of piety out of mere piety for the past is after all but ancestor worship. And such worship still abounds in New England—but it is not Puritanism. The success of the American Revolution and the coming of political independence was, therefore, a severe blow to the old faith. Puritan theology is a crisis theology and subsides as the crises pass. It is not yet absolutely dead, however, for our security is still insecure, and there are still large numbers of the population who find comfort, relief, and escape or, for that matter, courage in time of trouble by reviving a faith to which they customarily give only lip service.

(2) Enlightenment. Though the spread of the Enlightenment helped to kill Puritanism, I wish to emphasize that it did not kill it in the way usually assigned. The spirit of Puritanism was not a spirit of

"orthodoxy in Massachusetts"; it was nourished from the start by a philosophical theology and constantly sought new light from new science. The Puritans were not fundamentalists; they interpreted the Bible in terms of a very sophisticated, Platonic scholasticism. When the Newtonian and Lockean science made the old Calvinist scholasticism antiquated, the Puritans like Cotton Mather, Samuel Johnson, and Jonathan Edwards, had little trouble in adapting their faith to the new learning. Platonism and science have always been friends, and the Puritan form of Platonism was no exception. But it was precisely this eagerness for enlightenment, this enthusiasm for education, that convinced the Puritans themselves of the limitations of their heritage. The rapidity and ease with which Eastern New England discarded Calvinism as a result of its enlightenment is one of the wonders of religious history. Almost overnight Puritans were transformed into Universalists, Unitarians, Transcendentalists, Christian Scientists, and a score of other faiths, more or less enlightened.

(3) Pietism. During the eighteenth century there crept into New England from the South and West a subtle, fatal fever, which carried away large elements of the population, especially of the rural population. Presbyterians, then Baptists, then Methodists preached a "new light," an exciting form of individualistic and otherworldly salvation. Orthodoxy, evangelicalism, and fundamentalism spread like a plague of passion. Up the Connecticut valley along the College Highway, from Yale to Northampton to Dartmouth, and across the hills from the Hudson Valley there streamed into New England hordes of fresh Scotch-Irish farmers, honest, tough, pious, but simple-minded. These new immigrants mingled in those regions with the old New England farmers, whom frontier conditions had physically hardened and intellectually softened. In this frontier culture the Bible was food for the soul, not texts for philosophical sermons. Learning declined among both clergy and laity. And the spirit of congregational solidarity also declined; a religious and moral individualism or, perhaps better, a familism centering in the homestead took the place of the intensive culture of the Puritan town. For the same reasons that Puritanism succumbed to pietism in Western New England, it died out as New Englanders migrated westward. Puritanism could not

be transported to the frontier; it needed the New England towns, congregations, and schools, all three working in close cooperation to keep it alive. No amount of Western Congregational churches scattered among those of numerous other denominations, no amount of sectarian seminaries and colleges could promote the growth of Puritanism in the West. Though the New England emigrants planted the New England seed, the fruit somehow turned out to be of a different flavor. Puritanism failed to spread and when it declined at home in Boston it declined absolutely, for no other climate proved propitious. Or, as our modern sociologists would say, it needed a bourgeois culture.

In New England there survived as Puritanism's ghost the genteel tradition. Longfellow, for example, spoke of "the stern old puritanical character" which "rises above the common level of life; it has a breezy air about its summits, but they are bleak and forbidding." This looking back and up to the heroic days of the Puritan faith reveals the depths to which the Massachusetts mind fell in its so-called flowering. The blossom time of New England's literature was also the funeral procession for the Puritan faith. Puritanism while alive was *not,* as Longfellow and his genteel brood believed, "above the common level of life"; it was the very substance of the common sternness of common life. It was a people's faith, born of tribulation and nourished by a common vision of a commonwealth. The pudgy, flabby descendants of the Puritans had no taste for "the bleak and forbidding" weather of antique New England; they were basking in a Victorian sunshine.

But here and there, now and then, a solitary remnant of genuine Puritanism showed itself. Let me call your attention to two such belated vestiges of a once vigorous faith. Hawthorne understood Puritanism correctly, though he made "romances" out of it for the popular consumption of a genteel public. He knew that Puritanism implied conscientious democracy; to him it was the antithesis of class society, as he saw it flourishing in Old England and as he saw it rising in the New. It was an austere faith precisely because it was devoted to equality, to public service, and to honest labor. The somber, tragic conscience of Puritanism was to his mind a mature conscience, reflecting a genuinely social morality. It is true, Hawthorne failed to distinguish between the utilitarian, secular discipline of the Yankee, and the communal, Platonic conscience of the Calvinist—both were to him but different aspects of the same hard lesson of life. Nevertheless, he did more justice to the religious than to the commercial side of the Puritan ethic, even though he translated it into secular, psychological language.

Another eloquent and critical survival of Puritanism came from the family of a typical Hudson River pietist, whose business in Albany so prospered that he could send his children to Boston. Henry James, Sr., outgrew the pietist Calvinism of his youth, but understood well the Puritan philosophy of New England. He felt the full force of the Calvinistic distinction between morality and salvation, between civilization with its individualism and spirituality with its faith in human solidarity, and a rationalized version of this distinction remained the core of his philosophy. He once wrote to Emerson: "You don't look upon Calvinism as a fact at all; wherein you are to my mind philosophically infirm—impaired in your universality. . . . I believe Jonathan Edwards *redivivus* in true blue would, after an honest study of the philosophy that has grown up since his day, make the best possible reconciler and critic of this philosophy—far better than Schelling *redivivus*." And in his autobiography he wrote:

> It is a monstrous affront to the divine justice or righteousness that I should be guaranteed, by what calls itself society, a lifelong career of luxury and self-indulgence, while so many other men and women, my superiors, go all their days miserably lodged, miserably clothed, and die at last in the same ignorance and imbecility, though not, alas! in the same innocence, that cradled their infancy. Now, I had long felt this deep spiritual damnation in myself growing out of an outraged and insulted divine justice. . . . In fact, what I crave with all my heart and understanding,—what my very flesh and bones cry out for,—is no longer a Sunday but a week-day divinity, a working God, giving with the dust and sweat of our most carnal appetites and passions, and bent not . . . upon inflating our worthless pietistic righteousness. . . . Religion in the old virile sense of the word has disappeared from sight and become replaced by a feeble Unitarian sentimentality. The old religion involved a conscience of the

profoundest antagonism between God and the worshipper . . . and meant discredit and death to every breath of a Pharisaic or Quaker temper in humanity, by which a man could be led to boast of a "private spirit" in his bosom, giving him a differential character and aspect in God's sight to that of other men, especially the great and holy and unconscious mass of his kind. . . . Morality is the summer lustihood and luxuriance of self-love. . . . Religion is the icy winter which blights this summer fertility . . . in the interests of a spring that shall be perennial. . . . Religion's sole errand on earth has been to dog the footsteps of morality, to humble the pride of selfhood which man derives from nature.[1]

No more radical critique of liberalism has appeared in this country than that of Henry James, Sr., and it is especially significant in view of the radical challenge which it aroused in William James:

Any absolute moralism is a pluralism; any absolute religion is a monism. It shows the depth of Mr. James's religious insight that he first and last and always made moralism the target of his hottest attacks, and pitted religion and it against each other as enemies, of whom one must die utterly, if the other is to live in genuine form. The accord of moralism and religion is superficial, their discord radical. Only the deepest thinkers on both sides see that one must go.[2]

William James took up the challenge in favor of moralism: the monism of religion must go!

The James family are perhaps strange specimens of Puritanism, and I do not wish to leave you under the impression that the Jameses were the last Puritans. They were much besides Puritans. But they did break through the crust of the genteel tradition, and in their own idioms revitalized a philosophy of faith and struggle which had at least one of its roots in New England.

[1] *Literary Remains of Henry James,* William James, ed., Boston, Houghton Mifflin Company, 1885, pp. 90, 39, 48, 54–5.
[2] *Op. cit.,* pp. 118–19.

II

THE DISSENTING TRADITION [1]

BY

JOHN T. McNEILL, D.D.

Auburn Professor of Church History, Union Theological Seminary

In the 1670 version of the Constitution of Carolina, Article xcvii, it is set forth at some length that since the native tribes are strangers to Christianity and the immigrants are of variant religious opinions, for the sake of peace and to avoid offense to God and scandal before men, persuasion alone shall be used to establish the truth, and seven persons agreeing in religion shall legally constitute a church. The skilled hand of John Locke is easily recognized in this document, which anticipates by over a century the better known Virginia Bill of Rights adopted at Williamsburg, May 6, 1776. Section 16 of this historic utterance of the Virginia Convention reads:

> That religion, or the duty which we owe to our Creator, and the manner of discharging it, can be directed only by reason and conviction, not by force or violence; and therefore all men are equally entitled to the free exercise of religion, according to the dictates of conscience; and that it is the mutual duty of all to practice Christian forbearance, love, and charity towards each other.

This weighty sentence was phrased in its final form by Madison. It reflects what had long been the trend of American opinion on the relations of church and state. But it is more important to observe that it affirms what was to be a life-giving principle of public law

---

[1] I am much indebted to my friend and colleague Professor R. H. Nichols for valuable suggestions that have been utilized in the preparation of the manuscript of this lecture for the press.

in the new Republic—the "free exercise of religion according to the dictates of conscience." Some remnants of former establishments still remained in the component states of the union, but the step from complete toleration to complete disestablishment was not long delayed. So far as the nation as a whole was concerned, there was to be no establishment. In 1787 it was laid down in Article VI of the Constitution, as a simple determination and without reference to the philosophy of the matter, that "no religious test shall ever be required as a qualification to any office or public trust under the United States." The first of the ten amendments to the Constitution contained in the Bill of Rights of 1791 provides that "Congress shall make no law respecting an establishment of religion, or prohibiting the free exercise thereof."

These historic decisions, expressed with great brevity and clarity, illustrate the characteristic trend of church-state relationships in the American scene, where no church is established, all churches are free, and no citizen is compelled to adhere to any. America has professed to abandon all enforced orthodoxy and has largely made good this profession. The attitude of government toward religion is friendly; among the forms of religion it is indifferent. At the risk, no doubt, of impairing some values both political and religious, we have effectively severed the bonds which in the Old World tied church and state together. Most Americans would say today that this course of action has justified itself, in that it has both enhanced the freedom of the citizen and deepened the reality of the religion professed. Some of them may have misgivings as they look upon the confused ecclesiastical pattern of the present day, and the loss of unity and dignity entailed in this for both church and society. But such considerations will hardly counterbalance in their minds the experience of freedom the laws have given us, of the sense of the blessings of unforced church activity and of a citizenship unencumbered by the demands of a privileged ecclesiastical order. Recognizing the loss, most of them will say that the separation of church and state has resulted in more gain than loss. If in any degree we rejoice in the outcome of this great experiment, we ought to remember with gratitude those resolute dissenters whose principles and attitudes went far to bring it about—

the men who long ago battled against the established churches of the British Isles, or in Continental nations, and those who in the formative era of the Republic assailed establishments and denounced authoritarian ecclesiasticism.

The separation of church and state in America was not a foregone conclusion even in 1776. Most of the states that were to be federated exhibited phenomena of establishment and dissent. Active persecution had been only occasional, but serious discontent was frequently registered against the privileges of established churches and the disabilities suffered by dissenters. Of the thirteen colonies that revolted, nine had established churches: three of these were Congregational and six were Anglican. The Revolutionary period, with its enthusiasm for liberty and equality, saw the abandonment of the establishment principle in Maryland, Georgia, North Carolina, and New York. Where establishments were retained they were weakened and insecure. Christians recognizing the authority of the Scriptures were generally free to associate for worship as they desired. In South Carolina "fifteen or more male persons not under twenty-one years of age professing the Christian Protestant religion" might constitute a church. Virginia, after protracted agitation and controversy, enacted (1786) that "no man shall be compelled to frequent or support any religious worship." This measure substantially abolished the Episcopal establishment, but property privileges connected with it survived in law to 1802. The New England Congregational established churches were more tenacious of their status. The dates of disestablishment in that area are: New Hampshire, 1817; Connecticut, 1818; Massachusetts, 1833. It is thus one of the features of the varied American scene that communions established in one state were dissenting bodies in another. In "the northern provinces," declared Edmund Burke in 1773, "the Church of England is really no more than a private sect."

We do well, therefore, to use the term "dissenting" in our title with discrimination. The New England Puritan colonists in crossing the sea moved ecclesiastically from the opposition to the government side. Whether they came as separatists or as disaffected would-be reformers of Anglicanism, before migration they were critics of the ecclesiastical régime to which the majority gave assent. In New England the same persons exercised theocratic rule, and were in turn faced by a class of disaffected minorities including a few Anglicans, and others more radical than themselves. Toward the latter they showed a good deal of intolerance; but their intolerance was not well supported in principle. Burke shrewdly observes that they were unlike Roman Catholics and Anglicans in their tradition, since in their former environment they had lived "in opposition to all the ordinary powers of the world and could justify that opposition only on a strong claim to natural liberty." This is no complete explanation of the eighteenth century vogue of "the great Mr. Locke" in America. Puritans had behind them experiences that predisposed them to Locke's doctrines. Burke may have had in mind not so much the teaching of Locke as that of the advocates of toleration and liberal government in the Parliamentary and Cromwellian period, many of whom were associated with some branch of Puritanism. These were men who protested against Roman Catholicism, then against Episcopacy, then against Presbyterianism, and were opposed to any reliance of the church upon the support of the state. Some of them were, indeed, advocates of natural liberty. Such were John Milton, John Goodwin, Gerrard Winstanley; the Baptists, Leonard Busher and John Murton, reached a ground for political liberalism and religious liberty mainly on arguments from Scripture. Cromwell once replied to a critic of his policy of religious liberty: "The state, in choosing men to serve it, takes no notice of their opinions." It cannot be said that the pillars of the Puritan state-churches in America were advocates of views of this sort. Yet in the end they were quite unable to prevent the growth of dissenting groups. Burke, viewing the scene in transatlantic perspective, saw the religion of the colonists as one of the chief sources of their opposition to the measures of the British Parliament which offended them, one of the chief reasons why they must be "conciliated." This religion he calls "the dissidence of dissent," which under a variety of denominations agrees in nothing but in "the communion of the spirit of liberty."

Doubtless a more intimate view of the scene would have forced Burke to concede to the discordant denominations a fuller measure of agreement; but he has fairly discerned the political significance of dissent, and the point to which its variations converge. The spirit of liberty was, indeed, on the eve of the Revolution, the common denominator of the dissenting denominations, and its triumph in law and society was the very condition of their survival and growth.

With our eyes upon the objectors to official religion, it is easily possible that we may overlook or underestimate potent secular forces that were active in the making of America. The thesis of F. J. Turner and his followers is well known. The modern American is the product of frontier conditions from the Massachusetts Bay colony down. Individualism, adaptation of church polities, and voluntary association in religion are of a piece with the individualism, adaptability, resourcefulness, and cooperation of the frontiersman, and are products of the soil of the frontier. Turner affirms that "from the beginning the frontier regions have exercised a steady influence toward democracy." He cites a good deal of relevant data but some of it hardly supports his thesis. Of the Scotch-Irish he says: "Followers of John Knox, they had the contentious individualism and revolutionary temper that seem natural to Scotch Presbyterianism." Were the frontier characteristics then, after all, an importation? Turner seems to admit this when he writes, following a characterization of Andrew Jackson as the personification of frontier democracy: "The frontier democracy of that time had the instincts of the clansman in the days of Scotch border war." Something more than an analogy is implied in this language, which would take us back, for the sources of the frontier spirit, far beyond the days of Knox and the Reformation. Some details given by A. M. Schlesinger, Jr. in *The Age of Jackson* [2] would indicate that Jacksonian democracy drew its strength from an appeal to classes out of sympathy with the churches. In other connections this author takes exception to the views of the school of Turner: "The great illusion of historians of the frontier has been that social equality produces economic equalitarianism." (p. 209) P. G. Mode's study of *The Frontier Spirit in American Christianity* [3] reveals more of the adjustments of the denominations to frontier

---

[2] Boston, Little, Brown & Co., 1945, chapter xxvii.
[3] New York, Macmillan Co., 1921.

conditions, their mutual rivalries and responses, than of frontier religion as a creative social force. This author holds that the lack of reverence and the sheer self-reliance of the American arise from the experience of success on a frontier that "showers its bounties upon muscular prowess," and in this context remarks:

> Always fascinating to the seriously minded, jaded, economically anxious Europeans, because of his elastic step, radiant countenance and buoyant spirit, the American is nonetheless to them the embodiment of profane iconoclasm and a "destroyer of souls."

This report on European opinions of Americans may be supported from numerous sources, but some of the keener observers have viewed the American type in another light. Alexis de Tocqueville, for example, pointing out that "despotism may govern without faith, but liberty cannot," expressed pronounced respect for the religion of Americans of all classes and saw in this country (in contrast to France) the spirit of religion and the spirit of freedom marching together, while separation from the state placed religion in a position of safety through the rapid changes of party government.[4] And later Professor Hugo Münsterberg wrote: "The entire American people are in fact profoundly religious and have been from the day when the Pilgrim Fathers landed. . . ."[5]

Most historians, I am sure, would deny that the great majority of Americans at any time were either profane or pious. The American undisciplined in heart by religion has often been offensively aggressive and vainglorious: the American who is religious humbly thanks God for his liberties as well as for his salvation and defends with stout courage the rights of others, no less than his own, to the free exercise of their religion. This is not to say that religion is for him one of the electives of life: he may firmly hold that the only election in religion is on God's initiative alone. At any rate no government can take the initiative. So far as government is concerned, religion lies in a field of activity to be left to each man's voluntary choice.

The strain of tradition with which this lecture has to do was brought

---

[4] *Democracy in America*, Part II (1840), chapter v.
[5] *The Americans*, New York, Doubleday & Company, 1905, chapter xx.

into recognition in 1930 by the publication of Thomas Cuming Hall's *The Religious Background of American Culture* (Little, Brown and Company). According to Hall the trend of culture and the free relations of church and state in America grew out of the testimony of English dissent of which the true begetter was John Wyclif. He sets out to prove:

> that Lollardism survived until the time of the Reformation so-called under Henry VIII; that it deliberately rejected nearly all that characterized later Protestantism; that it has remained true to its essential character in England and still more in America; that it is still influencing thousands of Protestants of the Wyclif type in direct contrast to the Protestantism of the Continental type; and that in its struggle for supremacy it has a large chance of relative success. (p. 37)

He tries to establish a clear division of the Wycliffite dissenting type from Puritanism which received its essential characteristics from the Continent of Europe. He draws the contrast between the Plymouth colony and that of Massachusetts Bay. The members of the Pilgrim colony at Plymouth were the spiritual children of the Lollards. They were for years content with lay preaching only and with a meeting place which was only a fortified house of the rudest construction. In these matters, and in their indifference to the sacraments, their attitude was exactly that of the Lollard conventicle and exactly the opposite of the attitude of Calvinistic Puritanism. The Bible was their sole directive; they shared the Lollard naïve faith that every unlettered man by the help of the Holy Spirit is in a position to expound the Scriptures. Like the Lollards, too, they were more concerned with morals than with doctrine.

Dr. Hall sees in colonial Virginia "the sturdiest expression of that spirit of self-help and self-government, that rather intense individualism that marks American life." The clergy were dominated by the vestries. The mass of the settlers came from "a class that, so far as it had a religious tradition, was trained in Dissent." The English lower classes, from which the colonists chiefly came, had been "Lollardized." Episcopacy was not desired; it survived in Virginia, Maryland, and the Carolinas, only because it was too unaggressive to count. The stress upon the role of Wycliffite Dissent is carried through the later history. In New England the Scotch-Irish settlers were "absorbed by the dissenting tradition."

There is a suggestive discussion of the Great Awakening as "essentially a dissenting movement" marked by individualism, lay exhorting, emotionalism, and inheriting the English dissenters' quarrel with the upper-class power symbolized in the Revolution by the Royal House. The Wesleys came of a dissenting family; Whitefield from an environment of Dissent. The Salvation Army is viewed as a kind of revived Lollardry in its anti-ecclesiasticism and simple lay Biblicism. Dwight L. Moody and even Mary Baker Eddy are made to conform to the theme.

This book has been regarded as provocative rather than definitive: indeed the author seems to regard his task in this light. It is open to criticism at many points. There is, of course, no doubt that Lollardry survived in England to the Reformation and in its Biblicism and anticlericalism affected the currents of the Reformation in its early stage. But its influence on Separatism has not been established. So careful a student of Puritanism as M. M. Knappen, having examined the records of sixteenth century Lollardry, states that "little was to be expected from such people; and when absorbed in later English Puritanism, they contributed almost nothing except numbers and the memory of a great past." [6] There is some reason to think, too, that Professor Hall has drawn much too sharply the contrast between the Plymouth and the Bay colony. Nor can we be sure that the resemblances to Lollard principles at Plymouth are evidence of a filiation from Wyclif's movement, and not rather of a fresh, unsophisticated and untraditional acceptance of Bible guidance. S. F. Willison's *Saints and Strangers* [7] lends support to the latter view. As W. W. Sweet noted in reviewing his book, Dr. Hall seems unaware of the whole literature on the frontier influence upon American culture, knowledge of which might have modified his thesis. Hall is not able to claim that Wyclif taught a general toleration in religion, but only that this would be "the logical outcome" of the Lollard

---

[6] *Tudor Puritanism,* University of Chicago Press, 1938, p. 9.
[7] New York, Reynal and Hitchcock, 1945.

doctrine of the Holy Spirit. He seems not to realize how his argument ascribing toleration in America to dissent is damaged by the insertion of the document in which the Amsterdam directors of the New Amsterdam colony in 1663 required Stuyvesant to tolerate Quakers. One is obliged, I think, to recognize that Hall's data are inadequate and his argument strained. Nevertheless he has as good a thesis as any other that has been advanced to claim for any religious tradition the determination of the American culture pattern. One can only regret that his book was not written with more patient research and historic imagination: in that case it would be easier to evaluate the interpretation it is designed to present.

John M. Mecklin in his *Story of American Dissent*[8] offers us no high ancestry of dissent but confines himself almost entirely to the American scene and mainly to the colonial period. In general he is true to the definition adopted at the beginning of his study (p. 9): "Dissent is of course the general term for all groups who fought the colonial establishments," though he treats the word also in its "comprehensive sociological sense" as including "all forms of religious revolt against the established churches of Western Christianity," whether associated with sectarian groups or manifested in mystical individualism or in the amorphous mass movements growing out of social unrest. Professor Mecklin is a sociologist working with a good command of historical data. His basic objections to Dr. Hall's thesis are two. First, Hall shows no awareness of the fact that "fundamental changes in the cultural pattern may turn conservatives into liberals, dissenters into churchmen." Secondly, he fails to recognize the contribution of the frontier to the triumph of the dissenting-revivalistic form of Protestantism. It is remarkable that Mecklin himself fails to examine adequately the frontier question as it relates to his inquiry. He does present, however, an impressive interpretation of the data of dissent in each of the colonies and with reference to all the important dissenting denominations. We may assume, I think, that in dedicating the book "to two young dissenters, John and Mary," he is merely consistent with his concept that dissent is a relative term and is not sardonically suggesting that it is a juvenile phenomenon. He is aware

[8] New York, Harcourt, Brace and Company, 1934.

that denominations have traditions and that these are not canceled out suddenly in a new environment. But he does not always show complete familiarity with the tradition or adequately recognize its tenacity. And he unjustly discounts the tolerant principles of most later American Protestantism when he states: "Within the dissenting-revivalistic churches of today there is no place for tolerance." (p. 112). Mr. Mecklin likes the prophets of dissent but has not much admiration for those who build the tombs of the prophets while enjoying the comfort of a successful and socially well-placed denomination.

Mecklin looks upon the Protestant denominations in their later development as sects of large growth. A sect, sociologically defined, is a religious group which makes no claim to universality and is united by bonds that are solely voluntary. It arises in protest, it cultivates a spirit of criticism and dissent, and its ideals are imperiled by institutionalization. In its beginnings it demands toleration, but it does this in order that it may be free to cultivate a narrow and intolerant piety. This, at the most, leads to the admission of liberty between sects, not to liberty within them. According to Mecklin, in the expanded and powerful sects of today—the Baptists, Methodists, and Presbyterians—the spirit of dissent is dead. One seeks in vain among them any real interest in religious liberty. They merely attempt to force sectarian ethics upon the nation, as in the prohibition incident.

It is in this general framework of ideas that Mr. Mecklin sets the history of dissent in the colonies. The dissenting tradition is dead in the organizations which in their infancy were informed by its spirit. Dissent has become a secular matter. The judgment rendered upon contemporary American Protestantism fails of justice because it ignores vast areas of fact. But it is near enough the truth to be challenging and disquieting to any who believe that Protestantism has a social role to play. For our present purpose it is not so important to know whether the dissenting spirit has departed from Protestantism to socialism and communism as to learn what it accomplished while it was alive in our midst. Mecklin gives dissent against the colonial establishments a leading role in our history. The adoption of a policy of religious liberty in America is seen as the product of vigorous dissent. New England did not mother it; Massachusetts made no contribution to religious liberty and did not understand it; while Virginia, with its vigorous dissenting groups, obtained experience that prepared it to take the lead in framing the terms of religious liberty for the nation.

Let us now look a little more closely at some significant incidents in the battle against establishments in the colonies, chiefly in Massachusetts and Virginia. Roger Williams, Cambridge-educated refugee from Laudian England, was the great separatist of the northern colonies. His protests against the establishment and John Cotton's view thereof were based upon a radical philosophy of church and state. These have entirely separate spheres. The state is at once free from ecclesiastical controls and forbidden to demand and enforce any religious conformity. The church as organization ought to be voluntary and totally detached from the government. Toward the state it bears a relation comparable to that of an incorporated company. There are inconsistencies and weaknesses in the argument, and it was presented to the accompaniment of some needless vituperation; but it could not be met by stodgy affirmations of theocracy, nor could the leaven of Williams's ideas be held in check by his expulsion (1636) from Massachusetts Bay. Forty years later when he was deep in old age and misfortune, the General Court of Massachusetts revoked its sentence.

Williams founded the Providence community on the principle of a wide liberty of conscience. "I desire not that liberty to myself," he wrote in 1652, "which I would not freely and impartially weigh out to all the consciences of the world beside." The second charter of Rhode Island, 1663, in the spirit of Williams states that no person shall be anywise molested for religious opinions that do not disturb the civil peace. C. H. Moehlman has pointed out, however, that the charter, if not in 1663, certainly in 1699, excluded Roman Catholics from public office, and that the colony had a numerous slave class.[9] In sharp contrast to the then prevailing principles, but in startling anticipation of those which now prevail, Williams gave to Rhode Island, in the words of Professor R. E. E. Harkness, "free rights in

---

[9] "The Baptist View of the State," *Church History*, VI, 1937, American Society of Church History, pp. 24–47.

religion; separation of church and state; (and) a government derived from the people."[10] His community land policy, however, was not a model for later America. Williams was ever a fighter, and often an aggressive one. In 1672 the aged champion kept an appointment, at heavy physical cost, to engage in a hot debate with some Quakers, whom he was always equally prepared to defend from intolerance and to rebuke for error. He claims that he had not been too resentful when certain Quakers had poured out upon him "the curses and judgments of God." But evidently when in this contest he found himself one against many and was heckled and insulted, he became aroused and abusive. He afterwards described his most aggressive opponent as "a flash of wit, a face of brass, and a tongue set on fire from the hell of Lyes and Fury."[11] Both the Quakers and Williams, as W. W. Sweet dryly observes, were living up to their principles of freedom of speech.[12]

The persecutions suffered by the Quakers in New England were the most severe that can be charged to the establishment. It may seem remarkable that a few enthusiastic preachers of the "inner light" should have aroused a vigorous response of fear and hate on the part of those whose fathers had fled from an establishment. But Massachusetts feared their incursions from their shelter in Rhode Island and not very mistakenly regarded them as a potential solvent of the entire Puritan plan of life. One is reminded of the fate of Servetus who presented a similar threat to Calvin's Geneva. Martyrdom did not daunt these resolute dissenters. But in New England their success was limited. It was the Baptists who played the largest role among opponents of the establishment. In an act of 1644 "Anabaptists" were excluded from the Bay colony. Numerous Baptists suffered penalties. Obadiah Holmes was savagely whipped at Lynn; he responded: "You have struck me as with roses" (1651). In this connection John Clarke and others had opportunity to state their opinions, and the cause grew slowly. In 1679, Charles II commanded the

---

[10] *Church History*, V, 1936, p. 226.
[11] J. Ernst, *Roger Williams, New England Firebrand*, New York, Macmillan Company, 1932, pp. 461–78; S. R. Brokunier, *The Irrepressible Democrat, Roger Williams*, New York, Ronald Press, 1940, pp. 272 ff.
[12] *Religion in Colonial America*, New York, Charles Scribner's Sons, 1942, p. 155.

Massachusetts authorities to grant to non-Congregationalists liberty of conscience. Congregationalists as well as Baptists in England protested against the persecuting policy of the Standing Order in Massachusetts, and champions of the latter made spirited replies. According to Backus, Edward Randolph made eight visits to England to obtain action against the Baptists.[13] In 1691, after the English Toleration Act, all but Roman Catholics were freed from penalties. But the ministers of the establishment were still of course supported by public funds. In 1728, Baptists and Quakers living within five miles of their meeting places and regularly attending these were legally exempted from the tax for church support.[14] But the old system survived in practice to a large degree, and Isaac Backus (1724-1806), greatest of eighteenth century New England dissenters, persistently attacked it as taxation without representation. Magistrates were elected to deal with matters "civil and worldly," not spiritual. "Religion is a concern between God and the soul with which no human authority can intermeddle." These ideas he identifies with "Protestantism." Backus has generally been accorded warm praise. Says Professor Mecklin: "Patient, tolerant, wise, and brave . . . he illustrated principles which were later to become embodied in organic law and made the guarantee of our democratic liberties." Uttering firm protests against entrenched injustice, he avoided the spicy vituperation of Williams and the Quakers. Incidentally, his three-volume *History of New England* commends him as a pioneer of reasonably objective, well documented, American historiography.

Backus did not live to see the end of the establishment. But he witnessed the relaxation of its bigotry and also such multiplication of the number of Baptist and other dissenters through the Great Awakening as to render impossible the enforcement of their disabilities. Professor Moehlman in a revealing article cited above, cautions us against reading into the Baptist utterances of that period too much advanced political theory, and points to the absence in Baptist statements of the phrase, "separation of church and state." But the Baptist protest against discrimination undoubtedly helped to make such

[13] *History of New England*, I, p. 519.
[14] *Ibid.*, Appendix, p. 9.

separation inevitable. John Locke once wrote that the Baptists were consistent "propounders of equal and impartial liberty."

In the Revolutionary era Virginia was the scene of the growth of the Baptist denomination to a strength that told in politics. The Separate Baptists, inspired by Shubal Stearns, a former Presbyterian who established a community in Sandy Creek, North Carolina, in 1755, exhibited remarkable energy and multiplied in Virginia after 1770.[15] The Baptists vigorously attacked the Anglican establishment, and petitioned for relief from parochial dues. With other dissenting denominations they were exempted from the obligation in 1776, and in 1780 a limited number of their ministers were permitted to celebrate marriages. Their part in obtaining the passage of the Bill for Religious Liberty of 1786 was considerable, and they labored persistently thereafter to obtain the distribution of the property of the establishment. Madison and Jefferson from different motives were seeking the same ends; Madison apparently felt their influence, and Jefferson acknowledged in 1809 the significance of their aid in securing "the freedom and happiness for which we have labored." [16]

Through the able statesmanship of William Penn, Pennsylvania became a colony of refuge for a wide variety of religious groups under disabilities in the Old World. For three quarters of a century the colony was under Quaker political control. It was not in Pennsylvania that the Quakers were dissenters. They were, in a sense, the establishment. By peaceable means, the colonists wrested power from a governor appointed by Penn. The legislature became the ruling power, and it was composed mainly of Quakers. Quaker ideals were nonpolitical, and some of the leaders exhibited hesitancy about pursuing the necessary tasks of government. Compromises of their pacifism and a sense of the inconsistency of their position as a dominant minority in an increasingly heterogeneous population led to contention and discouragement and, finally, to the abdication of leading members of the Quaker government (1756), and the pro-

---

[15] W. M. Gewehr, *The Great Awakening in Virginia,* Durham, N.C., Duke University Press, 1930, pp. 108 f., 117.
[16] Moehlman, "Baptist View of the State," p. 44.

hibition, by the yearly meeting, of political officeholding under penalty of exclusion from the fellowship (1758). Professor G. H. Hershberger writes that their "pursuit of justice involved a struggle for power which sacrificed the principle of love." [17] But there is another aspect of the matter. The Quakers had followed their principle of tolerance and had avoided using their power for any kind of religious persecution. They had, however, earned the growing opposition of many of the new settlers, especially of the Ulster Scots or Scotch-Irish who settled in large numbers in the frontier counties during the first half of the eighteenth century. The Quaker governing minority failed to take needed measures to prevent massacres by Indians, from whom the newcomers had to defend themselves as best they might. Some of the latter settled beyond the limits of their legal claims. They were roughly removed from the Juniata valley in 1750, and their houses burned. They soon began to organize as a party of resistance to the political discrimination under which they suffered. In 1755, the Quakers had twenty-six of the thirty-six seats in the legislature, though they constituted only about one fifth of the population. The numerous German groups were divided, frontiersmen exposed to the Indians joining with the Scotch-Irish in objection to the ruling minority. The Anglican element was on the same side. The struggle did not end with the events of 1756–58. The three Quaker counties still held a majority in the legislature, and only step by step was this "flagrant piece of iniquity" redressed. The oligarchy met its final over-throw in 1776, when a new constitution for Pennsylvania was framed by a provincial convention. The political history of Pennsylvania continued to be stormy, but it was now truly democratic. It can hardly be said that the issue had been one of religious liberty at all, save in so far as one religious group, religiously tolerant, sought to retain as a minority the political privileges it had assumed when it was a majority.[18] Dr. Mecklin charges the "dissenting-

---

[17] *Church History*, VIII, 1939, p. 73.
[18] *Cf.* W. F. Dunaway, *The Scotch-Irish of Colonial Pennsylvania*, Chapel Hill, University of North Carolina Press, 1944, chapter viii, and E. S. Bates, *The American Faith*, New York, W. W. Norton, 1940, pp. 200 ff.

revivalistic" churches with having capitalized legal tolerance in the interest of spiritual intolerance. In the story of eighteenth century Pennsylvania we see something like the reverse of this: the spiritually tolerant Quakers were content for long years by skillful manipulation to deny to others political equality.

The Scotch-Irish who came to Pennsylvania had put in an apprenticeship as dissenters. Among them was an element of natives of Scotland, where Presbyterianism was established; but the series of secessions which mark the eighteenth-century history of the Kirk provided America with numerous seceders of one or another denomination. The Presbyterian Ulster Scots had fought a long and not too successful battle against the Church of Ireland (Anglican). The saintly Jeremy Taylor was among those responsible for the intolerant treatment of the Scots. He refused to recognize them as a corporate group. Their precious Covenant was held to be seditious. By a policy of passive resistance and reiterated appeals they had secured some relief.[19] But the eighteenth century brought them new distresses, religious and economic. They had left Scotland for Ireland while Scotland was still an independent nation and had not acquired a loyalty to London, much less to Canterbury. Already somewhat alienated from the British government by their experience with the established church, they came to America for freedom and food. They were energetic, vigorous, and aggressive frontiersmen, hungry for lands and homes. They were convinced Presbyterians, and as Presbyterianism got itself organized it brought its culture to their wilderness; but religious influences were weak at the beginning. The revivals of the time stirred their communities and made them a more church-loving people; and the leadership of their ministers was strong in the Revolutionary period.

It was in Pennsylvania that the role of these Scotch-Irish in Revolutionary politics was mainly determined. They claimed equal rights "as freemen and English subjects" with the people of the Quaker counties of Philadelphia, Chester, and Bucks. John Dickinson, the brilliant Quaker opponent of British policy, had furnished the very

[19] O. A. Marti, "Passive Resistance of the Scotch-Irish Presbyterians during the Period of the Restoration," *Journal of Religion*, VIII, 1928, pp. 581–602.

materials of the Scotch-Irish claims against the Quakers. I quote Carl Becker's *Beginnings of the American Peoples:* [20]

> Opposed to all attempts to infringe their rights "either here or on the other side of the Atlantic" they at last gained control of the anti-British movement, and made use of it, employing the very arguments which Dickinson and his kind had used in resistance to British oppression, in an attempt to overthrow the Quaker merchant oligarchy that had so long governed the colony in its own interests.

The tide of Scotch-Irish settlement reached the Alleghanies and was deflected southward. Virginia and Maryland offered cheap land. Presently we find these people prominent in the typical role of American dissenters in these states, and not long afterward in the Carolinas and Georgia.

It is impossible, however, to pass over the name of the Irish-born early pioneer minister, Francis Makemie (1658–1708). Makemie's labors as the leading founder of the Presbyterian church in North Carolina, Virginia, and Maryland, and his formation of the Presbytery of Philadelphia (1706) cannot be reviewed here. More significant for us is the fact that he fought for the right to preach in New York, told Lord Cornbury, the governor, that as a minister he dared not give bond that he would not preach, and was put in jail for six weeks (1706). Acquitted on trial, he was unjustly forced to pay the costs. The Act of Toleration of 1689 was claimed by Makemie, but was held not to be in force in New York. However, the Church of England was established only in four counties of the province, and the laws of the province favored the dissenter. During his able defense Makemie warned the court against a general persecution of dissenters, who outnumbered Anglicans. The record of the trial shows that he was allowed to argue his position at length and that he very ably took advantage of this.[21] The case weakened the position of the establishment by advertising the argument of an able dissenter.

It should be remembered that the victory of dissenters and of liberal

---

[20] Cambridge, Mass., Houghton, Mifflin Company, 1915, p. 242.
[21] L. P. Bowen, *Days of Makemie,* Philadelphia, 1885; *The Journal of the Presbyterian Historical Society,* Vol. IV; I. M. Page, *The Life Story of Rev. Francis Makemie,* Grand Rapids, Wm. B. Erdmans Publishing Company, 1938.

politicians in Virginia was conditioned by the weakness of Anglicanism. The Virginia Anglicans were not eager partisans of their church. Most of them were low-church, or indifferent to religion, or openly anticlerical. The clergy sent to the colony were prevailingly unfit, and even devoted Society for the Propagation of the Gospel missionaries were often unwelcome among those of their own communion. The establishment had less tenacity and resourcefulness than Massachusetts Congregationalism. Almost every encounter with dissent was a defeat for Anglicanism.

Through the pre-Revolutionary period the claims of dissent were not demands for disestablishment. They were rather couched in the form of appeals for religious toleration. This is the emphasis in the utterances of Samuel Davies (1723-61), who began work in Hanover County in 1748. His vivacious personality and polished and earnest eloquence attracted all classes including neglected Anglicans; but his interest lay primarily in meeting the spiritual needs of the Presbyterians in the colony. In 1738 Governor Gooch by large assurances of the free exercise of their religion had encouraged Presbyterians to begin settlement. Davies obtained license to preach in a few places. Like Makemie, he sought the recognition of the Act of Toleration, and an act of 1712 which modified it, as valid law. This was in a general way admitted; but how far could a dissenter be permitted freedom to preach? In England the "license of the place" was freely accorded. Davies obtained from the celebrated Nonconformist, Philip Doddridge, full information on the English practice, and from the Bishop of London a somewhat different view. The bishop was for reducing his license to one locality. Makemie had been called a "strolling minister" by his accusers, and Davies was held to be an itinerant when he entered parishes beyond Hanover. Dawson, the Commissary, wrote the bishop to complain that Davies had been "holding forth on workdays to great numbers of poor people," taking them from their proper work. The bishop regarded Davies as a mere intruder into an Anglican preserve, and claimed that the law gave him no right to "gather congregations where there were none." In 1752, Davies was permitted an associate, but an extension of licenses was long delayed. He paid a visit to Great Britain (1753-55) in the interests of the College of New Jersey, obtained golden opinions and rich cash gifts there, and returned with new laurels. Davies was a leader of the Virginia revival of the 1750's; Whitefield came in 1755, and Presbyterianism grew stronger, while the authorities were too busy with a frontier war to enforce restrictions. A presbytery was formed, new licenses were obtained, new settlements were entered, and opposition crumbled. The established clergy became unpopular because they protested the reduction of their incomes (which were paid in tobacco), an economy necessitated by the costs of war and the short tobacco crop. Davies later played the role of a political preacher and patriot, with superb eloquence arousing resistance to the Indians and the French. When in 1759 Governor Dinwiddie was succeeded by Francis Fauquier, Davies obtained for the presbytery the new incumbent's full assurance that he would support the application of the Act of Toleration with all its immunities. With no assault upon the establishment as such, Davies had made a permanent change in the attitude to dissent when in 1759 he left the colony to become president of the College of New Jersey.[22]

The struggle in Virginia entered on a second phase with the presentation of various memorials to the House of Burgesses by the denominations about 1770. But new restrictions were introduced in 1772 by the Assembly. In 1774, the Baptists asked permission to hold their meetings at night, a privilege denied them, though not restricted by English law, and were given liberty to preach "at all seasons." In this year also the Hanover Presbytery, grateful for its own liberties but fearing their loss, sought in a petition "to secure by law the religious liberties of all dissenters in the colony." These were to include the right "to go about doing good," and protection from violence. These Presbyterian dissenters do not answer to Professor Mecklin's definition of a sect. They do make a "claim to universality." They made their appeal as representatives of a series of Old World Presbyterian churches and not only of their growing American church. Their phrase, "a church neither contemptible nor obscure," is applied to ecumenical Presbyterianism. They include, too, an affirmation of

---

[22] G. H. Bost, *Samuel Davies: Colonial Revivalist and Champion of Religious Toleration,* part of a Dissertation, Chicago, 1944.

their concern for "the interest of American liberty" (November 11, 1774).

American liberty was indeed in the making in Virginia. The Convention meeting at Williamsburg adopted the famous Bill of Rights in May, 1776. The legislature meeting in October received a flood of petitions directed against the establishment from the dissenting churches. That of the Presbyterians in a long argument refers to the "violation of their natural rights," "religious bondage," and the retardation of settlement and temporal progress under the establishment. Counterpetitions were filed by the Methodists as "a religious society in communion with the Church of England," and by a considerable number of Episcopalians. The House, largely Episcopalian, "after desperate contests," as Jefferson said, abolished laws affecting religious opinions and exempted dissenters from church taxes. The struggle continued; but the end of it has already been alluded to at the opening of this paper.[23]

It is to be borne in mind that dissent in early America was from time to time aroused by, and enjoyed great increase from, revivals. The phenomena of American revivalism have been treated by numerous writers, notably by P. G. Mode in a book already cited, and more recently by Professor Sweet. Mode shows how naturally the revivalistic method fitted into frontier conditions. He also suggests that the reason the revivals fed the membership of Baptist and Presbyterian churches was "their staunch advocacy of republican ideas and their vigorous resistance in New England and Virginia to everything that savored of state-church favoritism." In *Revivalism in America*[24] Dr. Sweet shows the profound effect of the revivals of colonial times in promoting the growth of church membership, particularly in the dissenting denominations, and their influence in the individualizing of religion, the rise of educational institutions, and the improvement of morals. The churches that multiplied their numbers through the awakenings were those which had popular forms of church government. Strengthened by their large accessions, they were bold to de-

---

[23] Charles F. James, *Documentary History of the Struggle for Religious Liberty in Virginia*, Lynchburg, 1900, conveniently supplies the chief source documents.
[24] New York, Charles Scribner's Sons, 1944.

mand their corporate rights as well as liberty of the individual conscience.

In the decade preceding the Revolution, and throughout the struggle, the ministers of all the eighteen denominations in the colonies, with the exception of a fair number of Anglicans and most of the few Methodist preachers, generally supported the opposition to British colonial measures. The New England establishments did not owe their security to British rule and their ministers were among the most vocal of its opponents. Philip Davidson [25] points to the mistaken fear in New England that the British government planned to establish Anglicanism in all the colonies. He also calls attention to the adoption by dissenting pastors of the doctrines of John Locke. The support lent by the Presbyterians, who were also aroused against episcopacy, to the Whig cause, enlisted a large number both of the well-to-do and of the poor inhabitants, while the Baptist churches, identified with the underprivileged, were individually penetrated by Whig propaganda. Davidson's view is that the churches did not take the initiative but were persuaded and used by the political organizers of resistance. He quotes a letter written from Philadelphia by Joseph Hewes of North Carolina: "We have persuaded the Presbyterian ministers here to write to the ministers and congregations of their sect in North Carolina, and have also made application to the Dutch Lutherans and Calvinists to do the same." (p. 90) There is no doubt, however, that a great many of the ministers adopted the cause without awaiting the persuasion of laymen, and were themselves among the most energetic progagandists. Such were: the English Congregationalist, William Gordon, who preached on "Religious and Civil Liberty" in 1774; the Scottish Presbyterian, John Witherspoon, President of Princeton, who did not carry his politics into the pulpit until after the beginning of the war; George Duffield of Philadelphia, whose "whole career," according to Davidson, "indicates a purposive effort to arouse anti-British sentiment among the colonists"; and the younger William Tennent, who had been educated in his father's

---

[25] Reprinted from *Propaganda and the American Revolution* by Philip Davidson by permission of The University of North Carolina Press. Copyright, 1941, by The University of North Carolina Press.

celebrated Log College of Neshaminy and thus belonged to the first crop of American-trained ministers. Davidson cites numerous instances of the fact that in the North, on the background of the fear of an American episcopate, "sermons of the period 1767–1774 made a joint appeal for resistance to both civil and religious tyranny." Miss A. M. Baldwin's *The New England Clergy and the American Revolution* [26] shows at greater length the inspiration given to revolutionary progaganda by the preachers of New England Congregationalism.

It would be interesting to search out the use in American texts of the phrase, "God alone is lord of the conscience," which had found a place in the Westminster Confession of Faith (xx, 2). In that document it was presented in defense against the requirement of obedience to unscriptural rules regarding faith and worship. It was borrowed in the Pennsylvania Charter of Privileges prepared at the direction of William Penn in 1701, and in the Delaware Charter of the same year, in the form: "Almighty God being the only Lord of conscience." Here the inference is freedom from state compulsion in religious matters. The Presbyterian Synod of New York and Philadelphia in 1788 elaborated on the theme by saying that "the rights of private judgment in all matters that respect religion" are "universal and unalienable"; each church, however, may declare its own terms of communion. This is a notable brief statement of corporate as well as private rights in religion. Numerous historians, including E. F. Humphrey and W. W. Sweet, have observed that the national constitution of the Presbyterian church took its rise at the same time and in the same city as the constitution of the United States, and that these alike rest on the principle of "constitutional republicanism." John Witherspoon and George Duffield were among the leading framers of the Presbyterian Assembly. Witherspoon was a member of the Congress of 1776 and heartily advocated the Declaration of Independence. His political influence was immense. Duffield had many members of the Continental Congress for his listeners. The Presbyterian documents were drafted in 1786 and made final in May, 1788, while the Federal Constitution was written in the period

[26] Durham, N.C., Duke University Press, 1929.

May to September, 1787. It would of course be unjustifiable to say here: *post hoc ergo propter hoc*. But the Scotch-Irish Presbyterians were as a group among the most convinced supporters of the movement of which the Constitution marked the fulfilment.

Conclusion

Dissent in America cannot be understood under any exclusive thesis regarding its origin. The communions which best exemplify its characteristics had indeed suffered hardship as stepchildren of the establishments in Britain and Ireland; but their filiation from medieval dissent has not been proved. The Scotch-Irish emerged from the established church of Scotland only a century before they reached Pennsylvania. The frontier, with its premium upon individualism, was doubtless a favorable environment for the dissenting tradition. But without any frontier England in Cromwell's time produced a prodigious brood of highly individualistic sects arrayed "in pious enmity to all that demonstrated the inequality of man." [27] The revivals gave religious experience of the most personal sort to the common man, made him self-conscious and articulate. Professor R. H. Nichols points to the fact that the revivalist preaching lacked any specific doctrine of the church. He believes that both the Puritan and the Scottish elements at the outset had a traditional reverence for the corporate church and that this was "weakened by the individualism of the Awakening," and by the absence of book learning and contempt for theory on the frontier. Dr. Nichols holds that this trend has left a serious intellectual and religious weakness in American Protestantism, in a secular and parochial conception of the church.[28] This is undoubtedly a phase of the topic to which due weight should be given.

In estimating the influence of dissent we cannot safely be more dogmatic than in accounting for its origin. We cannot fail to recog-

---

[27] W. Y. Tindall, *John Bunyan, Mechanick Preacher,* New York, Columbia University Press, 1934.

[28] "The Influence of the American Environment on the Conception of the Church in American Protestantism," *Church History,* XI, 1942, pp. 191–92.

nize in the dissenting communions a creative political vitality strongly tending to democracy. But we may not credit our liberties exclusively to any, or to all, of these denominations. Sir Edwin Sandys, Lord Baltimore, Jefferson, and the much maligned Thomas Paine are among those to be thanked—men who owed little or nothing to American dissent. Individualistic liberty was exemplified to popular admiration by such pioneers as the knightly and worldly John Sevier, whose forefathers were Xaviers and French nobles turned Huguenot, but whose eminence arose from the fact that he could outrun, outfight, and outswear his fellows in Tennessee. The churches did something to bring this charming insolence under discipline, and to confront men with the claims of the Kingdom of God. Most of their members were, however, and long remained, indifferent or hostile to traditions of ecclesiastical order. While the denominations differed in their teaching, they were drawn together in a common interest to create in America what Burke happily named "the communion of the spirit of liberty."

III

THE ENLIGHTENMENT TRADITION

BY

RALPH HENRY GABRIEL, Ph.D.

Professor of History, Yale University

In the middle period of the twentieth century Americans erected on the banks of the Potomac in the city of Washington a memorial of white marble. It suggests the Pantheon in ancient Rome but its more recent inspiration was the Rotunda which Thomas Jefferson had designed as the intellectual center and the architectural climax of his University of Virginia. Within the walls of the memorial stands a statue of that country squire who wished to be remembered chiefly for having founded the university and for having written the Declaration of Independence and the Virginia statute establishing religious liberty. Not far from this memorial stand two others, that to Lincoln and the simple shaft which commemorates the name of Washington. The date of the Jeffersonian memorial is not without interest. It came late—almost a century and a half after the death of the master of Monticello. It was built to celebrate a man of agriculture by the citizens of a highly complex industrial age. Nor was the memorial the expression of the attitude of a minority group. It was evidence that Thomas Jefferson at long last had taken his place among the small group of American folk heroes of the first rank. But the event had more than significance for the memory of an individual man. Both Jefferson and Washington were men of the eighteenth century. But Jefferson alone in his outlook and in his contribution to thought and civilization can be called one of that small world company of *philosophes* who were the leaders of the Enlightenment. In raising Jefferson to a place of the highest rank in the American pantheon mid-twentieth-century Americans were doing homage to the Enlightenment. The reasons for this belated turning to the Enlightenment, if such it was, are worth exploring.

As the eighteenth century gave way to the nineteenth a young clergyman in New York City busied himself with the writing of a book, one among many that came from his hurrying pen. Samuel Miller, not yet thirty-five, was associated with two colleagues in a collegiate pastorate of the three Presbyterian churches: Wall Street, Brick, and Rutgers Street. In addition to preaching and writing he was wont to deliver several addresses each week, to make many pastoral calls and to carry on a voluminous correspondence. In 1803, this dynamic individual who sought to carry the élan of the eighteenth century into the nineteenth, published a two-volume work to which he gave the somewhat misleading title, *Brief Retrospect of the Eighteenth Century*. From a pastor's study in which the influence of John Calvin was a living force Samuel Miller looked back on what Voltaire in France and Gibbon in England had called the Age of Enlightenment. Miller agreed with their nomenclature. Neither Benjamin Franklin or Thomas Jefferson ever equalled the rhetoric of Miller as he depicted the foundations of the century just gone.

> At the close of the seventeenth century, the stupendous mind of Newton and the penetrating genius of Locke, had laid their systems of matter and of mind before the world. Like pioneers in an arduous siege, they had many formidable obstacles to remove—many labyrinths to explore—and the power of numberless enemies to overcome. But they accomplished the mighty enterprise. With cautious, but firm and dauntless steps, they made their way to the entrenchments of fortified error; they scaled her walls; forced her confident and blustering champions to retreat; and planted the standard of truth, where the banner of ignorance and of falsehood had so long waved.

Rather good for a Calvinist.

Newton and Locke were of the essence of Jefferson's thought. And, if Newton disclosed the reality of matter in motion, Franklin, completing a line of investigation begun by Farraday, disclosed a century after Newton the reality of electricity in motion. The

Enlightenment was the outgrowth in popular thought of the work of the two great seventeenth century Englishmen. Franklin and Jefferson were evidence not only that the Enlightenment, as a phase of thought, had made its way to English provincial society west of the Atlantic but that eighteenth century American culture was capable of contributing to it figures of world importance, one in science and the other in social and political philosophy.

Samuel Miller in his book caught the essential mood of the Enlightenment. Newton had applied mathematical logic—the eighteenth century called it reason—to the mechanical problems of the heavens. Observation had verified his results. The success of Newtonian physics gave rise to an élan that was a blend of triumph and of confident hope. The eighteenth century man was like a climber making his way at dawn up a mountain flank through the ground fog at the base until suddenly he found himself in the clean air and clear light of early morning. He felt that he had left superstition behind and below him. He was convinced that reason was an instrument that would ultimately enable men to discover the inmost mind of God, conceived of as a Great Engineer and as the Author of Nature. Within less than two centuries after Franklin's kite brought electricity to earth from the storm cloud, reason has enabled men to lay hold upon the elemental electrical energy of the cosmos. Two centuries are but a short time in the history of the race. The buoyant optimism of the Enlightenment has been justified. Men have, in fact, made a beginning in understanding the basic technique of the Cosmic Engineer.

John Locke turned his thought to the problems of man in society. He emphasized the individual man as endowed with reason and with certain natural rights that reason can discover. He pictured the human mind as, at birth, a *tabula rasa* which, as the years pass, gets its configuration and character from the sensations that flow in upon it from the encircling environment. Man, thought Locke and the Enlightenment after him, could manipulate this environment through the use of reason and, by so doing, effect improvement, perhaps perfection, in the quality of men. Locke and his American disciple, Jefferson, thought of this manipulation primarily in political terms. Men of reason by governing themselves could shape conditions to further the general progress. The idea of progress was central to the eighteenth century.

The Enlightenment produced, inevitably, not only a cosmology, the concept of a machine universe functioning perfectly, and a social philosophy, the doctrines of natural rights of environmentalism and progress, but also a religion, the religion of nature. There were many and varied expressions of this religion of nature in the old world and the new. Philip Freneau, lover of the sea, and fiery pamphleteer and poet of the American revolutionary epoch, managed to compress not only the religion but with it the cosmology and the social philosophy of the Enlightenment into a single verse:

> Religion, such as nature taught,
> With all divine perfection suits;
> Had all mankind this system sought
> Sophists would cease their vain disputes,
> And from this source would nations know
> All that can make their heaven below.

Men of the mid-twentieth century look back a little wistfully upon the Enlightenment. So much has happened and so much been learned since Freneau wrote. The world has seemed to grow old. A weary sophistication has replaced that exuberant optimism of two centuries ago. Fear spreads among a conquering generation.

In such an age we rebuild Williamsburg and develop it into an important center of research in the eighteenth century. We write popular and scholarly biographies of Jefferson. And we plan a gigantic publication of all the writings of this latest addition to the galaxy of our greatest folk heroes. Yet to the men of the middle of the twentieth century the doctrine of the perfectibility of human nature seems childishly naïve. Not even John Calvin had a deeper sense than we of the extent and the toughness of evil in the world. Are we then inclined to run away from an uneasy present and to clutch at an optimism made romantic by distance? I think there is more than this in the building of the Jefferson memorial. There are enduring values in the Enlightenment. There is even a kinship between the mid-twentieth century and the eighteenth in America.

The Enlightenment emphasized the individual man. And for this emphasis it was indebted in part to a long Christian tradition of which, in fact, for all its religion of nature, it was a part. It was the individual who had natural rights which the state was created to secure. It was the individual who had reason which entitled him to the dignity of participating in his own government. The eighteenth century man, following the seventeenth century philosophers, thought of government in terms of a social contract. Rousseau brought this concept to its full development. In the early years of the Enlightenment social thinkers in western Europe, under the influence of Newton and of the idea of the cosmos as an infinitely perfect machine, had thought of men as governed by natural law in almost a physical sense. The great German, Immanuel Kant, had moved away from the materialistic tendencies of the early post-Newtonian thinkers. For natural law in a physical sense he had substituted the idea that the substructure of society is made up of the laws of freedom or, as he preferred to call them, moral laws. For Kant the central social fact was the free individual and Kant's theory of history was that it is the struggle to achieve a civil society in which the individual is conceived of as an end in himself and in which the moral law replaces force as the supreme authority. The specific ideas of Kant were not important in America until the nineteenth century. But the drift of American thinking in the second half of the eighteenth century showed many similarities to that of the German philosopher.

Actions are usually more expressive than words of the ruling ideas of an age and place. An episode that took place in 1782 at Newburgh, where Washington had established headquarters, illuminates better than any formal pronouncement the character of American eighteenth century thought. The Revolution was nearly over. Americans looked upon the struggle just ending as a war to preserve the natural rights of men. Not long before, the Commonwealth of Massachusetts had written the doctrine of natural rights into a new constitution. Yorktown in 1781 had brought the fighting to a victorious conclusion, but the peace had not yet been secured. The new Articles of Confederation had drawn the outlines of a confederacy but had failed to establish a central authority that could command the respect of Americans. The Congress of the Confederation, made up for the most part of second-rate politicians whose vision seldom extended beyond the boundaries of their respective states, was without funds or the power to raise the funds to pay the officers who had led the armies of the Revolution through defeat to victory. Many of these were compelled to see their families plunged into want and suffering humiliating hardships. The angry murmurs of men unjustly treated by their government grew in volume until an anonymous paper passed from hand to hand announcing the date of a meeting at which a plan would be presented for a march on the Congress and a demand for justice by organized and armed men before they were stripped of their power by the demobilization of the army. Washington found himself faced with his greatest crisis outside the field of battle.

He was not taken by surprise. Not long before, a spokesman for a group of men who felt that governmental weakness was bringing the country to chaos and disaster had approached him with the suggestion that it was his patriotic duty while he still wore the sword to become the strong man who would lead his demoralized countrymen to peace and prosperity. He had administered to this representative of evil a sharp rebuke. Now he commanded his officers to assemble in the old church at Newburgh. Entering at the designated hour, he stood before them with all the prestige of the victorious chieftain. He called upon them to lay aside their arms and to put their faith in an impotent, drab, and timorous congress:

> Let me conjure you in the name of our common country, as you value your own sacred honor, as you respect the rights of humanity and as you regard the military and national character of America to express your . . . detestation of the man who wishes under any specious pretences to overturn the liberties of our country, and who wickedly attempts to open the floodgates of civil discord and deluge our rising empire with blood.

As significant as Washington's appeal is the fact that his officers heeded his voice. Their sense of the importance of the rights of humanity and of their obligation to secure these rights triumphed over the temptation to appeal to force even in a just cause. In the following year Washington, at the zenith of his power and influence, presented himself to a congress of mediocrities and surrendered the commission their more illustrious predecessors had given him.

The military leader of the Revolution was a man of faith—faith in the reason and in the rectitude of the common men of eighteenth century America. No man of his generation knew his fellow countrymen better. As commanding general Washington had seen them carry through deadly encounters with a stout courage. He had seen them also turn poltroons and run away with scarcely a shot. He had seen them loot the homes of their private enemies. He had watched them desert when the common cause hung in the balance. He had lived with them in camp as they remained steadfast and loyal through the long winter of Valley Forge. Washington knew the strength and the weakness, the stupidities and the wisdom of the everyday American. His thought and theirs were shaped by the same social philosophy. He was willing to trust the nation in the hands of its citizens. On this faith American democratic theory and practice are founded. Behind that faith was the belief in the reality of the rights of humanity and the ultimate efficacy of the moral law.

The men of the Enlightenment thought naturally in terms of universals as well as in terms of free individuals. They spoke of universal natural rights that they conceived to flow from the nature and dignity of man himself. It was the fashion in Europe and even in some quarters in the United States in that uneasy period between the two great world wars to think primarily of men in terms of their organization into rival nation-states. Tribalism in the twentieth century grew to terrifying proportions. There were some, even in America, who denied that the concept of humanity, of man in general, had any utility and who affirmed that nations or races are the ultimates in society. The so-called realists of the 1920's dismissed contemptuously the idea of universal values. They emphasized the particular, especially that particular power structure, the nation-state.

From such a philosophy it was but a step to the doctrine that in the relations between these modern supertribes the only reality is the never-ending struggle for power. Out of such doctrines grew the disaster which recently engulfed us. And from this holocaust our country has emerged possessed of power surpassing anything the world has known—and with that power a gnawing sense of apprehension as to what the consequences of that power may be. It is fitting and a hopeful sign that in such an age we should enshrine in a chaste and simple temple in our national capital the memory of a great champion of the rights of all men. And to put on the walls of that shrine the words of the Squire of Monticello: "Almighty God hath created the mind free. . . . I have sworn upon the altar of God hostility against every form of tyranny over the mind of man." The men of the Enlightenment believed that there are values of universal validity throughout mankind. This doctrine also came from ancient Palestinian tradition. It was an expression, in an age when many parts of the world were little known to Europeans or Americans, of the concept of men as forming for some purposes a single world community. Because we desperately need this concept in the modern world we turn our eyes back to the eighteenth century, when the concept was the beginning of social thinking.

The debt of twentieth century America to that small provincial eighteenth century community scattered along the Atlantic seaboard needs no emphasis. Since Freneau wrote of religion and nature we have passed through the romanticism of the first half of the nineteenth century, the crude materialism of the age of the robber barons and the disillusioned naturalism of the post-Versailles decade. In the 1930's we discovered with Freud that psychological reality, and with Pareto that social reality, lie in part in the irrational. We saw in totalitarian mass movements anti-intellectualism grow into a spurious crusade to bring salvation to the modern age. Tribalism, anti-intellectualism, the worship of naked power—these were devils that entered and threatened to take possession of the edifice of western civilization. At heavy cost they have been, for the moment, at least partially subdued. Now a generation that has concluded the greatest of all wars takes stock. What vestiges of romanticism remained before the invasion of Poland are gone. A stark realism born of fighting on all the continents and all the oceans characterizes the modern mind. Skepticism goes hand in hand with realism. And Fear darkens the outlook of the victors.

Wistfully we look back at the eighteenth century man climbing his mountain slope, looking down on the ground fog of superstition and thrilled with the triumphs that reason had already achieved and the vision of others to come. It is worth recording that the man of the middle-years of the twentieth century has also passed through the fog—the fog of wartime confusion and uncertainties. He has emerged into the clear, hard light of an unlovely day. He has used reason to achieve triumphs of technology and of organization and finally to unlock the elemental energy of the cosmos. He has overthrown the high priests of the worship of naked power and has lifted the burden of militarism from the backs of oppressed and exploited millions. He has begun the hard task of building a new order.

The age of the mid-twentieth century is close kin to that of the Enlightenment. It may, in fact, one day be called in retrospect the New Enlightenment. If our investments in technology and in scientific laboratories have evidential value, we, like the men of the eighteenth century, have put our faith in reason. If our wars of liberation have any meaning, we have put our faith in the reality and the validity of the rights of humanity. We know, as did the men of the eighteenth century, that we are making a new world. And we know far better than did the men of the Enlightenment the evils that must be constantly fought off if we are to make progress. What we do not have is the élan of the young Jefferson writing the Declaration of Independence or the young Washington leading the rebel armies in the fight for liberty. But I venture to suggest that we may have it tomorrow. We are still oppressed with the weariness of years of war. But we are on the threshold of an age whose possibilities for advance are beyond the imagination. I have faith that the collective reason of the peoples of the world will be able to control and to harness for useful purposes the energy which science has loosed. In the midst of dynastic and imperial wars and of political and social revolutions the eighteenth century man held fast to high hope. Can the man who has shared in the prodigious triumphs of the middle years of the twentieth century do less? We are well advanced up the mountain slope. The fatiguing and dangerous trail ahead beckons us!

IV

THE RELIGION OF THE FOUNDING FATHERS

BY

ROBERT C. HARTNETT, S.J., Ph.D.

Lecturer in Political Philosophy, Fordham University

In order to bring our topic into focus, we must define what we mean by the term "religion" and the term "the Founding Fathers."

One might well include under the heading of Founding Fathers at least the thirty-nine signers of the Constitution,[1] and probably the fifty-five signers of the Declaration of Independence. Only six names are repeated in this total of ninety-four names. One would have to include, too, men like John Jay and John Marshall who contributed mightily to the establishment of our political society without having signed either document. The number would run to well over a hundred, too many for us to examine into their religious beliefs even in a much longer paper. The best alternative seems to be to select a few of them for careful analysis.

Among the signers of the Constitution, at least six had so much influence that we must consider them individually. They are George Washington, James Madison, James Wilson, Gouverneur Morris, Alexander Hamilton, and Benjamin Franklin. Two signers of the Declaration only, John Adams and Thomas Jefferson, soon rose to the Presidency. For this and other reasons they also require careful attention.

---

[1] Sixty-five men were appointed as delegates to the Constitutional Convention, three of them to replace men who did not attend. Sixteen attended but did not sign, either because they opposed the Constitution or because they were absent at the end. Ten of the delegates never attended (*Documents Illustrative of the Formation* of the *Union of the American States,* ed. C. C. Tansill, Washington, Government Printing Office, 1927, pp. 85–86).

What do we mean by "religion" in this analysis? I mean belief in the existence of a transcendent Being, endowed with intelligence and free will, Who created the universe, Who governs it by His Providence, and Who will reward and punish human beings according to whether they carry out His will as it is known to them. Such a belief involves, of course, belief in human intelligence capable of grasping with certitude suprasensible realities, in human freedom of choice, and in the immortality of the human spirit.

Writers speak rather loosely of the "deism" of the Founding Fathers. The deistic movement was characterized by a "spirit of criticism aimed at the nature and content of traditional religious beliefs, and the substitution for them of a rationalistic naturalism . . ."[2] Deists were individualistic freethinkers. I think that deism, as distinguished from theism, must be detected by certain recurring symptoms such as intolerance of Revelation and all forms of institutionalized Christianity and the frequent use of such terms as "superstitions," "priestcraft," and "corruptions," in speaking of Catholicism and all forms of Protestantism. Deists had no special respect for Scripture, as they denied its divine inspiration.

Another symptom was this: deists seemed to regard their doctrines as a purely intellectualistic explanation of the universe. They admitted only a *general* Providence by the Creator over His creation, if they admitted anything at all beyond materialism. By excluding *special* Providence, they made intercessory prayer valueless. I think that anyone who believed in a special Providence and who reduced this belief to the concrete by resorting to prayer remained on the orthodox side of deism from traditional theism. Men who were serious enough about religion to pray, usually saw some good in organized religion since it provided for public and private worship.

In any case, it seems to me that the boundary marking off the individualistic and naturalistic rationalism of men who rejected Revelation, the divinely inspired Scriptures in which it was com-

---

[2] Francis Aveling, "Deism," *Catholic Encyclopedia,* New York, The Encyclopedia Press, Special Edition, 1913, IV, pp. 679–683. The author is a trained theologian. Deism ran "its short and violent course" in England through the writings of ten or twelve exponents in the seventeenth and early eighteenth centuries.

municated to men, and institutionalized Christianity by which traditional beliefs were made operative among men, notably through intercessory prayer, from the men who set some real store by these elements of traditional religion, is the most significant division one can make when speaking of the religion of the Founding Fathers. In some men deism is so conservative that it shades off into latitudinarian Christianity. From the point of view of public policy and religious liberty, the decisive difference is that between statesmen who are convinced that the institutionalized forms of religion in their country constitute a menace to national progress and those who are prepared to consider that, for all their real or supposed faults, they are making a real contribution to the national culture.

Like so many members of the "first" families of Virginia, George Washington was a vestryman of the Episcopal Church of Truro Parish (Pohick Church). Although this office admittedly had a semicivil character,[3] all the evidence of Washington's copiously published writings confirms the opinion that he was a sincere believer.

In the French and Indian War, for example, "he issued a standing order for church services on Sundays and saw to it that his troops marched to prayers." He took the same steps to secure the attendance of his Revolutionary troops at divine worship to thank Almighty God for victories and the help necessary to live decently and thus to deserve the support of Heaven in the struggle. After Braddock's defeat, he counted the bullet holes in his coat and acknowledged that a power higher than man had preserved him.[4]

After his marriage, according to the incomplete record of his diaries, he was a more consistent church attendant than before, and his churchgoing became more frequent whenever the country which depended so much on his strength and decisions was faced by periods of special danger.[5] On June 1, 1774, in accordance with resolutions passed in the Virginia Legislature to keep that day, the day the Boston Port Act was to go into effect, as "a day of Fasting, Humilia-

---

[3] William C. Rives, *History of the Life and Times of James Madison*, Boston, Little, Brown and Company, 1859, 2 vols. Second edition, 1866, I, pp. 46 ff.
[4] John C. Fitzpatrick, *George Washington Himself*, Indianapolis, Bobbs-Merrill, 1933, pp. 130–131.
[5] *Ibid.*, p. 131.

tion and Prayer, devoutly to implore the divine interposition for averting the calamity which threatens destruction of our Civil Rights, and the evils of Civil War," Washington went to church and fasted all day.[6]

The same religious attitude looms up in his public addresses. When he laid down his command before Congress at Princeton on August 26, 1783, he took occasion "to express my humble thanks to God and my grateful acknowledgments to my country, for the great and uniform support I received. . . ."[7] In his Inaugural Address of April 30, 1789, he acknowledged the benefits of God's "providential aids" at every step of our formation as an independent nation.[8] The Senate replied that "a review of the many signal instances of divine interposition in favor of this country claims our most pious gratitude. . . ."[9] The tone of Washington's Proclamation of a National Thanksgiving, October 3, 1789, is also very religious.[10]

But his most important public document, from a religious point of view, was his Proclamation of a Day of Public Thanksgiving and Prayer of January 1, 1795. In this he spoke of "our duty *as a people* . . . to acknowledge our many and great obligations to Almighty God . . ."; he recommended religious services "to all *religious societies and denominations,* and to all persons whomsoever . . ."; he urged them to render thanks and "humbly and fervently to beseech the kind Author . . . to *imprint on our hearts* . . . ; *to dispose us to merit* the continuance of His favors . . ."; and "finally, to impart all the blessings we possess, or ask for ourselves, to the *whole family of mankind.*"[11] Washington revealed in this declaration his appreciation

---

[6] Nathaniel Wright Stephenson and Waldo Hilary Dunn, *George Washington,* 2 vols., New York, Oxford University Press, 1940, I, pp. 312-313, and note.

[7] *The Writings of George Washington, 1745-1799,* ed. John C. Fitzpatrick, 39 vols., Washington, Government Printing Office, 1931-1944, XXVII, p. 117.

[8] *Messages and Papers of the Presidents, 1789-1897,* ed. James D. Richardson, Washington, Government Printing Office, 1896, I, p. 52.

[9] *Ibid.,* p. 54.

[10] *Ibid.,* p. 64. That Washington believed in the divinity of Christ is quite clear. In his Circular Letter of Congratulation and Advice to the Governors of the Thirteen States, June 18, 1783, he urged his fellow Americans, with obvious reference to Christ, to practise "the characteristics of the divine author of our religion."

[11] *Ibid.,* pp. 179-180 (italics inserted).

that man was a socioreligious being, that the American people *as such* should give thanks and ask pardon, and that they should do this through existing religious organizations. He also asked God for special illumination, and brought in the concept of merit. It was peculiarly American for him to ask the same blessings for "the whole family of mankind."

When Mrs. Annis Boudinot Stockton wrote that she had imposed upon him, Washington replied playfully that she talked as if he were her father confessor, but that in any case the transgression did not exceed the "venial" kind and that he would absolve her with a light penance to perform.[12] He was on speaking terms with "Romish" practices.

For a religious man of that day and age, Washington had a firm and delicate regard for the rights of others to practice religion in forms with which he did not agree. When he dispatched Colonel Benedict Arnold with one thousand men to penetrate into Canada in 1775, he ordered the troops to avoid all disrespect or contempt of the religion and ceremonies of French Catholics. His order is a model of the statesmanlike tolerance in religious matters which set Washington apart from so many of his contemporaries.[13]

We may accept, then, the judgment of his recent biographer that "those who are familiar with the whole body of his writings know that the [religious] expressions are not perfunctory, but a part of his habit of mind." [14]

John Adams of Massachusetts, signer of the Declaration and our second President, was a Congregationalist. He was so attached to his religion that he resented criticism of the "mild establishment" of Calvinism in his home state.[15] It is easy enough to produce evidence that he was personally a religious man and that as a statesman he

---

[12] Washington to Mrs. Annis Boudinot Stockton, September 2, 1783 (*Writings,* ed. Fitzpatrick, XXVII, pp. 127–128).

[13] Fitzpatrick, *George Washington Himself,* p. 182. *Cf.* p. 165.

[14] Waldo Hilary Dunn in Stephenson and Dunn's *George Washington,* II, pp. 259–260.

[15] *The Works of John Adams, Second President of the United States* ed. C. F. Adams, 7 vols., Boston, Little, Brown, 1865, I, pp. 398–400, (Diary for Sunday, October 9, 1774).

tried to promote the practice of the Christian religion as essential to the social and political well-being of the people of America.

In his *Diary* for the fall of 1774, when he was at Philadelphia for the opening of the Continental Congress, he records his regular attendance at religious services on successive Sundays. He showed great interest in the preachers he heard—Witherspoon, Sprout, Coombe, Duché, Percy, Allison—and compared them with a half dozen Boston preachers. Although he naturally thought the latter superior, except in the case of Duché, he always found something to praise in the sermons he heard. Sometimes he went to services both in the morning and afternoon. He attended not only Congregationalist places of worship, but Presbyterian, Methodist, Quaker, and even Roman Catholic. He was interested in the administration of "the Sacrament" by the Presbyterians and he found the liturgy and appointments in "the Romish chapel" so impressive that he wondered the Reformation had ever succeeded.[16]

We get an even better insight into his religious principles from his public addresses as President. One must remember the circumstances of his administration. The country was alerted for war with France. Adams took the Federalist view that the French Revolution was an attack on Christian principles and institutions. In his Inaugural Address of March 4, 1797, he professed as part of his qualifications to occupy the office vacated by Washington

. . . a love of science and letters and a wish to patronize . . . every *institution* for promoting knowledge, virtue, and *religion* among all classes of people . . . as the only means of preserving our Constitution from its natural enemies.[17]

In a special Proclamation on March 23, 1798, he declared that "as the safety and prosperity of nations ultimately and essentially depend on the protection and the blessing of Almighty God," *the people* owe Him the duty of a *national* acknowledgment. He thereupon appointed

---

[16] *Ibid.*, I, pp. 356–357, 364, 368, 378, 382, 392, 395, 397–400, 401. From August 28th to October 30th he absented himself from Sunday services only twice, October 16th and 30th. He spoke of Mrs. Skippen, the sister of Richard Henry Lee, as "a religious and reasoning lady" (September 3rd, I, p. 363).

[17] *Messages and Papers of the Presidents*, ed. Richardson, I, p. 231 (italics inserted).

May 3rd "as a day of solemn humiliation, fasting, and prayer." He urged all religious congregations to acknowledge their sins and transgressions as individuals and *as a nation,*

> ... beseeching Him at the same time, of His infinite grace, through the *Redeemer of the World,* freely to remit all our offenses, and to incline us by *His Holy Spirit* to that sincere repentance and reformation which may afford us reason to *hope for His inestimable favor* and heavenly benediction.[18]

The dogmatic implications of this public declaration should not be overlooked.

The accent on the social character of religion grew stronger in the remarkable words of his Proclamation of March 6, 1799:

> As no truth is more dearly taught in the Volume of Inspiration ... than that a deep sense and a due acknowledgment of the governing providence of a Supreme Being and of the accountableness of men to Him as the searcher of hearts and righteous distributor of rewards and punishments are conducive equally to the happiness and rectitude of individuals and to the well-being of communities; *as it is also most reasonable in itself that men* who are made capable of social acts and relations, who owe their improvements to the social state, and who derive their enjoyments from it, *should, as a society,* make their acknowledgments of dependence and obligation to Him Who hath endowed them with these capacities and elevated them in the scale of existence by these distinctions. ...

He sets April 25th as a day of solemn "humiliation, fasting, and prayer," and again employs the phrase, "through the Great Mediator and Redeemer...."[19] That the expression of such sentiments found a congenial response can be seen in the reply of the House of Representatives to his Third Annual Message.[20]

The country was wonderfully united in opposition to France in 1798, in contrast to the temporary division of opinion in 1793. But the Federalists were the ones who took specific exception to the anti-

---

[18] *Ibid.*, p. 269 (italics inserted).
[19] *Ibid.*, I, pp. 284–285 (italics inserted).
[20] *Ibid.*, pp. 294–295.

religious crusade of the French Revolutionists. That this alarm sprang from sincere attachment to institutionalized Christianity is further confirmed by an examination of the religious beliefs of Alexander Hamilton.

We have it on the word of Robert Troup, Hamilton's schoolmate at King's College, that the young collegian prayed on his knees every morning and evening and was deeply interested in Christian apologetics. He was, like John Jay, among the New York Anglicans who took the side of the Whigs in favor of the American Revolution. Hamilton inspired and drafted the proclamations of Washington for days of national prayer and thanksgiving. In the rules of behavior he drew up for his son Philip he laid down for Sunday, "Attend the morning church." Like Washington and Adams, he held a firm trust in divine Providence. He believed, and often declared in his State papers, that God blesses a nation in proportion as it adheres, in its public acts, to the divine law of morality and justice.

Two pieces of evidence which reveal Hamilton's religious beliefs deserve special treatment. One is the account of his death by Bishop Moore, who attended him. Hamilton was most anxious to "receive the Sacrament" before he died. Bishop Moore interrogated him regarding his belief in Christ's Redemption, his hope of the Redeemer's grace, and his sorrow for his transgressions. Hamilton's responses satisfied the Bishop. The Bishop's letter giving an account of his last visit to the dying statesman, as well as the Reverend John Mitchell Mason's account of his conversation with Hamilton at the end, may be found at The Grange, Hamilton's home, which still stands on Convent Avenue and 143rd Street in this city.[21]

The other piece of evidence consists of the two paragraphs in Washington's *Farewell Address* on the necessity of morality for civic well-being and necessity of religion as a "prop" to morality. Hamilton—

---

[21] The evidence relating to Hamilton's religious beliefs is given in full in an as yet unpublished dissertation by the Reverend Robert C. Hartnett, S.J., *The National Statesmanship of Alexander Hamilton* (available in the Fordham University Library), New York City, 1946, Part One, Chapter II, pp. 94 ff. Bishop Moore's account is given in Allan McLane Hamilton, *The Intimate Life of Alexander Hamilton*, New York, Charles Scribner's Sons, 1911, p. 406.

and Washington—discountenanced the attempt to establish a lay morality, *morale laïque*. They explicitly rejected the proposition, which is now a part of "the American way," apparently, that education is a sufficient substitute for religion as a means of inculcating morality. That Hamilton composed those two paragraphs without any suggestion in the previous drafts is now beyond question. What is equally interesting is that Hamilton's draft included a strong statement which Washington did not see fit to use. Hamilton's paragraphs ended with the question: "Does it [national morality] not require the aid of a generally received and divinely authoritative religion?"[22]

Allan Hamilton has reproduced a "fugitive scrap of paper" in Alexander Hamilton's apparently youthful handwriting in which the statesman-to-be professed his belief that the history of the Jewish people, as set forth in the Bible, bespoke a providential plan.[23] This is very little, indeed, but it is quite in line with Hamilton's consistent appreciation, in contrast to Jefferson, of the continuity of western culture and his respect for institutions stamped with the approval of the greatest men of our race.

Had James Madison been a stronger character and had the circumstances of his religious and political affiliations been different, he might well have taken a more clear-cut line on the relation of institutionalized religion to public welfare.

Certainly in religious literature he was probably the best read American statesman of his time. He was an Episcopalian. In his youth he read extensively among the great religious writers from the Fathers and the schoolmen onwards, and took minute and elaborate notes on the Gospels and Acts of the Apostles. For examples of his jottings, we may take these two:

Christ's divinity appears by St. John, ch. xx, v. 28.
Resurrection testified and witnessed by the Apostles.
Acts. ch. iv, v. 33.[24]

---

[22] Hamilton's "Original Major Draft," *Washington's Farewell Address* ed. V. H. Paltsits, New York, New York Public Library, 1935, p. 192.
[23] Allan Hamilton, *op. cit.*, p. 21n.
[24] Rives, *History of the Life and Times of James Madison*, I, p. 34n.

Although himself an Episcopalian, Madison as a young man thought he found "pride, ignorance, and knavery among the priesthood," [25] and he vehemently opposed any form of legal establishment of the Episcopalian Church in Virginia and the proposal of a general assessment for religious purposes.[26] A believer in complete religious liberty, he wrote in 1822 that religion had prospered in Virginia far more after the disestablishment than before.[27] He therefore defended his part in the disestablishment as a positive aid to the promotion of traditional religion among the people of Virginia.

Madison's natural theology merits a passing word. The backbone of his religious convictions was the proposition to which he firmly adhered all his days that the existence of God as Creator and Governor of the universe could be proved with certainty from the existence of contingent beings. He was not impressed by criticisms leveled at this proposition.[28]

Further evidence of his interest in traditional Christianity can be seen in the extensive catalogue of volumes he suggested for the Library of the State University of Virginia. He listed a number of volumes of the Fathers of the first five centuries, included the works of St. Thomas, Duns Scotus, and Bellarmine, and took care, when including a volume directed against a traditional Christian doctrine, to include a volume which tried to answer it.[29] When Madison was doing his wide reading in religious literature, he felt that "the defects and mis-

---

[25] Madison to William Bradford, Jr., January 24, 1774, Rives, *op. cit.*, I, p. 44. Rives thought Madison overdrew the picture (*ibid.*, pp. 45–51).

[26] Rives, *op. cit.*, I, pp. 599 ff.; *Letters and Other Writings of James Madison*, Congress edition, 4 vols., New York, R. Worthington, 1884, I, pp. 111, 112, 116, 130, 140, 144, 148, 154–155, 159, 175, 214.

[27] Madison to Edward Livingston, July 10, 1822, *Letters and Other Writings*, III, p. 276.

[28] Madison to Reverend F. Beasley, November 20, 1825, *Letters and Other Writings*, III, pp. 503–504. *Cf.* Madison to Dr. C. Caldwell, November, 1825, *ibid.*, pp. 504–505.

[29] Rives, *op. cit.*, I, Appendix A, pp. 642–644, gives the entire list. Jefferson, who requested the catalogue, said in his letter to Madison of August 8, 1824, that he knew Madison had in his early days bestowed attention on the subject and was acquainted with writers on "religious metaphysics" (*ibid.*). This letter of Jefferson to Madison does not seem to be included in the hitherto published editions of his writings. A new one is forthcoming.

representations of infidels had confirmed him in his religious orthodoxy." [30]

The religious opinions of Gouverneur Morris are not very important. Although he made great contributions to our political foundations, he was an earthy *bourgeois* of a rather skeptical and certainly very sophisticated turn of mind. He seemed to think that belief in a particular Providence was a species of self-love, although at times he succumbed to it. He said he liked real piety, but detested "the Grimace of that which is false." He did attend the services of the Episcopalian church of St. Peter's, Westchester, but his sex morality, at least while he was in Paris, is no credit to him.[31]

He thought religion essential to morality, however.

I believe that Religion is the only solid Base of Morals and that Morals are the only possible support of free governments.

And he sized up the French anti-religious movement in these terms:

But I have lived to see a new religion arise. It consists in a Denial of all Religion and its Votaries have the Superstitions of not being superstitious. They have with this as much zeal as any other Sect and are as ready to lay Waste the World in order to make Proselytes.[32]

Not being of a philosophical or speculative turn of mind, he can probably be put down as a definitely tepid and worldly Christian who, as a statesman, saw that institutionalized Christianity was essential to social order. He was against the establishment of religion on the ground that "God is sufficiently powerful to do His own Business . . ." and favored leaving it "to the Supreme Being to influence the Thoughts [of men] as He may think proper." [33] This declaration is not consistent with disbelief in a particular Providence, but Gouverneur Morris seems not to have bestowed enough thought on religion to have worked out a consistent position.

---

[30] Rives, *op. cit.*, I, pp. 35–36, in a letter to William Bradford, Jr., 1774.
[31] Gouverneur Morris, *A Diary of the French Revolution,* ed. Beatrix Cary Davenport, 2 vols., Boston, Houghton Mifflin, 1939, Introduction, pp. xvii–xx.
[32] *Ibid.*, Morris to Lord George Gordon, Paris, June 28, 1792, II, p. 452.
[33] *Ibid.*, February 28, 1790, I, p. 430.

In James Wilson of Pennsylvania we come upon a statesman who, in my opinion, rose head and shoulders above all his contemporaries as a political philosopher.[34] Unfortunately, it is impossible to describe his religious beliefs in detail. His life and letters have never been published, although they have been prepared in manuscript for the purpose.[35] We must therefore rely on his public lectures on law and on his general political essays.[36] For our present object these really suffice.

A native of Scotland, Wilson was a Presbyterian. But as he rose to prominence in Philadelphia he identified himself with the Episcopalians. This shift is not surprising, as his political philosophy and indeed, his total philosophy, have much in common with that of Hooker and even, as Mr. Randolph Adams has noted, with that of St. Thomas Aquinas.[37]

Wilson's religious beliefs were to a large extent traditionally Christian. He took the Sacred Scriptures at their face value as the Word of God, and the words of Christ as infallible.[38] He believed in the original state of justice and the fall of man.[39] He accepted the existence of angels and what he called the glorious immortality of "the souls of the just, made perfect."[40] That he believed in a particular Providence and in the value of intercessory prayer becomes an inevitable inference from his unhesitating acceptance of New Testament Christianity whole and entire. His total philosophy of man, as an individual and as a member of society, puts him in the scholastic tradition.[41]

His appreciation of the social nature of man and of the role of institutions naturally made him a friend of organized religion. But

---

[34] Randolph Adams marveled that Wilson's writings had not received the attention they deserved (*Selected Political Essays of James Wilson*, ed. Randolph Adams, New York, Alfred A. Knopf, 1930, "Introduction," p. 3).

[35] *Ibid.*, p. 4.

[36] *The Works of James Wilson*, ed. James DeWitt Andrews, 2 vols., Chicago, Callaghan and Company, 1896.

[37] *Selected Political Essays*, pp. 7–8.

[38] *Works*, I, pp. 31, 91, etc.

[39] *Ibid.*, p. 31.

[40] *Ibid.*, p. 49.

[41] *Ibid.*, Chapter VI, "Of Man as an Individual," and Chapter VII, "Of Man as a Member of Society."

what distinguishes Wilson from his contemporaries is his grasp of traditional metaphysics. His attack on Locke's theory of ideas and the two opposite philosophies to which it gave rise—skepticism and philosophical idealism—would do credit to Maritain, if not to the founder of Thomism himself.[42]

Compared to the systematic and consistent profundity of the writings of James Wilson, those which Thomas Jefferson has left us strike the student as an ideological crazy quilt. He insisted, of course, that *he* was a "real Christian," that is, a disciple of Jesus as Jefferson understood the teachings of Jesus.[43] The question is, how did Jefferson understand those teachings?

A recent specialist on the subject of Jefferson's philosophy has termed him a "conservative materialist." [44] The designation is justified by the evidence of Jefferson's letters. He declared that God was "an ethereal gas," and that this was the teaching of "the ancient fathers generally of the first three centuries." [45]

But Jefferson was not only a patristic scholar—of sorts. He was also a textual critic of the New Testament. He set out to judge for himself what parts of the New Testament embodied the genuine teachings of Jesus and what parts represented later accretions. His method was extremely simple. He selected the teachings which appealed to him because of their moral simplicity and arranged them in what is now known quite properly as *Thomas Jefferson's Bible*. He said that he got them all into "an octavo of forty-six pages, of pure and unsophisticated doctrines." These were as easily distinguished "as diamonds in a dunghill" from what he called "the *deliria* of crazy imaginations," referring to the theology of St. Athanasius, no less.[46]

---

[42] *Ibid.*, Chapter VI, pp. 233–243.

[43] Jefferson to Charles Thompson, January 9, 1816, *The Writings of Thomas Jefferson*, ed. A. E. Bergh and A. A. Lipscomb, 20 vols., Washington, The Thomas Jefferson Memorial Association, 1903–1905, XIV, p. 385. *Cf.* the same to Benjamin Rush, April 21, 1803 (*ibid.*, X, p. 380).

[44] Adrienne Koch, *The Philosophy of Thomas Jefferson*, New York, Columbia University Press, 1943, p. 34.

[45] Jefferson to John Adams, August 15, 1820, *Writings*, XV, pp. 274–275.

[46] Jefferson to John Adams, October 13, 1813, in *The Complete Jefferson*, ed.

Jefferson's self-assurance, which carried him so far as to make himself out a first-class expert in the assaying of theological diamonds that he could write off the great Greek genius as an imbecile, is characteristic. Newman has written something about those who "see no difficulties in the most difficult subjects."

The Sage of Monticello wrote one lady that he had been variously charged with being "atheist, deist, or devil," and he countered these accusations by declaring that it was nobody's business what he was, religion being "a concern purely between our God and our consciences for which we were accountable to Him. . . ." [47] He was a fanatical individualist who avowed: "If I could not go to heaven but with a party, I would not go there at all." [48] Quite a few of his contemporaries thought that this self-chosen alternative would have suited him properly. Although he dissociated himself from all sects, he declared himself an Epicurean in philosophy, adding that he meant Epicurean in the genuine and original sense.[49] He was not a crude materialist, in other words, but a comparatively refined one. But he insisted that he was a materialist, according to the "genuine" teachings of Jesus, of course.

Indeed, the clue to Jefferson's religious beliefs seems to be this intemperate individualism. In contrast with all the great Founders whose religious attitudes we are canvassing, Jefferson detested every form of organized religion, although he attended church. He threw overboard everything remotely resembling Revelation. He could not mention religion without emotional outbursts about "Platonizing priests" and their endless catalogue of alleged corruptions and deceptions. One gets the impression that whenever Jefferson, whose mind loved what was simple, came upon any doctrine which he found difficulty in grasping, he dismissed it as a "Platonic" corruption. The

---

Saul K. Padover, New York, Duell, Sloan, & Pearce, 1943, pp. 950–951; and the same to Dr. Benjamin Waterhouse, June 26, 1822, *ibid.*, pp. 956. These last two letters are in his *Writings*, XIII, p. 390, and XV, pp. 383–385.

[47] Jefferson to Mrs. Samuel Harrison Smith, August 6, 1816, *Writings*, XV, pp. 59–61.
[48] Jefferson to Francis Hopkinson, March 13, 1789, *ibid.*, VII, p. 300.
[49] Jefferson to William Short, October 31, 1819, *ibid.*, XV, p. 219.

best he could make out of the Trinitarian doctrine was that its adherents believed in three Gods.[50]

His manhandling of the New Testament shows what scant respect he had for the sacred writings of Christianity. Besides, he swallowed uncritically the sensist psychology which came out of England and France in the eighteenth century.[51] For these reasons it is impossible to regard him as other than a deist, steeped in naturalism, of materialistic leanings.[52]

It would be a mistake, of course, to take his philosophical and theological opinions as seriously as he took them himself. It seems unfair to ignore them, however, as ideological historians often do when they assume that the Federalists hated Jefferson because he loved "the people." They also hated him because he regarded as puerile "nonsense" the Christian beliefs which his opponents held sacred. For a man who preached tolerance, his fanatical intolerance of revealed and institutionalized religion is amazing. But it is not surprising that the Federalists reciprocated the contempt in which Jefferson held them, especially since he never wrote a line which showed any real talent for philosophical or theological thinking.[53]

When we turn to Benjamin Franklin we notice immediately how sharp is the contrast between his urbanity and respect for the beliefs of others, and Jefferson's high-strung bitterness. Young Ben was baptized in Old South Church, Boston, being the son of Nonconformist parents.[54] The effect of reading controversial arguments *against* deism was to make the young man a deist himself, but when he was wronged by his freethinking friends, ". . . I began to suspect that this doctrine,

---

[50] Jefferson to Dr. Benjamin Waterhouse, June 16, 1822, *ibid.*, XV, pp. 383–385.

[51] Jefferson to John Adams, August 15, 1820, *Writings*, XV, p. 274. Miss Koch has documented the French influence very carefully. Priestley was the chief English influence, together with Locke.

[52] Abundant references to Jefferson's religious beliefs may be found in *The Complete Jefferson*, ed. Padover, and in *Democracy By Thomas Jefferson*, ed. Saul K. Padover, New York, D. Appleton–Century, 1939, Chapter VI and index, besides in Miss Koch's work.

[53] Charles A. Beard has adduced abundant evidence to show that Jefferson was not even a tolerably consistent political thinker, either, *Economic Origins of Jeffersonian Democracy*, New York, Macmillan, 1915, Chapter XIV.

[54] Carl Van Doren, *Benjamin Franklin*, New York, Viking Press, 1938, p. 7.

tho' it might be true, was not very useful." This new insight led the very practical young Ben to wonder whether some fallacy had not insinuated itself into his earlier reasoning by which he had adopted the pleasure-pain criterion of right and wrong.[55] Franklin was able to submit the experience of his very full life to shrewd analysis.

He has summed up for us himself the general religious attitude he held throughout his life:

I had been religiously educated as a Presbyterian; and tho' some of the dogmas of that persuasion, such as *the eternal decrees of God, election, reprobation, etc.,* appeared to me unintelligible, others doubtful, and I early absented myself from the public assemblies of the sect, Sunday being my studying day, *I was never without some religious principles*. I never doubted, for instance, the existence of the Deity; that He made the world, and govern'd it by His Providence; that the most acceptable service of God was the doing good to man; that our souls are immortal; and that all crime will be punished, and virtue rewarded, either here or hereafter. *These I esteemed the essentials of every religion; and, being to be found in all religions we had in our country, I respected them all,* tho' with different degrees of respect, as I found them more or less mixed with other articles, which, without any tendency to inspire, promote, or confirm morality, serv'd principally to divide us, and to make us unfriendly to one another.[56]

Although the "essentials" of Franklin's religion were the hall-mark of many deists, two elements in his religious convictions set him off from that group. The first was his friendly bearing toward organized religion. He always retained a sense of the propriety of public worship, and he consistently contributed his "mite" to the erection of new churches. He even paid his annual subscription for the support of the only Presbyterian minister in Philadelphia, and owned that had this preacher given better sermons, he (Franklin) might have continued to attend services regularly. Unlike the typical freethinker, the great statesman was ready to acknowledge that his conduct in absenting himself from the meetings of his sect for the reason given might have

---

[55] Benjamin Franklin, *Autobiography,* New York, Random House, Modern Library edition, 1944, pp. 8-11.
[56] *Ibid.,* p. 21 (italics inserted after first set). *Cf.* p. 41.

been "blamable." [57] Franklin was too social-minded to object to going to heaven "with a party" if, in the dispensation of divine Providence, that was the way to get there. He saw nothing contrary to human nature in such an arrangement.

Secondly Franklin found that his program of moral perfection proved more arduous than he had anticipated; so he added a prayer of his own composition to solicit the assistance of God, "the fountain of wisdom." He always carried this prayer with him on his travels, and ascribed to his system of daily examination of conscience and resort to intercessory prayer, "with the blessing of God," the happiness which attended him into his seventy-ninth year, when he wrote his *Autobiography*.[58] If we were right in assigning as a symptom of deism a lack of interest in religion as a concrete guide to conduct and especially a lack of belief in special Providence, implying disbelief in the value of intercessory prayer, then Franklin on these counts, too, was no deist.

At the end of his life he was asked about his religious beliefs. Concerning Christ's divinity, he said that he had "some doubts . . . , though it is a question I do not dogmatize upon, never having studied it. . . ."

> I see no harm, however, in its being believed, if that belief has the good consequences, as it probably has, of making his doctrines more respected and better observed . . . [59]

Franklin's interest in religion was almost exclusively moral, not doctrinal. He was not much of a philosopher or theologian. But he has engraved on the annals of our history one of its most noble religious declarations. When the debates in the Constitutional Convention had become hopelessly snarled, it was the venerable figure of Franklin who made the following proposal:

> In this situation, groping as it were in the dark to find political truth . . . how has it happened, Sir, that we have not hitherto once thought of humbly applying to the Father of lights to illuminate our understanding?

---

[57] *Ibid.*, pp. 91-92.
[58] *Ibid.*, pp. 92-101, 107.
[59] Franklin to Ezra Stiles, March 9, 1790, *The Writings of Benjamin Franklin*, ed. Albert Henry Smith, 10 vols., New York, Macmillan, 1905-1907, X, pp. 84-85.

This was a strange intervention from a man alleged to have been a deist. He went on:

> In the beginning of the Contest with G. Britain, when we were sensible of danger we had daily prayers in this room for the divine protection.—Our prayers, Sir, were heard, & they were graciously answered. All of us who were engaged in the struggle must have observed frequent instances of a superintending providence in our favor. . . .

Then he came to the point:

> And have we now forgotten this powerful friend? or do we imagine that we no longer have need of his assistance? I have lived, Sir, a long time, and the longer I live, the more convincing proofs I see of this truth—*that God Governs in the affairs of men*. And if a sparrow cannot fall to the ground without His notice, is it probable that an empire can rise without His aid? We have been assured, Sir, in the sacred writings, that "except the Lord build the House they labour in vain who build it." I firmly believe this; and I also believe that without His concurring aid we shall succeed in this political building no better than the Builders of Babel.[60]

Franklin therefore moved that "one or more of the Clergy of this City" be requested to lead prayers in the Convention every morning. The members did not take up this suggestion, Hamilton and others fearing that to adopt the practice at that stage would be to advertise abroad the *impasse* to which they had come. But the circumstance of its not being acted upon in no wise detracts from the significance of Franklin's plea, for it breathes a profound spirit of Christian faith, which was conspicuously one of the wellsprings of the early American achievement.

Since we have limited ourselves to the outstanding personalities in this brief canvass of the religious beliefs of the Founding Fathers, a few words should be added about some of the men we have passed

---

[60] *The Debates in the Federal Convention of 1787*, by James Madison, ed. Gaillard Hunt and James Scott Brown, June 28th, in *Documents Illustrative of the Formation of the Union of the American States*, ed. C. C. Tansill, Washington, Government Printing Office, 1927, pp. 295–296. Roger Sherman and Edmund Randolph seconded the motion.

over. Charles Carroll of Carrollton was a Roman Catholic, although possibly not always a practicing one. Daniel Carroll and Thomas Fitzsimons, both signers of the Constitution, were, I believe, good Catholics. John Jay was prominent as an Anglican, a group to which Rufus King also belonged. In fact, Jefferson assailed his opponents as being members of the "Anglican monarchical aristocratical party."[61] Dr. Witherspoon, President of Princeton and a signer of the Declaration, was, of course, a Presbyterian. The catalogue could be almost indefinitely lengthened and one would find that an overwhelming preponderance of the Founding Fathers were identified with one or other form of organized Christianity. One has to go outside the ranks of Founding Fathers to find freethinkers to accompany Jefferson (if he was wholly a freethinker), for instance, men like John Taylor of Carolina, probably, and Thomas Paine. The fact that the latter were so vocal should not distract us from seeing that they were pitifully few and that none of them had a hand in the framing of the Constitution.

Conclusions

Among the leading statesmen who established the United States of America as a national political reality one finds varying shades of Christian orthodoxy. Washington, Hamilton, John Adams (at least while his political influence amounted to anything) and James Wilson were sincere Christians who believed in Revelation, inspiration of the Sacred Scriptures, and church organization. They believed in public worship and the efficacy of intercessory prayer. They stood their ground without yielding to the spirit of eighteenth century rationalism or materialism. Although Madison crossed swords with the Episcopalian Church on the question of legal establishment, he, too, was dominantly *traditional* in his religious outlook.

Even Gouverneur Morris took the side of institutionalized Christianity. Like his fellow Federalists, he held that morality was the

---

[61] Jefferson to Phillip Mazzei, April 24, 1796, *The Life and Selected Writings of Thomas Jefferson*, ed. Adrienne Koch and William Peden, New York, Modern Library, Random House, 1944, p. 537.

backbone of a republican form of government, and that religion was the backbone of morality. Franklin inclined to the same position, though not so actively.

Only Jefferson bore the earmarks of deism: the rejection of Revelation and of the inspiration of Scripture, a ferocious individualism in all that concerned religion, and a fanatical opposition to what he kept calling the "corruptions" of Christianity at the hands of the clergy. Of all these great men, he alone surrendered without a fight to the sensism of Locke, Hume, and Priestley, and that long after he drafted the Declaration. That landmark in western political thought gave undying expression to the theistic and indeed Christian political philosophy which was common to men of the revolutionary generation in America. It is to Jefferson's credit that he never claimed originality for its substance, though he was rightfully proud of the literary form he imparted to it.[62] It should never be forgotten that Jefferson himself took no part in the framing of the Constitution. It was the handiwork of men who thought quite differently from him in politics as well as in religion.

Although Jefferson was not entirely secularist in his point of view,[63] he gave momentum to the movement of secularization, especially in his program of public education. Can a secularized people understand and carry on the democratic system of government which was informed by the religious beliefs of its founders? That is a question disturbing the minds of many thoughtful Americans today. To those who fear that they cannot, the knowledge that "the American way" was blazed by believers should bring courage to keep alive in the souls of Americans the flame of religious faith which lighted the torch of American democracy from the beginning.

[62] Jefferson to James Madison, August 30, 1823, *Writings,* M.E., XV, p. 462; same to Henry Lee, May 8, 1825 *ibid.,* XVI, p. 118. As he disclaimed credit for the ideas expressed and still prided himself on the authorship, it was for the literary style.
[63] George Harmon Knoles, "The Religious Ideas of Thomas Jefferson," *Mississippi Valley Historical Review,* XXX, September, 1943, pp. 187–204, substantiates the account of Jefferson's religious beliefs given in this paper, but calls attention to the fact that he attended church and contributed to the support of churches of more than one denomination, p. 188.

V

THE IDEAL OF RELIGIOUS LIBERTY—
A PROTESTANT VIEW

BY

O. FREDERICK NOLDE, Ph.D.

Professor of Religious Education, Lutheran Theological Seminary

The ideal of religious liberty must be conceived in terms of man's experience in society. Definitions of religious liberty and of the grounds whereon it rests may be set forth in abstract forms. Agreements among religious groups to permit the attainment of their separate aims and to protect the freedom of the individual may be couched in careful language, and with praiseworthy purposes. The laws of national states and of a world organization may be drafted to safeguard man against coercion and discrimination. While all these have profitable place, the ideal of religious liberty is achieved or thwarted in the stream of living. Any description of the ideal must find its focus there. Ethical, theological, social, and political considerations cannot be disregarded. They are important. They will make their significant contribution only when each is appropriately related to the highly complex and variegated experience of man in society.

Viewed as an ideal to be achieved in the stream of living, religious liberty does not stand by itself. It is indissolubly related to all other human rights and fundamental freedoms. The exercise of religious liberty, in its fullest sense, becomes possible only when accompanied by freedoms of speech, press, assembly, and the like. The right of conviction and expression in religious matters loses much of its meaning unless accompanied by the right of belief and expression in social, political, economic, and cultural relationships.

When religious liberty, with its close relation to all human rights, is located in experience, attention is immediately centered upon the contemporaneous scene. Convictions of long standing find particular meaning in present circumstances. Four motives combine to prompt study and level-headed activity toward the end that religious freedom may be preserved and extended in our own time.

First, there are inalienable rights of man. As the world comes to be more closely knit together, our sympathies are sharpened with those who are in suffering or distress of any kind, wherever they may be. We cannot rest satisfied so long as our brothers—brothers in faith or brothers in humanity—are denied rights which the dignity of man as the highest of God's creation prescribes. *Because we believe in man's inalienable rights, we seek the ideal of religious liberty in society.*

Second, religious freedom holds a significant place in our democratic tradition and life. Democratic practice has permitted the individual citizen to make his own decisions in matters of religion and has allowed him wide liberty in shaping his behavior by conscience. *Because we believe in a democratic way of life and because we humbly desire that the good therein be made available to the people of this and following generations, we seek the ideal of religious liberty in society.*

Third, a brotherhood of nations, cooperating for their mutual well-being and advancement, represents not only a Christian ideal but an ideal which must commend itself to all men of good will. So long as human rights are suppressed, conditions favorable to anarchy and disorder will prevail. So long as freedom of religion is denied, man's conscience cannot operate adequately in criticism or in commendation of national and international policies. *Because we believe in the goal of world order and security, we seek the ideal of religious liberty in society.*

Fourth, the Christian recognizes as imperative the commission to preach the Gospel of Jesus Christ to all men everywhere. Acceptance of the Christian message by those who hear it is a matter of personal faith and any effort to force acceptance is contrary to the very nature of the Gospel. The Christian's commission can and, if there is no other way, must be obeyed in the face of opposition and persecution. We are convinced, however, that among the inalienable rights of man is the right to hear in order that he may decide for himself what his response shall be. *Because we believe that all men should have the opportunity to hear and to accept the Gospel, we seek the ideal of religious liberty in society.*

Impelled by these motives, we must direct our efforts toward the refinement of human relationships. For relationships constitute the reality of life in which religious liberty may be achieved. To move toward the ideal we must first of all gain a clear understanding of what man as a member of the human family needs in order that he may have religious freedom and of what man, in the process of exercising religious freedom, owes to himself and to the human family. We must then view the relationships among religious groups, composed of individuals with similar convictions, to determine what freedoms they may rightfully exercise and what obligations they are required to meet in the interest of religious liberty for all. Thereafter, we must define the necessary interplay between the individual and the religious group, on the one hand, and social institutions and governments, both national and international, on the other. The development of these considerations will reflect a Protestant point of view in so far as Christian faith is concerned. In so far as the development concerns the functioning of man in society, it approaches validity only by being acceptable in circles beyond the Protestant Christian community.

I. *The ideal of religious liberty is achieved in society when the individual, by freely but responsibly combining his own resources with the spiritual inheritance of the human race, may seek the highest development of his own personality and, at the same time, contribute most richly to the well-being of his fellow men.*

This proposition centers attention upon *individual* man in society. He is one of a vast host of men living on the face of this earth—some two billion, two hundred million. In looking at him, the Christian sees what the biologist, the sociologist, and the psychologist see. But he finds something more than human science alone can discern. To the Christian, every man on the contemporaneous scene is the concern of an eternal God. Beset by the demands of living in a complex world, man may yield to confusion or lower self-interest; or, utilizing most effectively the resources which God has placed at man's disposal, he may become "a living sacrifice, holy and acceptable unto God." Whether viewed from the standpoint of science or of an eternal dispensation, to every man is given an appointed potentiality. The realization of his potentiality rests with man and with society. Every man ought to have the chance to become what God intended him to be. Upon society rests the responsibility to give every man that chance.

To realize the opportunity which is due him, man must bring into proper balance the diverse and somewhat contradictory factors which operate in his growth. These factors find parallels in the paradoxes of life. The individual must be in a position to act freely, but he must also act responsibly. He must use his own resources, but he must combine them with the spiritual inheritance of the human race. He must seek the highest development of his own personality, but he must also seek to contribute most richly to the well-being of his fellow men. These factors, which on the surface appear to be contradictory, must become complementary. This is man's responsibility. The ideal of religious liberty requires that he be given an opportunity to meet it.

Before proceeding to consider what man needs in order that he may be free in matters of religious conviction and expression, it is well to recognize quite honestly that in some respects man can never be free. He is born into this world with the limitations of biological inheritance. Not only in physical structure, but also in mental and emotional competence, his boundaries are fixed. To say that all men should be free does not imply that all men are to be equal. Freedom is forced to operate within the limits of each person's biological inheritance. Man is also born into this world with the limitations of environmental inheritance—religious, cultural, political, economic, social. While these are not perforce permanently binding, they cannot be ignored. Man may rise above the environment of his birth and childhood. Nevertheless, the obvious reality of environment—as a minimum influential and as a maximum determining—makes it impossible to hold all-inclusive claims to religious liberty. Another limitation—to be sure, of a far different kind—needs to be added to those imposed by heredity and environment. It grows out of the point of view with which we insist that religious liberty shall be sought for all men. The freedom we seek is not intended to open an inviting door to the lowest levels of conviction and action. Rather, it is intended to encourage an achievement of the highest that is possible for each individual and for the world society of which he is a member. Religious liberty is ideally achieved only when faith and love combine to make a free man his brother's servant. This limitation, while not inherent in the nature of man and of society, is one which we insistently impose upon man's freedom by virtue of the Christian view with which we approach the issues of religious liberty.

Here, then, is man in society with his personal and social limitations and with an imposed ethical obligation to himself and to his fellow men. What does he need in order that he may be in a position to exercise the religious freedom which is his right? To answer this question, the broad functions which man must be free to perform are sketched. No effort at defense is attempted. A brief discussion of each function is intended to bring to light the completing factors which are necessary to make the freedom personally possible and the limiting factors which are necessary to make the freedom socially beneficial.

1. *Man is his innermost, personal life should be free to determine his own beliefs.* Here is involved that aspect of the conscience which touches the individual alone—the operation of conscience as it was previously formed and the shaping of conscience in the contacts of life. Belief grows out of voluntary acceptance and therefore cannot be the result of compulsion or force. It is frequently claimed that freedom of conscience, in so far as it concerns only individual beliefs and not social actions, cannot be denied. This is untrue. For, while a person is free to believe as he sees fit within the scope of the information at his disposal, the kind and the amount of information open to him decidedly limit the decisions to which he commits himself.

A first requirement for freedom of belief therefore is the right of access to information. To say that an individual may believe as he desires and at the same time to prevent him from coming into contact with ideas to which he may react is an empty gesture. The opportunity to hear must be the forerunner of acceptance or rejection. Freedom of access to information should be sought for all men with a clear understanding of its reasonable limitations. Parents have the right to determine the kind of religious influence to which their children shall be exposed during childhood. A religious group has the right to determine the kind of beliefs and action it seeks to cultivate, subject to a recognition of the rights of other religious groups and to the claims of the larger community to which it belongs. A nation, with representative government, may determine its policies and practices in the light of the religious outlook which at any time is predominant in its constituency, provided its government permits criticism from its own constituency and from peoples of other countries. Neither the religious organization nor the state has an obligation to *provide* information beyond that which it has customarily made available except when a consistently open-minded study of "foreign" points of view reveals a worth previously unavailable to its constituency. Both have a responsibility to *permit* the mature individual to relate himself to sources of information in such a way as to allow personal decision and belief.

If the right of access to information as a first requirement for freedom of belief is to be personally and socially beneficial, the individual, in exercising his right, must meet related requirements. His mind must be open to entertain new points of view, or, when dissatisfied with beliefs he holds, he must actually seek additional information. In the process, he must be held free to change his beliefs. He must use judgment in appraising the information to which he has access or he must rely upon the judgment of others in whom he has confidence. In the process of reaching decisions, he must consciously take into account his higher self-interests and the implications of his beliefs for the well-being of his fellow men.

2. *Man in his innermost, personal life should be free to enjoy the fruits of his belief*. Here is an area where the individual can enjoy his freedom to the utmost. A Christian description of the experience may be given in the words of Galatians 5:22, 23: ". . . The fruit of the Spirit is love, joy, peace, longsuffering, gentleness, goodness, faith, meekness, temperance; against such there is no law." The only serious obstacle which arises to interfere with this enjoyment is the impossibility of access to information which a person considers necessary to the refinement, strengthening, or modification of his belief. While no force external to the individual can grant or deny freedom of personal

enjoyment, it must be included to make the pattern of individual religious liberty complete.

3. *Man should be free to join with those who hold similar beliefs with a view to carrying on such activities as do not involve direct participation by others who believe differently.* Freedom to organize with people on the basis of common beliefs should carry with it freedom to worship according to conscience, freedom to preach, freedom to educate members of the group and their children, freedom of fellowship and service. The rights of the individual must then be extended to the group. Pursuit of the group's activities will require that it be granted, through its members, freedom of speech and of press; freedom of organization and of public meeting; and freedom to acquire and hold such property as may be necessary to corporate life.

In exercising his freedom to join with others who hold similar beliefs and in becoming party to their activities, the individual must be alert to implications for himself, for his children, and for the broader society in which the group moves. On grounds of personal belief or on grounds of community good, he should always have the right of withdrawal from a religious group without suffering loss of any privileges beyond those which rightfully attached to his previous membership.

4. *Man should have freedom to express his belief in a social and political group where differing religious convictions are held.* Many communities are not characterized by cultural or religious homogeneity. The more closely the nations and peoples of the world become interknit, the more diverse will the complexion in communities tend to become. Freedom of conscience in its wider sense demands that man as an individual—whether he stands alone or as a member of a religious group—have the opportunity to express his beliefs in all social and political relationships. Objectively conceived, this gives the proponent of one religious view no position of advantage over the proponent of another religious view. The strength of any religious conviction must ultimately be found in the truth upon which it rests. A social or political community may thwart the effective application of a truth. When the ideal of religious liberty is spun out in society,

that risk must be run. Notwithstanding, the individual must be free to express his belief. This freedom is his right. It is also an imperative for social growth. Progress is made not so much by adjusting the conduct of an individual to the accustomed standard of the community as by adjusting the conduct of the community to a standard higher than that which it had previously accepted.

In order that this freedom may be real, man needs freedom of speech as involved in the spoken word and in publication. Free speech, by way of criticism or commendation, is essential in order that man may make his contribution in shaping the conduct of the community. It is also essential to enable him to propagate his own beliefs; or, looking at progagation from the side of the recipient, freedom of speech is necessary in order that others than the speaker may have access to the information and beliefs which he holds. The community in which this freedom to propagate beliefs is to operate must not be narrowly conceived in terms of municipality or nation; it must move from the smallest social unit ultimately to include the world community of nations. In addition to freedom of speech, the individual should have the right to govern his conduct in the political and social group by conscience. The opportunity to act in accordance with belief is indispensable in full freedom.

Individual freedom of speech and action in a society of differing religious convictions becomes possible only when social and political institutions play their part. The right of man to determine what he says and what he does by conscience must first of all be a recognized premise for interrelationships in the community. Responsible people in social and political institutions must be disposed as a matter of principle to heed the stand which the individual has taken and to appraise fairly the conviction on which the stand is based. They must grant immunity from discrimination and from legal disability on grounds of a person's conviction at least to the point where recognized community interests are adversely affected. Their judgment of what actually constitutes community interests may be warped, and progress may be accordingly retarded; but their judgment, in so far as it reflects the will of the people whom they represent, is the only criterion by which they can shape policy and practice.

To this situation, the individual must bring a measure of competence to justify his freedom. Obviously, he must recognize that other people who hold different beliefs have the same right of expression which he claims for himself. He needs the courage of his convictions. He must have respect for authority even when his conscience forces him to take issue with the positions advocated by authority. The representation of his beliefs should be accompanied by an open-mindedness which will make him seek to appreciate other views and by a willingness to modify his position when justified. With full recognition of the complementary rights of the individual and of society, he must be ready, if need be, to suffer persecution and deprivation to be true to his conscience.

In directing our study to man in society, we have attempted a functional analysis of the ideal of religious liberty for the individual. (1) Man in his innermost, personal life should be free to determine his own beliefs. (2) Man in his innermost, personal life should be free to enjoy the fruits of his belief. (3) Man should be free to join with those who hold similar beliefs with a view to carrying on such activities as do not directly affect the lives of others who believe differently. (4) Man should have freedom to express his beliefs in a social and political group where differing religious convictions are held. The effort to place in proper functional relationship the various factors which may foster religious liberty in a complex society, has forced an anticipation of factors which fall appropriately in the functional consideration of religious groups, and social and political institutions. This need in no sense be disturbing. In fact, it is unavoidable when the ideal of religious liberty is viewed in the stream of living.

II. *The ideal of religious liberty is achieved in society when any religious group, fully recognizing the rights of other religious groups and the requirements of social well-being in a community, may freely but responsibly pursue its chosen activities among its own members and, at the same time, proclaim its way of life to others for their acceptance or rejection.*

In the make-up of contemporary society, whether viewed on a world scale or in the narrower compasses of national states, appears a multitude of different religious groups. Humanly viewed, they have come into existence because they came to profess distinctive beliefs, because they were convinced of the inadequacy of formerly held beliefs, or because they viewed earlier beliefs as inaccurate. In many instances, the conviction of divinely revealed truth attaches to origin. At times, national and racial affiliation has been instrumental in the process of formation. Most religious groups, while influenced strongly by tradition, justify their continued separate existence on the ground that they advocate a distinctive interpretation of a truth which in its general form is held by other groups or on the ground that they alone hold and proclaim the highest truth which has been divinely revealed and humanly apprehended. Honesty compels us to recognize that each group either believes that it alone is right or that it is more right than any other group. Each group, therefore, seeks to pursue a program of life that will not only affect its own constituency but will also win new adherents to its faith. The intensity of the effort at self-propagation and growth varies considerably. Nevertheless, it must be assumed as valid that when an individual or a group holds convictions strongly enough, the desire to have others hold similar beliefs is inevitable.

To achieve the ideal of religious liberty for the individual, the claims of competing or cooperating religious groups must be adjusted. Two areas of possible conflict should here be noted: man in relation to various religious groups and the religious groups in relation to each other. How can the rights of man be respected? How can any religious group with firm convictions allow freedom to other religious groups with different convictions? Protestant Christianity with its central emphasis upon the Gospel need have no difficulty in resolving these apparent contradictions.

As far as the individual is concerned, a starting point lies in the recognition of man's right of access to information. In obeying the commission to preach the Gospel to all men everywhere, a commission which roots in the experience of the earliest Christian community, the Christian Church places at man's disposal the information it possesses. The evangelical conception of the message thus proclaimed prohibits compulsion or the use of force. Man is free to accept or to reject. Individual freedom of religion is not impaired.

In determining relations among religious groups, imperfection in man and in society must be taken into account. In the provisional dispensation which imperfection establishes, many different religious points of view will inevitably be held and proclaimed. When Protestant Christianity claims freedom for itself it must also grant freedom to others. It can do this and remain faithful to its trust only because it has faith in the fundamental correctness of its message and confidence that truth will ultimately be victorious. While it credits other religious groups with equal sincerity, it will jealously guard its heritage and seek continuously to refine that heritage with the help of God. It will use all its resources to place what it cherishes at the disposal of all men. At the same time, it must grant equal right and freedom to other religious groups. To the extent that its conduct exemplifies this point of view, it can reasonably expect that other religious groups will proceed with similar animation.

The freedoms claimed for religious groups are rooted in the freedoms claimed for the individual. The individual should have the right to organize with others. As he affiliates himself with those who have similar convictions, his individual rights become corporate rights. Freedom for the religious group should be interpreted to include freedom to worship according to conscience and to bring up children in the faith of their parents; freedom for the individual to change his religion and his group affiliation; freedom to preach, educate, publish, and carry on missionary activities; and freedom to maintain and to develop an organization, and to acquire and hold property, for these purposes.

Each of these freedoms in varying degree impinges upon, or presupposes the recognition of, certain civil and social rights. Governments and social institutions, in so far as lies within the province of each, have an obligation to see that these rights are observed. Freedom to worship, interpreted to include public worship, is dependent upon the right of public meeting and, to a certain extent, of organization. It may involve freedom of speech and freedom of press. Freedom to bring up children in the faith of their parents, if it is to include education beyond that which the home provides, is dependent upon freedom of speech, of the press, of organization and public meeting. Freedom for the individual to change his religion will call into play most of the civil and social rights as soon as the individual practices the religion which he has come to profess. Freedom to preach and to educate demand freedom of speech, of press, of organization and public meeting. Freedom to publish is identical with freedom of the press. Freedom to organize with others and freedom to acquire and hold property are in themselves social and civil rights. Freedom to carry on missionary activities basically bespeaks the right to testify to one's conviction in any chosen locality. It may involve all or many of the other freedoms. By its very nature, however, it carries implications which the other freedoms may not contain. These implications grow out of the historical fact that missionary activity more frequently and specially involves the nationals of foreign states, their ingress, egress, and activities as aliens. It is justified in the first instance on the right of individuals everywhere to access to information. It therefore requires that social and political institutions permit freedom of access and exposure to the cultures, ideas, and beliefs of other peoples and freedom of cultural exchange.

As religious groups are granted the freedoms here indicated, they will recurringly be brought into close relationship with each other and therefore will encounter the dangers of competition and friction. Acceptance of an ethical code would tend to minimize or remove tensions. The following principles are offered as a step toward a voluntary code to guide such behavior and action as have bearing upon relationships of religious bodies, either at home or abroad.[1]

1. *Emphasize positive values.* Constructive spiritual and moral effort, helpful living and service to the community, positive witness to the truth vouchsafed, rather than controversy and conflict of religious enterprise, are the method of true religion.

2. *Cooperate in tasks of community welfare.* Willingness to cooperate with members of other religious groups and with community

[1] M. Searle Bates, *Religious Liberty: An Inquiry,* New York, International Missionary Council, 1945, pp. 562-3.

organizations in voluntary tasks of common welfare is the practice of brotherhood.

3. *Respect the conscience of others.* Regard for the conscience, the sense of moral values, the cultural and religious traditions of those who do not share the same religious allegiance, is required by love for one's neighbors.

4. *Deal open-mindedly and fairly with men of other faiths.* Full faith will temper assurance and conviction of the truth and witness to it with continual practice and teaching of respect, fairness, and love toward those who believe differently. "Dogmatic intolerance" carries a heavy obligation to make sure that it is not applied in practice as enmity toward men of other groups.

5. *Recognize for others the liberty and regard desired for self.* Full mutuality and reciprocity will continually be sought in matters of religious liberty and of all relationships among religious bodies. Surely the Golden Rule is operative in matters of religion, if anywhere. General dislike and distrust of another religious group is a sure sign of the failure of love within the suspecting persons, whether or not there is excessive fault in the disliked.

6. *Promote good citizenship in state and world.* Furtherance of good citizenship in the fields of character and service, which are the proper concern of religion, with regard also to the universal relations of man to man, is a religious duty.

7. *Give due heed to law and custom.* Willingness to observe the requirements of law and of respected custom in the community—or, if informed conscience requires violation of them, to accept in good spirit the corresponding penalties—is the obligation of a Christian.

8. *Make clear the purposes and procedures of religious enterprises.* There is every reason for deliberate and thorough openness in all procedures, making clear the purposes of every religious organization and undertaking.

9. *Practice sound respect for ties of family and community.* Christians will practice conscientious regard for the ties of family and of other significant human relationships. Persons under sixteen years of age (or such age as is established in the community for freedom of

religious attachment) will not be received as members of the religious body without the consent of parents or guardians.

10. *Keep the appeal of religion free from material influence.* Social, educational, and medical service, as well as all forms of material assistance, will be provided for the sake of their own values, as an integral part of the expression of Christian faith, not primarily to win converts. Such witness should not require listening to a religious message as the price of receiving the advantages offered. Regard for spiritual liberty will be watchful that religious contacts in the course of such services be genuinely voluntary.

III. *The ideal of religious liberty is achieved in society when governments, both national and international, assure all citizens, in their individual and group relations, freedom from direct or indirect compulsion in matters of religion and guard them against discrimination and legal disabilities on account of religion.*

The purposes and prerogatives of government may be defined in many different ways. When viewed in the light of religious liberty as a fundamental human freedom, governments bear a clear responsibility to the individual man as a member of society. Negatively, it is not within their province to prohibit or to curtail the exercise of religious liberty by their citizens. Positively, they have an obligation to create conditions which are favorable to the freest development and expression of conscience consistent with the best interests of the entire community under their jurisdiction. Historically, governments have in varying degree failed to meet this responsibility under two broad conditions: (1) when governments as a matter of consistent policy claimed that the people existed for the state, not the state for the people; and (2) when governments, under adverse pressure from other states, found it necessary to protect the interests of their people and, in the process of aggressive or defensive action, limited or prohibited the exercise of normally recognized rights. Conversely, governments have tended to meet their responsibility (1) when, as a matter of consistent policy the state was known to exist by virtue of and for the sake of the people; and (2) when national states were relatively undisturbed by political or economic threats from other national states.

At the risk of over-simplification it may be stated that representative government and international order will be conducive to the recognition of religious liberty and, in fact, of all human rights. Since the ideal of religious liberty is being viewed in terms of man's experience in society, due account must be taken of the present situation. Not all governments represent the will of the people and international order has not become a reality. Nevertheless, representative government is being sought in many countries, and nations are moving to bring about world order through an international collaboration which may result in some form of world government.

In face of the present situation, the exercise of religious liberty as a human right must in the first instance be made possible through the action of separate national states.

Many of the requirements upon government have already been indicated in relation to the exercise of religious liberty by the individual and by the religious groups. They are here brought together to reveal the part which governments should play.

1. Governments should assure to all citizens—as individuals and in their corporate relation as members of a religious body—freedom of religious belief and action to the point where community interests are adversely affected. This will require the right of access to information, freedom to worship according to conscience, freedom to bring up children in the faith of their parents; freedom for the individual to change his religion; freedom to preach, educate, publish; freedom to carry on missionary activities; and freedom to organize with others, and to acquire and hold property for these purposes. These rights and freedoms should be equally assured to majority and minority groups. The group which claims the freedoms when it is a minority in a country, should also grant the freedoms when it is a majority in another country. Where such rights and freedoms are granted without distinction, people will be free from external compulsion in matters of religion.

When political authorities reach the conclusion that the exercise of freedoms adversely affects the community well-being, they have the right to interfere. However, such interference should not be with the purpose merely of granting one religious group a more favored position than another body. It must be on the basis of community well-being. It must be with a consideration of man's place in the human family and not of his place in relation to the majority religious body. As has been previously pointed out, the judgment of political authorities or the criterion of judgment whereby they conclude that action is harmful to a community may be wrong. This risk cannot be avoided. It will be minimized when, through closer relations among the peoples of the world, a higher "world morality" is achieved.

2. Governments should create conditions favorable to the exercise of the freedom in religious belief and action which has been granted to the individual and to the religious group. A first contribution of government will be to safeguard its citizens against discrimination and legal disability on account of religion. It is true that a person who holds a conviction strongly enough will continue to hold it in face of threatened discrimination and legal disability. Notwithstanding, at least indirect pressure is bearing upon him when he must anticipate or endure the results of discrimination because of religious conviction.

In seeking to create conditions favorable to religious liberty, a government should recognize the part which intermediate social agencies play. It should safeguard the rights of the family and the home. It may demand an ethical level in business—both management and labor—in education, in civic organizations, in newspapers, in the theater, and in radio. It should seek for its citizens an atmosphere which is in harmony with the religious complexion of its society and which, at the same time, keeps the door open for continued growth.

When a strong majority of citizens in any country with representative government are affiliated with a religious body, it is to be expected that their point of view will color the outlook and policy of the government. In the main, Protestant Christians believe that the function of the church is to place Christian insights at the disposal of government leaders. Historically, the procedures that have been followed to do this fall into two broad categories. In the first category, the churches have limited their representations to general principles and have allowed Christians as individual citizens to press for particular applications. This has tended to minimize the danger of pressure blocs and has maintained the separation of the church and state. In the second category, churches have had direct part in government through official positions traditionally granted to specified members. The dangers inherent in this procedure—which fortunately have in most instances not materialized in Protestant practice—would make profitable a periodic review of the system whereby church and state are related. This would seem to be especially advisable in the light of changing forms of government and changing proportions in the religious society of any nation. Whichever system is followed, the rights of minority groups must be consistently recognized. As a minimum, the majority group or the group which has representation in government is called upon to grant the same rights to minority groups which it claims for itself elsewhere, when it is in the minority. The conception of religious liberty must never overlook man's experience—every man's experience—in society.

The people of our day seem bent upon writing a new chapter of history. It carries as its distinguishing mark an apparent desire to work out a system of international collaboration for the well-being of all nations—for world order and security. The closing paragraphs of this chapter, when they come to be written, may describe an operating world government. The Charter of the United Nations recognizes that one of the major purposes of the world organization shall be "to achieve international cooperation in promoting and encouraging respect for human rights and for fundamental freedoms for all without distinction as to race, sex, language, or religion." The Charter requires the Economic and Social Council "to set up commissions in economic and social fields and for the promotion of human rights." In this latter commission will center largely the responsibility to determine the human rights for which respect is to be encouraged and the means whereby observance of them may become a reality. As the prerogatives of national sovereignty yield to the demands of world order and security through international collaboration, national states and the world organization must cooperate to secure to every man his inalienable rights. In anticipation of this need and recognizing the fundamental aspect of religious liberty, the Federal Council of the Churches of Christ in America and the Foreign Missions Conference of North America formally adopted a Statement on Religious Liberty. This

Statement, while concerned specifically with religious liberty, is drawn on the background of all the human rights and fundamental freedoms of man in society. It is intended to interpret the meaning of religious freedom and to fix responsibility for creating conditions which will permit its reasonable exercise. The second and the third paragraphs are somewhat specific in that they set forth in detail certain rights which should be guaranteed against adverse legal provisions and administrative acts. The first and the last paragraphs are somewhat general in that they call upon the government and the people—each in its appropriate fashion—to assume responsibility for achieving in practice the right of individuals everywhere to religious liberty. The text of the statement follows.

We recognize the dignity of the human person as the image of God. We therefore urge that the civic rights which derive from that dignity be set forth in the agreements into which our country may enter looking toward the promotion of world order, and be indicated in treaty arrangements and in the functions and responsibilities assigned to international organizations. States should assure their citizens freedom from compulsion and discrimination in matters of religion. This and the other rights which inhere in man's dignity must be adequately guarded; for when they are impaired, all liberty is jeopardized. More specifically, we urge that:

> The right of individuals everywhere to religious liberty shall be recognized and, subject only to the maintenance of public order and security, shall be guaranteed against legal provisions and administrative acts which would impose political, economic, or social disabilities on grounds of religion.
>
> Religious liberty shall be interpreted to include freedom to worship according to conscience and to bring up children in the faith of their parents; freedom for the individual to change his religion; freedom to preach, educate, publish, and carry on missionary activities; and freedom to organize with others, and to acquire and hold property, for these purposes.

To safeguard public order and to promote the well-being of the community, both the state, in providing for religious liberty, and the people, in exercising the rights thus recognized, must fulfil reciprocal obligations: The state must guard all groups, both minority and majority, against legal disabilities on account of religious belief; the people must exercise their rights with a sense of responsibility and with charitable consideration for the rights of others.

VI

THE IDEAL OF RELIGIOUS LIBERTY—
A JEWISH VIEW

BY

LOUIS FINKELSTEIN, Ph.D.

*Rabbi; President and Solomon Schechter Professor of Theology
Jewish Theological Seminary of America;
Director, Institute for Religious and Social Studies*

A problem of religious liberty, similar to that of our own time, arose in the third century before the Christian era. In earlier days, there had been occasional persecution of prophetic followers of the God of Israel by idol-worshipping kings, and there had been occasional efforts to suppress idol worship on the part of devout kings. But, generally speaking, the struggle between the two groups in Israel, those loyal to the God of their people, and those following the gods of other peoples, had been carried on in free discussions. The utterances of the Prophets, preserved in Scripture, offer evidence of this. The Prophets were usually free to speak their minds and worship their God; and so were their opponents.

When Ezra came from Persia to Palestine, he was clothed with authority to establish the law of Moses as the law of the land. But apparently neither he nor anyone else interpreted this right as giving him authority to interfere with foreign worship by those outside the ranks of Israel. The law of Moses was the law of the land so far as the Jews were concerned. The rest of the population did not have to heed this law.

The charter given the Jews by Antiochus III, in the year 200 when the Syrians came into power over Palestine, seems to have gone beyond this authority of Ezra. It recognized Jewish law as the constitution not only of the Jewish community but of the country. At any rate, we may take it that this end was sought by the Jews of the period. (Indeed, perhaps it had been attained even before, when the Egyptian Ptolemies ruled.)

About this date we hear for the first time of a code of laws which Judaism considered binding not only on its own members, but also on all peoples. Jews were naturally expected to live according to the law of Moses. But what of the heathen? What did a Jewish state expect of them? Obviously, they were not to be compelled to become Jews; for enforced conversion, or even conversion under special persuasion, was repugnant to the whole spirit of Judaism. Yet neither was it right that there should be worship of idols in the land of God.

Out of this conflict there arose the conception of the Noachic commandments, mentioned for the first time in the Book of Jubilees (which, in company with a number of other students, I am now convinced was composed early in the second century B.C.E.). These Noachic commandments were six in number. They are said to have been revealed by God to Noah, and therefore to be binding on all his descendants, that is, on all mankind. They include the prohibition of idolatry; of blasphemy; of murder; of unchastity; and of theft; also the injunction to observe the civil law. The heathen who accepted these injunctions and followed them was, from the Jewish point of view, a *ger toshab,* a member of the large community of the righteous worshippers of God, though he was not of the Jewish fold.

As the doctrines of the resurrection and of personal immortality began to win wider recognition at about the same time, it was natural that the heathen who observed the Noachic laws should also be thought to have won for himself complete salvation, identical with that of the Jew, who observed all the 613 Mosaic commandments. A document which is described in the Talmud as belonging to that period, enumerates seven historical persons who have no share in the future life. Six of these were of Israelite descent; but the seventh, Balaam, was of heathen descent. The fact that Balaam is specifically excluded from the eternal reward of the righteous, indicates that the heathen generally might acquire immortality. They could acquire immortality, as a later scholar stated, by observing the Noachic laws.

In this early solution of the problem of the heathen in the land of Israel, we notice an approach to the problem of religious liberty which is exceedingly important and interesting, but rare in our own time. The ancient Jew did not regard liberty of worship as an end in itself. Freedom of worship did not theoretically include the freedom to worship idols; for the worship of idols is the negation of the most important single fact in human existence, namely, the fact that the world is essentially spiritual, and that it is one. There could be no compromise between Judaism and idol worship; nor could there be tolerance of idol worship on the ground that in matters of religion a man ought not to be interfered with, regardless of his actions. The ancient Jewish teacher recognized that spiritual religion, with its emphasis on the invisible and transcendent God, was vital to mankind; and he would not yield an iota in his insistence on the acceptance of that doctrine. Neither would he tolerate blasphemy against God. He would not tolerate murder, unchastity, or theft; and he insisted on the observance of the civil rights of men. But granted these basic principles, he had no other demands to make on his fellow inhabitants of the Holy Land.

Nor did the ancient Rabbi object to deviation within his own group. It is clear that many differences of custom which became the subject of sectarian controversies in later generations, originated in the early days of the Scribes. But then the varieties of observance and of belief existed side by side without conflict. The Book of Psalms contains some which unequivocally assert that man is immortal, and that after death he will be resurrected. They also contain the beautiful psalm of thanksgiving in which the psalmist declares that, "The heavens are the heavens of the Lord, but the earth hath He given to the sons of men. The dead praise not the Lord, neither any that go down in silence." Apparently at least this psalmist did not accept the widely current view that the dead do praise the Lord; and that the heavens as well as the earth belong to the children of men. Immortality of the soul was for him a concept quite different from what it was for many other writers. While the various psalmists took such different views of their faith, the ancient Rabbis saw no difficulty in singing both psalms, in receiving them in the same canon, in regarding them both as the sacred word of God. There were similar differences in apparent meaning between Ezekiel and the Book of Leviticus, between different parts of Job, between different verses of Proverbs and Ecclesiastes.

There were pious Jews who observed the Pentecost on the fiftieth day after the first day after Passover, as Jews do today; there were equally pious ancient Jews who observed it on the fiftieth day after the Sabbath of Passover week, as did the Sadducees.

The Passover service contains an ancient homily, probably composed in the third century before the Common Era, which maintains that God appeared in visible form at the Red Sea. To many Jews of that and of later periods, this concept was almost blasphemous; but nonetheless this homily, beautiful and interesting for other reasons, was included in the Passover service, and handed down to us.

Intolerance of opposition within Judaism developed largely under the influence of Hellenistic philosophy. The Greeks, being polytheistic, were tolerant of all faiths. They could accept any new god or religion in the spacious courts of their pantheon. But those Jews who were tutored by them, found such tolerance difficult. Accordingly, when the issue of the beliefs in the resurrection and immortality of the soul became vital issues, the Saducean group of Jews—far more deeply imbued with Greek influence than their opponents—virtually excommunicated the Pharisees. Indeed, the word Pharisee means literally "heretic."

But it is in the nature of intolerance to give birth to more intolerance. The Pharisee replied to his exclusion from Judaism by the Sadducee with a counter-exclusion. If the Sadducee declared that belief in immortal souls was inconsistent with Judaism, the Pharisee replied that the denial of the belief and not its assertion was the heresy.

The ancient struggle between the Sadducees and the Pharisees changed the contour of religious thought at a moment crucial in western civilization. With this quarrel came the introduction of dogmatics as tests of piety in Judaism, and a new development in the concept of religious liberty.

Yet though the Sadducees and the Pharisees each bitterly denounced the other's views, for many years they continued to work together in common causes. The high court of the Sanhedrin included Sadducees as well as Pharisees; the high priest was generally a Sadducee, yet the Pharisees continued to worship at the Temple under him. The two groups were on such good terms, that Sadducean ladies, and presumably their husbands, are recorded as having often gone to Pharisaic teachers for guidance in the law.

But the spiritual decay of the ancient world, which centuries before the fall of Rome heralded the downfall of the whole Mediterranean civilization, could not but exert a profound influence within Judaism itself. The Pharisaic group discovered internal differences. These were not only tolerated, but encouraged. The two schools—which later came to be known by the names of Shammai and Hillel—far from regarding each other with animosity, apparently believed their views supplementary. Even when they contradicted one another, they held that "both views are the words of the living God." How it was possible to interpret the Law in two opposing ways, and to hold both interpretations correct, they did not say. But they apparently felt that the word of God is subject to more than one interpretation; and that it was possible to obey it according to either interpretation and still be a good Jew.

Though the differences between the Schools of Shammai and Hillel were in many respects more profound than those between most modern religious denominations—extending to such issues as the legitimacy of marriages—each school refused to denounce the other's usages. "Though these declared pure what the others declared impure; and though these declared permissible marriages which the others declared prohibited, they did not hesitate to eat in one another's homes, or to marry into one another's families, fulfilling the verse, 'Love ye truth and peace.' "

But in the course of the first century of the Common Era, the Shammaitic School apparently began to question the very doctrine of this ancient tolerance and fellowship. We are told that when, on one occasion, the Shammaites came into control at the Temple, they for the first time seemed to insist forcibly on conformity with their views; and would not, in accordance with the older practice, permit Hillel himself to worship according to the usages he held correct. On another occasion, again finding themselves in a majority, the Shammaites issued the famous "eighteen decrees" which demanded obedience to the views they had expressed.

In the first century of the Common Era, the last generations before the fall of the Temple of Jerusalem thus witnessed a struggle within Judaism with regard to the problem of religious liberty itself. The Shammaites rejected the ancient Hasidean and Pharisaic doctrine that pagans attain immortality if they accept the Noachic commandments. Disagreeing both with tradition and with their contemporary Hillelite scholars (as well as later Judaism), they maintained that only those who accepted the whole Mosaic law would have a share in Paradise.

Fortunately for Judaism, the Hillelite view won over that of the Shammaites, "A heavenly voice was heard in Jabneh declaring that the rule of the House of Hillel was to prevail," says the Rabbinic metaphor which records this historical fact.

Yet while Shammaism was defeated, it was by no means extirpated. Moreover, the social and intellectual world forces which had produced Shammaism within the Jewish fold did not cease to operate. The ancient Hellenistic world was decaying. The extension of the Roman empire to include the whole Near East could not arrest this process. On the contrary, the loss of political independence, and the subjection of the Hellenistic peoples to a new, overwhelming force resulted in a lower degree of culture than that which they formerly possessed, and weakened even further the power of ideas in their midst. The respect for force begotten by the astonishing victories of Alexander and the continuous wars among his successors was now augmented by admiration for the prowess of Rome, the embodiment of force.

The ancient willingness to tolerate and encourage deviation was out of accord with the spirit of the later generations. Fierce conflicts in the infant Christian Church had their analogues in almost equally bitter struggles among Jewish groups. Rabbi Eliezer ben Hyrcanus was excommunicated because he insisted on adhering to views which were rejected by the majority of his colleagues. In a later generation, Rabbi Meir barely escaped the same fate. When Rabbi Tarphon, who in some respects preferred Shammaitic to Hillelite practices, once found his life in danger through a ritual observance, a colleague remarked to him, "Your peril was deserved; because you violated the precepts of the Hillelites."

Despite such occasional lapses from the tradition of freedom of opinion, all through the Middle Ages the synagogue remained astonishingly hospitable to deviations from the norm. Every effort to create a central authority, empowered to compel unquestioning obedience to its decisions, failed. Through a curious chain of circumstances, and without deliberate intention, there developed a system of checks and balances, in which any living source of authority would find itself matched by some other equally effective. The academies in Palestine, which claimed authority by virtue of their location, were challenged by those of Babylonia, which were generally recognized as superior in learning. Within the Babylonian system, authority of the academy of Sura was often challenged by its sister academy in Pumbedita. The authority of the heads of the academies was, when necessary, challenged by the lay heads of the Exile. In the course of time, new academies developed in the various countries of North Africa and Europe; and while all of these recognized the transcendent authority of the Talmud, they were unwilling to recognize the authority of any living Talmudic interpreter.

Yet while deviation and argument were common, there was no anarchy. Judaism remained a unit, despite the diversity of belief, practice, and attitude within its fold. Maimonides, the foremost scholar of the Spanish tradition, differs very widely in many significant details of the law from his French contemporaries. He declares prohibited what they permit; and he permits what they prohibit. But he undoubtedly would not have hesitated to partake of their food, had he visited his French colleagues.

The deviations permitted in theoretical, theological, and metaphysical interpretation of Judaism were even greater than in the realm of practice. Indeed, except for outright atheism or polytheism, and the denial of human spirituality and the Divine inspiration of the Holy Scriptures, there is hardly a theological view, which has not found support in traditional Judaism. Rabbi Levi ben Gershom, a great scholar and saint, maintained the eternity of the material world, which seems contrary to the letter of the Law, and which had been denied by Maimonides. Maimonides insisted that anyone attributing physical form to God was heretic; but he was himself rebuked for this by Rabbi Abraham ben David of Posquierres, who agreed with his view regarding anthropomorphism, but denied the right of anyone to exclude other Jews from the fold for disagreement on this issue.

Curiously enough, Maimonides' works were the first in the history of Judaism to be banned because of the philosophical views they expressed. But even in that instance, it was the books and the views, and not the man, who was declared out of accord with Judaism; and the ban was quickly removed, when the scholars who had declared it interpreted as punishment for their offense the frightful calamities which befell the community soon afterward. Excommunication of a person because of his theoretical beliefs occurred for the first time in the case of Uriel Acosta and Benedict Spinoza. The conditions under which these excommunications occurred were of course abnormal; a considerable section of the Jewish population in Holland was of Marrano background, and had been reared without an immediate appreciation of the Jewish tradition. Just as the Babylonian authorities declared certain customs as "originating in the time of persecution" and therefore not to be followed, so also it may be said of the excommunication for doctrinal deviation, that it arose from the conditions peculiar to persecution.

The bonds which held Judaism together were (a) common recognition of the authority of the Talmud, especially the Babylonian Talmud, as interpreter of the Jewish tradition and of Scripture, so far as ritual practice is concerned; (b) mutual respect of scholars for integrity in the interpretation of the Law; and (c) an unspoken but undoubtedly real apprehension on the part of the greatest scholars that they might be in error in their own interpretations. The three attitudes of mind did not prevent lively arguments, but they did prevent most arguments from becoming open quarrels.

This development within Judaism has much in common with the processes by which scholarly and scientific truth generally are achieved. No matter how bitterly scholars may be opposed, so long as each recognizes (a) common tests of validation, (b) the other's integrity and (c) the possibility that he may himself be in error, they cannot oppress one another. Their arguments take the form of discussions, rather than of battle.

Just as Judaism holds that there are basic values which no religion may flout and still be recognized as a religion, so there are basic values which no type of Judaism may reject and still be entitled to call itself by that name. There is wide room for variation among the dialects of Jewish worship; but that does not mean that there is no unity in the language. It is not, however, for any person to read another out of Judaism because the latter's dialect seems foreign. Such rejection must be left for generations of scholars, as the suspicions of the early groups become confirmed in the course of time.

We know too little of the cross-influences of thought in antiquity and in the Middle Ages to estimate with accuracy the extent to which the wide tolerance and scholarly approach of Judaism affected other human thought. Ideas, like words and myths, spread in curious ways; and the existence throughout the Roman empire of groups of people loyal to the scholarly tolerance of Hillelite Judaism may well have affected the attitudes of others. But whether or not Judaism was able to bring these spiritual influences to bear on human thought generally, it has retained them within itself. To this day, deviation of practice and even of belief, within specified limits, are recognized as entirely consistent with adherence to Judaism.

VII

THE SPIRIT OF THE FRONTIER

BY

HAROLD RUGG, Ph.D.

Professor of Education, Teachers College, Columbia University

The concept "frontier" brings to mind pictures of physical regions where few men have trod. I shall explore briefly the traits of men who succeed in coping with such a frontier, but it will be merely for the purpose of employing these characteristics in a study of the frontier of the imagination on which the Americans are now compelled to live.

The physical frontiers of the earth have been jungles of disorder and an important history of civilization could be written around man's effort to bring order out of their chaos. The theme is particularly pertinent to our times, for we live today in a social jungle of anarchic disorder. Our production of commodities and services is stunted because it is based upon selfish and warring competition. Government is socially inefficient because it is conducted by the continuous warfare of political parties whose chief purpose is to acquire and to keep office. Our state papers accept the principle of human equality, but our practice of living rejects it in many areas of life. The right to a place on the land and the right to social credit are denied to more than half of the population. Today, as in the 1890's when Frederick Turner first said it, "economic power secures political power," and there is a strong suspicion that might still does make right. In short, we are living today in a jungle of human disorder reminiscent of the moving geographic frontiers of the past two centuries. But I propose to have us concern ourselves with frontiers far different from the frontier of the land which the Bureau of the Census warned sixty years ago was rapidly disappearing. The Superintendent of the Census would have been well advised to warn our fathers then to gird themselves for the pressures that would shortly push them on to baffling social frontiers of the imagination.

No major people on earth, unless it be the European Russians of the Soviet Union, have come to our own harassing day with a spirit born of as much experience of frontiers as the Americans. For two hundred and fifty years our people never lived apart from geographic frontiers and these, in fusion with the world conditions that put the people on this continent, built in them a unique spirit. I am convinced that the way of life which evolved from the process embraces the peculiar ingredients of the spirit needed to cope with the baffling social problems of today. More is needed, of course, than spirit; knowledge of man and culture, imaginative insight, the capacity to take thought and to design are needed also. But the traits of the spirit are foundational to the conquest of every kind of frontier. So it is important that we take ourselves back to the geographic frontier for a moment to assemble these traits, beliefs and values for our special use today.

Manifest Destiny

I think they can all be summed up in the phrase that was much used by our own early American masters of forensics—Manifest Destiny. The spirit of the frontier and of American life to this very day has been that of Manifest Destiny. Cooper's description of it in 1830, or Turner's famous essay of 1893 would need little paraphrasing to be apt today. Turner showed that on the moving frontier of two centuries, the traits were built that we have since come to associate with the term the "pragmatic mind." They are—a coarseness and strength combined with acuteness and inquisitiveness; a dominant individualism of buoyancy and exuberance driven by restless, nervous energy; practical inventiveness, alertness in finding expedients; in general, a masterful grasp of the material life. Our people became Thing people. Correlated with these traits was a deep-seated fear of control; a spirit of "Don't tread on me" . . . "Keep off each other and keep each other off" . . . "Live and let live." Although it was lacking in the artistic, it became powerful to effect great ends. Through it all coursed a good-humored spirit of adventure, a feeling of limitless opportunity and capacity both in the people and in the continent. Even today our business leaders find it expressed in a spirit of risk-taking for the chance of the higher return that contrasts sharply with our British cousins' tendency to accept a low-order guaranteed security.

These are the traits which, in a hundred years, conquered the continent that Mr. Jefferson said could not be cleared in a thousand. Working in a favorable milieu of isolation from Europe's intrigues and destructive wars, they built the machinery for the highest standard of living that man has ever envisaged but the most tangled social jungle that he has yet confronted. Deeply embedded in the American climate of opinion, these traits were passed on from generation to generation down to our own day. Even in the 1940's, while the world sneered at America's fat softness, the spirit of Manifest Destiny continued to work its wonders. When our people, committed traditionally to peace and to aloofness from quarreling Europe, were faced by the gigantic tasks of arming half the world and training and equipping youth of hitherto slipshod habits and restless insecurities, the bewildered American giant rose in his might and threw off his lethargy. From being soft he became tough, from being weak he became energized. Habituated to license he took on discipline. Giving up part of his treasured Bill of Rights—but only for the duration—he dropped peacetime work and girded himself for war. Jazz-mad youth toughened in six months, conquered gigantic physical obstacles. Business and labor, ostensibly burying the hatchet, pulled together well enough to design and build and transport overseas the paraphernalia of a gargantuan war production. Thus, confronted by physical danger, Manifest Destiny still runs true to form in our people.

Manifest Destiny—On the Social Frontier?

But when, in our own times, the Americans were faced by social danger—for example, by technological unemployment that displaced millions of workers, or by the necessity of collaborating in diplomacy and mutual understanding with devotees of a completely alien ideology—the political leaders that the Americans had chosen did not present convincing proof that they were strong men of cooperative design and construction. Naturally so, for nothing in their environment—except lip service—has ever demanded group thinking and the social principle. Not their informal education, nor their community way of life, nor their formal schooling had taught them the nature of the world that our fathers built and in which we now must live. Hence, when confronted by the intellectual jungle of a worldwide industrialism, which now is caught in a grim succession of Great Depressions and World Wars, their characteristic response was a baffled, tantrum-like castigation of convenient scapegoats. All the evidence that we can bring to bear from the past generation shows that in these foundational aspects of life the rank and file of Americans, including most of their business and political leaders, have behaved like adolescent, unsure men. Our history made them so. Throughout two centuries and a half, their attitudes were marked by slavish worship of Britain and Europe and the classical past. Their schoolmen built the curriculum by copying the trivium and quadrivium of academic Europe's seven liberal arts. Their architects debauched the continent by scattering over it tens of thousands of eclectic Greek-Roman-Gothic-Georgian-Tudor buildings. Their dance was classic Italian-French-Tsarist ballet. Their theater, their law, their language, and their letters were British.

The reasons lie in our history, and are twofold. The first is the fact that ours was a new and youthful society mushrooming up with dizzy speed. Our fathers were really "first builders"; having no antecedents to follow, they had to improvise. In the initial stage of a dynamic era, the order of the day was, "Try something, try anything . . . once . . . and see if it works. If it works, it is a success." "Its truth will be measured by the tests of its consequences." The sanctions of life, in theories of thought as well as behavior, were pragmatic; as with all innovators and improvisors, perfection was not demanded. "Get it built and on time," was the slogan. Thus, in every walk of life, in every area of the culture, the "slack" provided by Nature's vast surface was so great that the people did not need to sit down and plan together.

In the second place the concepts with which they thought about their problems were appropriate only to an individualistic social order. Every phase of the culture exhibited the *laissez-faire* idea—take off the lid, and the competition of strong men will produce the maximum possible national wealth and income. "I" was riding "We," and the *laissez-faire* idea worked well enough in an infant pioneer society. All the basic concepts of democracy were interpreted in a similar nominalistic theory of particulars and of action. Freedom was defined as absence of restraint. Property was thought of as the thing, not the use to which it was put; hence it could be used or even withheld from use at the owner's discretion. Our state papers proclaimed that men were created free and equal, but the limitations of the concept were never delineated, and its inner significance was not actually implemented. Hence, when confronted by novel enterprises in which swift improvisation, hitting the bell five or six times in ten, would suffice, the frontier strength, efficiency, and initiative of the Americans got by.

But throughout our own times, although most of our people and their political and business leaders did not know it, we were swiftly leaving behind the jungle world of every man for himself. We were entering a world in which men would have to plan together every social enterprise of the culture. These lusty Americans, anaesthetized by their riches but still muttering "Manifest Destiny" were being whirled into a new day that would demand a new spirit and new ideas—cooperation rather than individual competition, concept as well as percept, thought before action, appraisal and design before building. Hence we must not lose sight of the fact that to meet the problems of a new day we need a new man who can deal with novel problems with new ideas. Veblen made that clear thirty years ago. It is true that the vigorous constructive traits bred on the physical frontier are important—a Paul Bunyanesque mood of buoyant confidence, and a naïve refusal to conceive of failure, an ability to discover hitherto unknown reservoirs of power—all backed by the stamina required to get up off one's knees when beaten down to the ninth count; all these are needed if one is to clear any jungle, whether it be social or physical.

But these traits alone will not solve the staggering problems on the present social and psychological frontiers, as is shown by the current impotence of most of our leaders when confronted by the economic-political impasse of the twentieth century. Pertinent knowledge of factors and forces and intellectual power are needed prior to action if sound design is to precede reconstruction.

Creative Americans and the Philosophy of Experience

In every deep crisis of American history a small nucleus of creative men have come forward with these very abilities; a few great mutants have produced creative works, some of political thought, others of intellectual composition and esthetic design: witness the original architecture and community planning of the eastern seaboard in the late seventeenth century and, a hundred years later, our Founding Fathers' brilliant state papers, passionate defenses of property rights, declarations of the rights of man, and designs for democratic government. Certainly the American spirit was vigorously in action on the social frontiers of those days.

I am convinced that it is even more alive and competent in our own times, although the practices of our business men and politicians have demeaned it; with such rare exceptions as the nucleus of a national council of design which Roosevelt created at Washington in the 1930's, it has not been utilized in practical government. The Americans of the 1890's were perhaps too humble in the presence of Europe to have much prevision of their own world destiny. But, whether or not they were aware of it, their culture was to become within the next half century the chief sustaining soil for the modern philosophy of experience, which was to produce a new psychology and sociology, esthetics and ethics, each of which would be appropriate to the changing times and the nature of our culture. History, I am confident, will acclaim this as a great achievement. In the 1890's Europe was breaking up; the disintegration of the unified culture of medieval Europe was almost complete. Industrialization of the continent had built thirty competing, suspicious nationalisms in one of the world's garden spots where a single, European people should have been cultivating a great society of economic and spiritual abundance. Within the next half century, they well-nigh destroyed the first structure of that society in a second horrible Thirty Years' War.

Partly, therefore, because Europe was becoming impotent, partly because the strong seed of the creative and democratic spirit had been sowed in North America, and partly because conditions here were most favorable for its growth, *the philosophy and psychology of experience that matured in the twentieth century* was thoroughly American. We must understand this tremendous fact, because we now have laid upon us a magnificent opportunity and a sobering responsibility. The mood of the physical frontier—"We can lick the world"—must give way to the call of the world's social frontier—"We can lead the world." I assert the coming American contribution in no chauvinistic mood; rather in the spirit of grateful humility at the opportunity and in eager acceptance of the obligation which is now presented to our people. It seems probable that what our people do in the next few years will set the world's norm for at least a generation.

What our greatest men of thought have done is magnificent. In the period between 1880 and today, a new view of the human individual and of his industrial-democratic culture was born. In fifty years our creative Americans have laid bare a dozen concepts which are the nub of what I shall call the philosophy and psychology of experience. This is our own phase of the main line of modern thought and feeling that has been building for three centuries. My readers hardly need reminding that its true beginnings lie far back in history; certainly it was clearly revealed as early as the sixteenth century when seminal minds launched a creative revolution which affected every strand of the culture. In the next two hundred years a dozen philosophers completed the destruction of the ancient rule of authority and laid the foundation for a philosophy and psychology of experience. Ten were British—Hobbes, Locke, Berkeley, Hume, Brown, Hamilton, the two Mills, Spencer, and Bain—and two were German—Kant and Herbart. These pioneers turned thinking men away from the rule of authority, laid the foundation for a naturalistic interpretation of the nature and behavior of the living creature, built a receptive attitude toward objective observation, and turned the limelight on human experience as the only real source of the data of psychology. And they brought psychology through the first step to the verge of becoming a science; both subject matter and method were empirical by the middle 1800's.

Five Frontiers of the Imagination

Then, after 1880, Manifest Destiny marched again, but this time on social and psychological frontiers. Two scores of thinking Americans put the modern philosophy of experience to work, in a Great Tradition that suffused no less than five distinctive frontiers of thought and feeling:

1. *On the Social Frontier,* through a profound study of man and his society, the foundations of every aspect of the culture—its economics, geography, anthropology, sociology, politics.
2. *On the Human Frontier,* through the physiological and psychological study of man, his nature and conduct, as a part of the expanding study of the organic life of the living creature—his health and its betterment through a better agriculture, medicine, hygiene, sanitation and diet.
3. *On the Frontier of the Expressive Arts,* through the study of man's esthetic statement of his view of life, and his attempt to portray it through every conceivable medium of expression.
4. *On the Frontier of Philosophy and Religion,* through the study of man's objects of allegiance, his methods of inquiry and ways of working.
5. *On the Educational Frontier,* through the application of the foregoing in the conscious design and construction of better schools.

Forty creative workers stand out above all others, but four truly great and original minds led them all:

Charles Sanders Peirce, mathematician and logician, the founder of the current operational psychology and the primitive form of the philosophy known as "pragmatism," or "experimentalism."

William James, author of the first fully integrative psychology of experience.

John Dewey, first to make a full statement of the organic, experimental, and functional psychology, and the first to found a laboratory elementary school on a consistent theory of psychology.

Thorstein Veblen, America's first social psychologist and pioneer student of the economic system.

I center attention upon them, not only because they made the most original contributions and were thorough products of the American spirit; in addition they personally taught the others. James, Veblen, Dewey, and a host of lesser figures stem directly from Charles Peirce. James created the first great psychological synthesis which laid the foundation for our functional psychology of experience. Veblen gave hundreds of social analysts of western culture the initial concepts of a functional and social productive system and of a social psychology. Dewey carried the experiential concepts into psychology, philosophy, and education. In a sense, sociology and psychology became one under these innovators, for the sociology was permeated with psychology, and the new psychology became increasingly social.

I see these forty original Americans laying, in a half century, four solid foundations for a great education that could be built in the post-war world. From their concepts has emerged already the structure of a new psychology, a new study of culture and society, a new esthetics and a new ethics. Peirce, James, Dewey in the vanguard, and Mead, Veblen, Baldwin, Thomas, as their early collaborators, built the new psychology. Veblen, Thomas, Boas, Turner, Robinson, Beard, Patten, Cooley and others laid the foundations for the new study of society that, in the hands of Ogburn, Linton, Kardiner, Lynd, Warner and others of the third generation has given clear promise of a maturing science of culture. Sullivan and Wright, Duncan and Graham, Steiglitz, Stein, Cheney, and others, built the new esthetics out of the most creative half century of expression in the arts of modern times.

These creative Americans, after 1880, felt intuitively and documented scientifically the very concepts and attitudes and ways of thinking and expression that would be needed on the baffling social and psychological frontiers of our times. If the best of our thinking men knew today merely what the best of their predecessors knew seventy-five years ago—assuming that the technological and political trends had moved to their present status—there would be little hope that the world could manage itself in an orderly and peaceful fashion.

But it so happens that while man's physical scientists have taken enormous strides in unlocking the secrets of the physical energy of the universe, his social and psychological scientists have taken comparable ones on their frontiers. As a consequence a growing body of our people know enough today to design human and social controls for the gigantic physical forces which are now at their command for either dreadful destruction or magnificent construction.

The Outlines of a New Science of Man's Behavior and Culture

From the intellectual trail-blazing on these frontiers we can see emerging today, in the frame of the philosophy of experience, the chief concepts of a new psychology of man and his behavior as well as the outlines of a science of culture. It is a functional, social psychology and an organic conception of behavior. Peirce first cleared the ground with his great operational principle, namely, "that beliefs were nothing more than rules of action," that "the whole function of thought is to produce habits of action," that "differences in meaning are but differences in practice," that "our conception of an object 'consists of the practical effects . . . we conceive the object to have.'" And Peirce and Wright gave us a profound clue to *the true role of concepts, namely that they are the finders of laws, not merely their summarizers.*

A clear prevision of most of the basic ideas of individual and social behavior was in James' great *Psychology*. He knew and dramatized the concepts of experience, the self, organism and the organic nature of response, habit, the moving body as a sounding board responding to the world as feeling, knowledge of a thing as knowledge of its relations. John Dewey built up a powerful logic for many of these ideas—especially the scientific method of inquiry, that is, of problem-solving thinking; growth as the characteristic of life; the human act as organic, general, unified, and a social process; mental development as a social process of participation; the Self as the unifying, motivating agent, the Complete Act as the Self in expression; most of life seen as problem solving, and education as a "freeing of individual capacity in a progressive growth directed to social ends."

A dozen important concepts are embraced in this total philosophy of experience but three are of such major significance that more than mention should be made of them: the Darwinian evolutionary concept, the conception of all living things as organisms, and the function concept.

Manifest Destiny and the Darwinian Idea

These American pioneers on the frontiers of thought all embraced the four Darwinian notions: the geometric multiplication of offspring, variation in structure and capability, competition for the means of existence, and the survival of the fittest. These concepts were made to order for the American spirit of Manifest Destiny. The idea of the growth of the living creature, learning by his own efforts to cope with his world and to become master of his destiny, not only fitted perfectly into the belief of the American in himself and in his people; it came also to orient the new interpretation of individual and social living. Societies as well as individuals came to be understood as growing, adjusting, and creative organisms.

From Mechanism to Organism

Meanwhile all the learned disciplines shifted from mechanistic to organismic views—a shift that spread throughout the entire culture. From the moment when the French physiologists first stumbled upon the idea of the general effects of the endocrines on the whole organism, through the later work of the Briton, Sherrington, the Russians, Bechterev and Pavlov, and the Americans, Cannon, Franz, Coghill and Lashley, to name only a few—a mountain of scientific data was piled up to establish the integrative principle. Contemporaries confirmed their findings for the study of culture and society. All societies of living creatures, as well as individual human acts and the interaction of organism and environment were seen as unitary wholes. Witness the lengths to which contemporary biologists and students of society go in the application of the organic concept: Joseph Needham, distinguished British biologist, gives it as his "profound conviction that we are standing today at a turning point between two civilizations, one of those turning points in history not unlike the first or second Christian century, the Renaissance, or the seventeenth century

England." He concludes: "In scientific words, the time has come for the atomistic, inorganic, chaotic community to give way to the organized, living, planned community."[1] And in another place, he documents elaborately the concept that "organizing relations . . . were to become the object of scientific study."[2] The fundamental thread that seems to run through the history of our world is a continuous rise in level of organization."[3]

And so, also, witness Whitehead's well-known statement:

Science is taking on a new aspect which is neither purely physical nor purely biological. It is becoming the study of organisms. Biology is the study of larger organisms, whereas physics is the study of the smaller organisms.[4]

And, later, he adds:

there are also organisms of organisms. Suppose for the moment, and for the sake of simplicity, we assume, without any evidence, that electrons and hydrogen nuclei are such basic organisms. Then the atoms and the molecules are organisms of the higher type, which also represent a compact definite organic unity. When we come to the larger aggregations of matter, the organic unity fades into the background . . . when we come to living beings, . . . the organic again rises into prominence.[5]

And in another source he adds:

the universe achieves its values by reason of its coordination into societies of societies, and into societies of societies of societies.[6]

We must not lose sight of the fact that the first premonitions of the organic concept were felt in the sixteenth century in the physical sciences; but for three hundred years after Galileo most scientists still saw the universe, man, his behavior and his society as Things. Then, in the nineteenth century three great steps were taken, each at an

[1] Joseph Needham: *Time: The Refreshing River*, New York, The Macmillan Company, pp. 88–89.
[2] *Ibid.*, p. 183.
[3] *Ibid.*, p. 185.
[4] Alfred North Whitehead, *Science and the Modern World*, New York, The Macmillan Company, p. 150.
[5] *Ibid.*, p. 161.
[6] *Adventure of Ideas*, New York, The Macmillan Company, p. 264.

interval of a generation, toward the understanding of the *organic* nature of even the physical world:

First, Faraday's experimental discovery of induced currents (1831) and Oersted's studies of the deflection of the magnetic needle (1820).

Second, Maxwell's formulation of the equations which stated the structure of the electro-magnetic field (1873).

Third, Hertz's demonstration of electro-magnetic waves and that their velocity equaled that of light (1885-1889).

Showing the profound significance of the first step Einstein and Infeld say that Oersted's and Faraday's discoveries constituted "the two most important pillars of support for the theory of the electric and magnetic field."

This was the first step which enabled physics to give up mechanical explanations in terms of particles of matter and to grasp that a magnetic field is a "field of force" and a "store of energy." Mr. Einstein calls the field concept "the most important invention of our time."

The Role of the Function Concept in American Life

No single idea was, in my judgment, more truly the mainspring of creative understanding in the American people generally and in their intellectual leaders than the function concept. Interpreted simply, it asked about any phase of the culture: "What is it for? Of what use is it to the people?" It was revealed both in what the people did and in the rationalizations of the scholars. After the Civil War the repressive effects of *laissez-faire* industrialism on the living of the farmers and the city workers led to the increasing imposition of restraints on the individual. Men began to say: "More government"—rather than less government—"the better." The Social—We—took its place beside the Individual—I. A cluster of new ideas came to rule over the social practices of the people as well as over the rationalizing theories of the scholars. After 1870, these exploding concepts of function—use to the people—were articulated in popular movements, got themselves expressed in new national and state legislation, and gradually taught the people to understand their conditions and problems more clearly. An advancing social democracy was in the air, felt dimly by the people perhaps, but revealed in their growing protests. As a result, by the 1920's the function concept had come to grip the Americans in every area of the culture. They applied it to American housing and produced modern architecture. Sullivan and his pupil Wright built their houses in the concept of House Functioning, asking of every building, every room, every strut, "What's it for—what function does it serve?" The key to land conservation and reconstruction became "Land in Use"—witness the TVA and other social enterprises of regional rebuilding. After Dewey, Mead, Thomas, Veblen had finished their first ten years at Chicago, the key to the new psychology became "mind in use," "mind functioning." Similarly, the concept of property ownership as implying the right to preemption, even to withholding land from use, gave way to the meaning of ownership as the obligation to develop, to use the land. Privilege gave way to obligation.

The Crux: "I" and "We"

The comments I have made about the function concept point straight to the central cleavage of our time. This is the great dichotomy, "I" and "We." Call it what you will—Self and Society, the Individual and the Culture, the Private and the Public—it is the age-long problem of freedom and control that from time out of mind has baffled the ingenuity of mankind. Today it sets the basic problem of democracy: *How provide, in a framework of maximum personal freedom that every individual shall rise to the highest stature of which he is innately capable and yet maintain the total group life on the highest level of abundance that the natural and human resources can produce?* "I" and "We" poses the crucial problem of every phase of our culture—the problem of discipline in home and school, work and play, occupation and government. It is central to every problem of growth: How much expression? How much control? The struggle over the structure and operation of democratic government turns upon it. It poses the issue over the destructive exploitation of the world's natural resources and the acceptance of the principle of the Sustained Yield. The failure of the people of the industrial nations to solve it was the chief cause of our modern Thirty Years' War. Full employment at abundance level cannot be maintained in the postwar world except through its solution. Because it is the problem that torments men in every phase of our culture I call it The Crux—the problem of "I" and "We."

On the economic-political level it reveals itself in the current stalemate between the six competing factors of our social system—namely, the men who control credit, the producers and buyers and sellers, the farmers, the workers, the cooperatives, and the government. It underpins the problem of full production and full employment at a high standard of living: how much shall we rely on private enterprise? How much on cooperatives? How much on government?

It was not a crucial problem on any of the geographic frontiers of American history. "Every man for himself" was a successful, pragmatic principle for the preemption and conquest of our physical resources. With the reservation that it produced ruthless exploitation of land and people, and tragic waste of both, it worked. But in the complex industrial communities that have mushroomed up behind every geographic frontier, it can hardly be said to have worked at all and for perfectly clear psychological reasons. Given three critical factors of the American frontier in the nineteenth century—the lure of gain from the virgin continent, the public sanction of *laissez-faire,* and the law of individual differences—the problem of the power and the glory was bound to emerge all over again in man's history. These three subtle psychological factors reinstated by the conditions of our time, must be studied together as a single interrelated unit if the problem of freedom and control in modern life is to be understood and solved.

As a consequence of this profound cleavage between the individual and the culture, the community in which the American child grows up today continues to divide itself in a deep dichotomy. In reaction to every political, economic, social and moral problem, the people scatter themselves over a scale of convictions and loyalties from diehard Right to die-hard Left. For convenience of thought and discussion we shall divide them at the middle, posing Center-to-Right against Center-to-Left. In general, the Center-to-Right believes in the Exploitive Tradition and interprets freedom as minimum restraint; it is in short for the predepression, prewar *status quo.* The Center-to-

Left believes in the Great Tradition, would design social reconstruction by the direction of social trends, believes that we shall never go back to anything predepression or prewar, concludes that we are in a cultural revolution and that now is the moment to guarantee our children a free and abundant world. On each side, of course, there are considerable differences from a middlish-near-the center to an extremist-right-or-left.

As a consequence, the children of America are being brought up between two warring camps. On the scenes of American life, opposed concepts clamor for adherents.

On the economic scene; the "I" concept of the private, preempted, restricted use of productive property opposes the "We" concept of its public development and maximum use for all the people.

On the political scene: How much government in economic life? sets the issue. The "I" concept—"the less government the better"—opposes the "we" concept—"enough government to keep the system going at abundance level."

On the esthetic scene: Expression versus Regimentation. Shall I say what I see, my way—assuming competence to meet rigorous criteria of Form; or shall I reproduce standard classic styles? Shall I put down my view of the profoundly formative forces of life or merely photograph the superficial contours of the external shape?

On the ethical scene: The conflict centers around the deep-seated Structure of Power and the respective roles of authority and self-determination.

Such a statement of I and We leaves little doubt of its crucial importance and, in bringing our discussion to a close I shall ask you to project the current trends a bit into the future. If we do so we cannot fail to deduce from them the continued encroachment of We upon I, of Society upon the Individual. The trends of technological invention and industrial production document it, and they are confirmed now by our success in harnessing atomic energy. If still further confirmation is needed, it is provided by the utter inefficiency and wastefulness of the doctrine of Freedom-as-absence-of-restraint and the lag of the acceptance of the Sustained-Yield principle behind the principle of greed-for-immediate-profits. The spirit of the social frontier speaks in tones that will not be downed. I can draw no other conclusion from the century-long curves of culture than that the socialization of the quantity production of standardized goods and services will markedly increase. Current signs are convincing that the people of the United States will be the last of the major industrial ones to do it, as the Russians were the first. But that this outpost of exploitation will fall in a generation, and a world of magnificent physical abundance will become an actuality I am convinced.

But I confront the acceleration of the encroachment of We upon I in the spiritual field with infinite anxiety for the life that our children will live. For the problem of their generation will be: How to preserve the Individuality of the Person in the midst of a society that has collectivized the production of standardized commodities and services? For the spirit of the American frontier also built a concept of the Person that is basic to the Great Tradition. By the Person I mean the mature personality who is aware of others as Persons and of his basic interdependence with them. I mean one who, while insisting obdurately on the integrity of himself, recognizes and accepts the dignity of every other human being, admires the honesty and beauty, the authentic inner truth that emanates from another mature personality. On the creative side it means the unswerving determination to say what he sees of life, in his own unique way, and with rigorous competence of statement. But to say it in spite of social pressure, no matter from what source. The mature personality sets before himself the old adage "Know thyself," carries off his behavior with a ready sense of humor, with special reference to himself. But above all, the Person has psychological ballast in a thought-out philosophy of life which gives consistency and a steadiness of direction to his behavior. The Person is he that has confronted society's questions of value and has endured the ordeal of making his own statement in answer to them.

I know no more subtle distinction in the body of modern, psychological concepts than that of the Individual and the Person. From birth to death, the human individual endures the struggle to become a

Person. The nub of it, I think, is in the ever-widening radius of awareness of the relation of each Self to other Selves. Every individual knows himself, as Waldo Frank says, to be

a focus of concentric cycles of wholes: his family, his calling, his nation, mankind, and—last and first to round the cycle—the whole of Being whose atmospheric touch upon his body in his hours of meditation he will recognize as God.

And the problem is not simplified by recognizing that the Person develops best in a society which is devoted to the public welfare. As Frank says:

A society where, not the individual but *the potential person* is the norm of value, is one in which all intelligence is dedicated intrinsically . . . to the public welfare. For the act of social justice is in the heart of the potential person who knows himself *a* heart of all men and of the universe; and whose knowing—however stumbling and full of error—is action. Not the individual, not the individual economic class or nation which is the sum of individuals, but the person and the group of persons is the valid integer for social justice.[7]

So I reiterate the menace of the powerful trend of socialization against the maintenance of Personality.

All too briefly stated, this is the chief creative problem confronting our people today on the American spiritual frontier. Speaking as an educator, I say one next step we can and must take—we must make a grand synthesis of these detonating concepts of the frontiers of the mind and the imagination. It has long been known that if the wealth of modern creative thought could be assembled, twentieth-century man would command sufficient wisdom to guide the world. Educational workers know that its result would be the School of Tomorrow brought to life today. Enough is known of our culture to design the content of that education. Enough is known of man, his knowing and his behavior to organize its teaching. Enough expressive experience has been lived to guarantee a high order of esthetics. Enough is known of the first principles of conduct to solve the problem of freedom and

---

[7] Waldo Frank, *Chart for Rough Water,* New York, Duell, Sloan and Pearce, pp. 128, 132.

control. The four foundations of education—a Sociology, a Psychology, an Esthetics, and an Ethics—lie scattered in many places, the makings of a great education. But these makings have never been organized in a single synthesis and that is necessary if they are to be focused directly on the problems of man. Let us make that great synthesis as the creative contribution of our time.

VIII

THE SPIRIT OF AMERICAN PHILOSOPHY

BY

JOHN HERMAN RANDALL, Jr., Ph.D.

Professor of Philosophy, Columbia University

I

At a recent gathering a distinguished American philosopher was setting forth his view of the function of ideals. He started with a technical exposition of what is known, in the jargon of the professionals, as "Value Theory"—one of the more abstract and formal disciplines invented by his German teachers for dealing with the most real and concrete of living human problems. He went on to develop the ideas of his Harvard professor, Josiah Royce, on "loyalty to loyalty"—we should extend our loyalty to our own ideals and highest commitments to embrace the loyalties of other men and groups to their ideals, provided their commitments in turn are such as to impel them to be loyal to our loyalties. And the speaker pushed Royce into a philosophy of "cultural pluralism," within a framework of mutual cooperation between groups.

The assemblage to which he spoke was typical of our gatherings of cosmopolitan intellectuals. I remember particularly a gifted and sincere Irish Catholic, who happens to be writing a dissertation on the philosophy of cooperation. There was a brilliant Irish anticlerical—a member of the Longshoremen's Union, a lecturer on psychoanalysis, an admirer and personal friend of John Dewey. There was a Greek, a close friend of the Orthodox clergy in the city. There were several Italians, including an Italian Baptist. There were a number of theological students from Union Seminary, and a sprinkling of secular evangelists from Teachers College. And since, after all, this was a group of intellectuals and students of philosophy, there were present a good many Jews, of all persuasions, including several theological students. There was even a man from Princeton.

The speaker, the philosopher himself, was a Harvard Ph.D.; he had been a Rhodes scholar, and a student at the University of Berlin in its great days. At present he is a professor of philosophy at Howard University. He happens to be a Negro.

This, I take it, is an illuminating illustration of "American philosophy," both in the theory of cultural pluralism the speaker developed, and in the typically American experience of cultural cooperation it exemplified—the kind of social experience out of which that theory had taken form. For I am assuming that *"American* philosophy" is not quite the same thing as "philosophy in America"; and that the contribution of America to philosophy is by no means identical with the contributions of philosophers in America.

The latter has had a long, interesting, and significant history. It began with the philosophy of the Puritans—with "Ramism," a Calvinistic philosophy of the sixteenth century. As Perry Miller has recently made clear, the Puritans of New England, like their British colleagues, were greatly addicted to the views of the Frenchman Peter Ramus. His death in the Massacre of St. Bartholomew's had endeared his thought to Calvinists in every land. And thus was initiated the history of European ideas on American soil. For Americans have always drawn on Europe for the materials of their thinking. They are the heirs of the great heritage of the classic tradition of Western thought, and in their education and their intellectual life they have preserved an unbroken continuity with the ideas of their European ancestors. And they doubtless always will, whatever further ideas they may also come to draw upon—from the great Oriental civilizations, for instance. That is why it is impossible to understand American philosophy and thought, and American moral and spiritual ideals, without a thorough knowledge of that classic tradition of Western Europe. In an inescapable sense American philosophy and thought, like American culture in general, began in Palestine and Greece.

But philosophy is the attempt to understand the meaning and significance of everything man has learned, of himself and his world and his God. And you can understand what is significant and important in what other men have learned in their long experience—you can find out what it all really means—only by bringing those lessons to bear on your own experience, and by reflecting on both in juxtaposition. You can make a real contribution to philosophy only if you use your own experience to modify and reconstruct and extend what has been learned by others.

Americans long worked over European ideas, as Jonathan Edwards and Samuel Johnson worked over and elaborated the thought of Locke and Berkeley, without American experience contributing very much to their thought. Hence for several centuries they were able to make little real contribution to philosophy, since the novel currents of American life contributed little through them. It is instructive to note that this seems to have remained pretty much true of Latin-American thought down to the present. Thinkers south of the Rio Grande have made interesting minor additions to the stream of European thought. But they have displayed little fresh insight or originality of their own; for their thinking has remained largely a kind of exotic veneer, almost completely divorced from the realities of Latin-American experience. Just such a colonial situation long prevailed in the North American colonies as well.

The distinctive experience bred of the new American conditions first began to modify European ideas in political thinking. Hamilton and Madison developed the political philosophy of federalism; Jefferson, in addition to his Virginian agrarianism and his novel American version of democracy, laid great emphasis on local decentralization. This tradition of a widely distributed political responsibility, bred of American conditions, still makes the European type of centralized "socialism" very difficult for Americans to stomach. Our social experience has led, not to a state socialism, but rather to syndicalism and decentralized group responsibility—to various forms of economic federalism.

But though Americans have long displayed independence and originality in political theory, it was not until the last generation that a series of great thinkers began seriously to reconstruct European philosophical ideas to fit American experience. These men succeeded in working out a distinctive "American" philosophy which gives genuine intellectual expression to the American spirit and temper of mind. Since it has been the problems of man and society that have furnished the starting point of their reflections, they are probably most widely known for their contributions to social science; they are responsible for raising American social science to its position of unique originality and promise. But the fact that they have devoted much attention to social problems and to elaborating novel intellectual tools for understanding and dealing with them hardly deprives them of their stature as genuinely philosophical thinkers. For they have managed to develop certain distinctive ideas and characteristic approaches to intellectual problems which many of them have generalized and raised to the level of a comprehensive philosophical attitude and way of thinking. In them, though their materials are European and though they are masters of the Western intellectual tradition, something new has happened as a result of American social experience. It would be quite impossible to mistake the background against which they have pushed that tradition in their own distinctive direction.

This original and characteristic American philosophy—as distinguished from philosophy in America—has in fact developed largely from reflection on the basic ideas underlying American social science. The dean, and still by far the most representative of American philosophers, is John Dewey. His thought has been aptly called "American anthropology critically aware of its presuppositions and leading principles." So true is this that any serious attack on Dewey's thought involves breaking lances with Franz Boas and his pupils, as well as with a host of other social scientists. A series of great figures—William James, Charles S. Peirce, Thorstein Veblen; Charles H. Cooley, Wesley C. Mitchell, Charles A. Beard, Franz Boas; George Herbert Mead, John Dewey, Walton Hamilton—have now for two generations been bending and reconstructing European ideas to reflect the lessons of American life. Their thought forms the background of all serious philosophizing today that can be called distinctively "American."

It is not, of course, the major inspiration of all important philosophy in America. There have been many able American thinkers, relatively insulated from the main currents of American experience and thought, whose intellectual interests have focused on the problems of the European philosophical tradition. There were the Cornell idealists of the past generation, like Creighton and Thilly, minds quite the equal of their European contemporaries. There is the unique Santayana, whose thought has been stimulated if not inspired by his New England experience. There are the many competent Neo-Thomists who have continued a great tradition. There are the Logical Empiricists, like the Prussian systematizer Carnap and the more tolerant Austrian Neurath, inspired by the international stream of natural science, and negatively provoked by German irrationalism. But whatever important contributions these vigorous individuals and schools have made to philosophy, America has contributed little to their thought—save by welcoming them, tolerating them, and letting them pursue their various intellectual enterprises.

Other figures, certainly as brilliant and undoubtedly more original, have made their very significant contributions to the classic tradition of Western philosophy because they have reflected deeply on American experience as well—because they have brought the "American spirit" to bear on that classic tradition and have used each to fertilize the other. Consider how differently German transcendentalism developed in its native home and in the hands of Emerson and his circle. The ablest of the idealists of the past generation, Josiah Royce, soaked as he was in German philosophy, used that thought to give intellectual expression to many of the characteristic themes of American life. The sources of William James were largely British and French, yet no thinker has ever been more American; the same is true of Peirce. Whitehead, Woodbridge, Morris R. Cohen, Dewey; are all distinguished equally for their mastery of the history of ideas and for their vigorous expression of the American spirit. It is such thinkers that come to mind when we consider "American philosophy."

II

Just what do we mean by "the American spirit," by "expressing the lessons of American social experience"? What is this temper and attitude of mind that has received technical development in the more original strains of American social science, and philosophical expression in the outstanding American thinkers?

The essence of the American spirit is to be cosmopolitan, to be free from the provincialism, the parochialism, and the prejudices of European lands, with their tight unified national traditions bred of a millennium of competition and warfare. That spirit is found at its best in our metropolitan cities, like San Francisco, Chicago, or New York. Our fellow countrymen often say that such cities are not like the rest of America; they sometimes insist that Chicago or New York is not truly "American" at all. On the contrary, I am profoundly convinced that our great cosmopolitan cities are the most "American" of all our many communities. They have learned to understand best just what America really means.

For America is not a nation, but a continent—a continent in process of growing into a community. It is not a "nation": it is not bound together by those ties which European nations cherish—a common origin, a common "stock," common traditions, a common religion. America, thank God, is united by no common and shared faith, to make it intolerant of other faiths and loyalties, as faith so often does. America has always been a welter of differing faiths, in which each has had to learn first to let the others alone, then to respect them, and eventually to cooperate with them. Hence for Americans a man's "faith" has been not a "public" but a "private matter"—an attitude quite incomprehensible to Europeans, for whom "faith" has normally served as a club to enforce public uniformity.

America is united in no common tradition—save that of living and working together. America faces forward to a shared task, not backward to shared memories. It is willing to learn—and what is still harder, to forget, to scrap prejudices, and to experiment with what is new. The United States is bound together not, like European nationalities, by a common past, but by a common future—by common interests, common enterprises, and common methods of getting along with each other. It is unified, not in a common religion, which would inevitably look to what has already been, but in a common education, which looks to what is yet to be.

Our cosmopolitan cities understand these essential facts of American life rather better than the smaller and less urban communities. Now that the Western frontier has disappeared, they probably understand its meaning best of all—or rather, the true "American frontier" has now definitely found its home in our great metropolitan centers; they have become the locus of that social experience which is distinctively "American." Indeed, the latest crop of historians, correcting the enthusiasm of F. J. Turner and his followers, have recently been assuring us that it has been so from the beginning. It was our coastal cities as well as the agrarian frontier that served as the meeting place where men and women of the most diverse origins came together to work upon the common problems of creating a new world.

The least "American" parts of our country are probably to be found in the Southeast—because men there are more backward-looking, and preoccupied with remembering the past, not with facing the future. And this is in large part because in those regions there are to be found so few who have come consciously seeking America that the rest fail to appreciate fully what they possess. In our cities there are so many who have been looking for it! They have been seeking not only freedom *from* everything that makes European lands integrated nations: common origins, common stock, common traditions, a common religion, a common faith—together with common prejudices, intolerance, persecution, fear, and war. They have come looking for the freedom *to* better themselves—to make money, to raise their standard of living, to learn more themselves and to give their children an education, above all to give them "more opportunity." They have been seeking, in a word, just what all our American social programs have always set as our American goal.

It often seems that those understand best what America means who have grown up in the homes of such "seekers," and have had ingrained in their youth what their parents hoped and learned. That is why it is so fortunate for America that the recent tragedy of Europe has once more brought to her shores so many fine men and women, carrying with them so much that we need, the very best of Europe. The result is bound to make America more American—in the precise sense in which we have been trying to define the American spirit.

The one universal American faith is the faith in certain *methods* of working with other and different men—in certain ways of co-operating with others. It is the faith in the method of Liberty—which for Americans has always meant primarily, "Let the other fellow do what he wants." It is the faith in the method of Democracy—which means for us, "Let him have a voice in deciding where we shall go." It is distinctly *not* the faith in any common pattern or goal—the kind of faith that always makes men cruel and ruthless toward dissenting minorities.

III

Something like this has been the lesson of American social experience. And in expressing this "American spirit," in our generation our American philosophy, whatever European ideas and intellectual traditions a thinker may have set out with, has come to exhibit certain of the pervading and controlling traits of our culture and our temper of mind. Running through the thought of the outstanding American philosophical thinkers today is (1) a pluralistic temper, (2) an experimental attitude, (3) an egalitarian spirit, and (4) an institutional approach. With Royce, that thought talks of "loyalty to the loyalties of others." With Peirce, it speaks of "chance, love, and logic." With James, it recounts "the varieties of religious experience." And with Dewey, it sets forth "a common faith"—in the intelligent cooperation of men of different traditions and experiences. Each of these characteristic titles bespeaks American authorship; it is hard to imagine any one of them coming out of another background.

1. American philosophy received its widely shared stamp of pluralism from the protest of James and Dewey against the "block-universe"—the monistic thought of the absolute idealism that dominated academic circles around 1900. Long taken for granted in technical philosophy, this pluralistic temper has recently received renewed significance in political terms. For in a social context pluralism means the opposition to any form of totalitarianism, and thus preserves a continuity with the political thinking in which the effect of American experience was first felt. The tradition of political "federalism" has today broadened into an emphasis on various forms of economic

federalism, and indeed into a generalized philosophic "federalism" or pluralism.

Throughout their thinking, our social scientists have come to place the emphasis heavily on a pluralistic approach—on particular contexts and perspectives, on specific problems and situations. Like all Americans, they prefer to consider strains and difficulties as they arise, so far as possible in their own appropriate terms rather than within the framework of a general social and philosophical theory. In contrast, the German social thinker has always prefaced his analysis of "the State" with a theory of the whole universe; the French, and even the English, have tended to think in abstract and general terms, like those of classical political economy. European anthropologists are prone to set forth an all-embracing theory of cultural development or diffusion; Boas and the Americans examine the specific traits of different "culture areas." A recent British study was published with the title, "*The* Money Rate in *the* Money Market." An American economist would have been much more likely to write on "Money Rates in Money Markets." For example, Walton Hamilton defines property as "an abstract symbol for a shifting miscellany of equities." This is the expression of a wholly different and characteristic philosophy.

Americans are convinced they are living in a complex universe containing in disordered profusion quite a mess of miscellaneous stuff. Its various parts, to be sure, are not wholly disconnected; each sets up a train of reverberations in the rest. But they can be isolated, and examined and dealt with by themselves. There is no discoverable neat logical pattern, with a fitting pigeonhole for everything. There are differences, irrelevancies, oppositions. Things are "relative," but not in the sense of a vague relativism. They are always "relative *to*" some ascertainable context or situation, to some specific problem; and the American is resolved to consider each in terms of its own peculiar setting. Technically, this attitude appears in our philosophies as an "objective relativism" or "contextualism." German thinkers also have been anxious to recognize oppositions and contradictions in experience. But they have usually transformed the brute fact of antagonism into a "principle of contradiction," and erected that "dialectic" structure into the pattern of the cosmos. American thinkers, strive as they may, have never been able to take such a wholesale "dialectic" seriously.

The roots of this pluralistic attitude lie deep in American experience. There is, first, the fact that American thinkers have always been able to enjoy a certain perspective on the various cultures of Europe. They have been bound to no single intellectual tradition, but have been free and usually eager to gain a knowledge of all the major currents of European thought. In consequence, American thought at its best has escaped the restrictions of the relatively isolated national traditions of Europe. It is not provincial, like the French, or insular, like the British.

Secondly, the fact that America is a continent and not a nation has long led to an emphasis on "regionalism," on the wide differences between the various sections of our vast country. Regional and sectional conflicts have formed the very substance of our history, as men like Turner and Beard have made clear. And these sectional differences have been reflected in cultural, fully as much as in economic, divergencies of interest.

Thirdly, there is the deep-seated and traditional religious pluralism of American life. From the very beginning Americans have been forced to recognize the fact that religious revelation differs from sect to sect and even from man to man. Equally good men look out upon the world through different windows, and have beheld diverse visions of God. Long accustomed to this diversity of faiths in the most important matters, Americans have found other diversities equally natural.

Finally, there is the historical pluralism, the emphasis on the temporal succession of quite different customs and beliefs, fostered by the extraordinarily rapid changes in American life since the coming of industrialization. The idea was originally formulated by the Germans and was taken up by Veblen and the institutional evolutionists; but American experience served to make it seem natural and popular. In its German version, as in Spencerian evolution, there was but a single significant stage at any one time. For Hegel, the *Weltgeist* settled and made its home in one country after another. To American thinkers this notion of a unilinear development has always seemed alien and uncongenial. And equally alien has appeared the German idea of a single "class-conflict"—two unified blocs of culture focused on a single issue. Such a view violates all American experience of conflict and social antagonism as almost infinitely plural and specific.

2. Intimately bound up with this pluralistic attitude is the experimental temper that has come to characterize American philosophy. That attitude leads naturally to investigation of the specific situation and problem, to enquiry into the precise circumstances. Pluralism hardly fosters the deductive and rationalistic procedure of hitting upon some more or less happy idea and then confidently elaborating its implications for everything else. The pluralist has to proceed experimentally to find out under just what circumstances that idea is relevant and valid. American thought does not take kindly to the abstract analysis of the "typical case." In a complex world no case is really typical, each is ultimately unique. Americans show little concern with abstract forms and structures. Thus Walton Hamilton does not conduct an inquiry into "Capitalism" in general; he produces instead a classic on a specific phase of production, *The Bituminous Coal Industry*.

American social thinkers are concerned to elaborate techniques of inquiry for particular fields; they show little interest in constructing elaborate formal frames of reference for society in general. Often, indeed, this means the intensive gathering of "data" without any leading ideas or guiding principles, the sheer description of "facts." We like to boast that this is being "hard-boiled" and "realistic." We pile up mountains of statistics without direction, and effect a host of meaningless "correlations." Much of this labor, of course, gets us nowhere, and for all our pains we find the data inadequate. Yet even this devotion to sheer fact can puncture facile European speculations, and a Boas can easily dispose of the diffusionist theories of a Rivers' *Children of the Sun*.

But though this "experimentalism" often expresses itself today in praise of the "experimental" or "scientific" method and in the worship of the "scientific temper of mind," it hardly leads to what its critics call the cult of "scientism"—rest in the present "conclusions" of science. Indeed, the experimental attitude of American philosophy, as it finds expression in the thought of James or Dewey, goes far deeper than mere admiration for natural science. It is really a product of the Romantic temper, the openness to all kinds of experience, and of the American confidence in the future—however discouraged, we feel there is always more, the chance of new discoveries and fresh opportunities. Above all, we can always hope to *do* something about any situation.

Thus, confronted by philosophies born of the agonies of European culture—by "Neo-Orthodoxy" in theology, by "the new sense of sin," by the "Existential" philosophy—by what Reinhold Niebuhr calls "the persistence of Sin in the lives of the redeemed," and by what the psychoanalysts, following Kierkegaard, call *"Angst,"* nameless dread—Americans show no desire, like the Germans, and now, apparently, the French in turn, to revel in a kind of *allgemeine Weltschmerz*, a "tragic sense of life." They are inspired instead to take active steps to do something about it all. They convert Kierkegaard, if they can take him seriously—few Americans can—into the demand for an adequate psychotherapy, and proceed to explore eagerly the appropriate techniques for getting over it.

3. Thirdly, there is the pervasive spirit of egalitarianism in American thought. Our philosophies display a keen sense of differences—between diverse groups, institutions, points of view, wants, needs, etc. Yet they welcome all of them with interest and sympathy, as possessing an equal value to begin with. All of them have to be taken into account and explored; no one can be neglected save at our peril. The practical problem is to harmonize and adjust them in some working fashion. But there is no desire to organize them into a neat system in which each will have its predestined and appointed place. James is eager to explore the many varieties of religious experience. But he makes no attempt to decide which is the "best" variety—except in his typically American prejudice against any variety that has been too neatly systematized into an ecclesiastical scheme that must inevitably become "second-hand." And James founds his whole ethical theory on the principle that at the outset, until inquiry has proved otherwise, "every claim is an obligation"—whatever any man demands must be given due consideration and somehow adjusted, so far as possible, to

the equally valid claims of everybody else. As Dewey puts it, every impulse, every demand, every experienced good has a *prima facie* right to recognition in moral deliberation. The task of moral philosophy is to suggest such a reconstruction of the pattern of living and of our social arrangements as will give them all the fullest possible fulfilment.

This egalitarian attitude likewise has its background in American social experience. Practically, it springs from the American method of conducting affairs by means of compromises, bargains, and deals—by the method of what we cherish as "politics" and glorify as "democracy." We manage to get on with each other by giving any group enough of what it insistently demands so that it will not object too loudly. There is in this process plenty of struggle and conflict, plenty of jockeying for position. But we feel that this is right and just, provided the bargaining and compromise take place between groups whose strength is relatively equal. All of our great popular political programs—all that have captured the imagination of enough men to become genuine forces in American life—have aimed in the end at keeping different groups equal in power. Under changing conditions the balance has to be redressed by some new effort to reestablish parity—by the Square Deal, the New Freedom, or the New Deal. We are under no illusions that we can ever permanently "solve" all our problems, or establish the perfect society. But we are convinced that we can set up the conditions under which different groups can bargain more equitably and fairly.

Intellectually, this egalitarian or democratic attitude has led to a distrust of all systems which attempt to assign everything its proper place, and to give every group its own station and duties. Instead, we are concerned to work out fluid techniques for adjusting inevitable differences and conflicts of interest. In contrast, since the days of Auguste Comte the tradition of French social thinking has been antidemocratic; it has sought order rather than adjustment. The German tradition has been predominantly paternalistic—it has thought in terms of "experts" telling people what to do, running things efficiently for them, planning for "the proletariat" or "the masses."

Expert knowledge must always direct activity *for* the nation—it must lead them, use them for their own good, perhaps "capture" them in order to do it.

Such an attitude leads to a very definite and characteristic kind of social theory—whether "conservative" or "radical" seems of secondary importance. And the American thinkers we have been analyzing will have none of it. German social theory, even Marxian theory, they regard as inherently undemocratic. To them it seems to lead, not to inquiry into what men want, but to persuasion to what is already known to be good for them. In American social theory there are no "masses" and no "leaders" in this Continental sense. Jacksonian democracy, to be sure, developed the idea of strong political leadership. But the American "leader" never owes his position to the fact that he knows better than they what is good for men, and can secure it for his unquestioning followers. His powers are very definitely delegated powers; he is a leader because he can express and crystallize the group experience. And when he ceases to do that, Americans show no hesitation in repudiating him. We do not forget the fate of Wilson. And Franklin Roosevelt, who never claimed to know better than his countrymen what was good for them, was most successful when he did not forget the democratic roots of his strength.

4. These permeating traits of our most original American social science, to which our outstanding philosophers have given generalized intellectual expression, are brought to a focus in a distinctively American version of that institutional approach to questions of social analysis to which industrial conditions have led all serious philosophizing today. Since Hegel we have all recognized the fundamentally social character of human action and human thinking; we have remembered once more what the Greeks knew, that individuality and freedom are social and group achievements, and are realized only through active participation in the institutions of an organized society. But American institutionalism, though it owes much to Hegelian ideas, is a distinctively pluralistic, experimental, and egalitarian institutionalism. With Walton Hamilton it regards socal institutions not as sacrosanct, but as "clusters of usages," as social arrangements that happen to have become established. With Dewey,

whose *Human Nature and Conduct* still remains the best exposition of the importance of institutionalized habits, it takes them as accustomed ways of doing things. This American emphasis on habit as the basis of social institutions is largely a reading in social terms of James's famous chapter on "Habit." William James, in fact—the James of the *Principles of Psychology,* not the James of "The Will to Believe"—is the starting point of most serious American social science. James never really happened in Europe; there is almost no background of experimental psychology in European social thinking. Psychology there means mainly psychoanalysis with its therapeutic mythologies. To Americans, this fact makes most European social philosophy, whatever its suggestive insights, seem already antiquated.

Americans, when they think in institutional terms, see society as a complex of crystallized habits; they see all change, all social action, as operating ultimately upon and through institutionalized behavior. Hence all reflection on society is dealing ultimately with "psychological" factors—though "psychological" in the biological, experimental, and functional sense. Its subject matter is human behavior—the habits of men and their ways of modifying them. This does not mean that American thinkers are "behaviorists" in the sense of having a mechanistic and physiological concern with muscle-twitches. It means rather that they are seeking overt, public, observable, and verifiable types of behavior. They do not emerge, like the Germans, with social "forms," *Gestalten,* "styles," *Geister,* or "spirits." These are all structural concepts which lend themselves much more easily to intuition and *verstehendes Denken* than to observational and experimental procedures. Our thinkers prefer to deal with ascertainable habits and ways of feeling and believing—which are functional and public concepts. All social and institutional "structure" is indeed a generalization from institutionalized habits. This conviction explains the American reliance on that great instrument of generalization, statistical method. Such attitudes are easily combined with a fundamental pluralism of approach, with a sense of the uniqueness, the equal worth of all habits and institutions.

Such institutional thinking leads our present-day philosophies to regard knowledge—any enterprise of organized science, for example, like our body of social science—as an institutionalized set of ways of acting and behaving. Hence in our philosophies "pure theory" and "practice" are not divorced, but rather indissolubly united. All "theory" is functional in character; it is, in the first place, an instrument of furthering inquiry and, in its broader uses, of bringing knowledge to bear on action. Science is ultimately to be understood as one institution in a complex culture, the way developed in that culture of dealing with the kind of problems that have led to the working out of that particular organized method of securing and testing valid beliefs.

Religion likewise seems to American philosophers most fruitfully treated in such institutional terms as a complex set of institutionalized ways of feeling, acting, and even believing, with definite functions of its own to perform in the culture that pursues it. Particular religions are best understood as comprehensive expressions of particular cultures—in some cases, as themselves particular cultures or civilizations. Such an approach leads naturally to a philosophy of cultural and religious pluralism, in which the problems of competing faiths find an intellectual solution in the cooperative fellowship of a community of religions.

American philosophy thus culminates in a method—a method of dealing with specific problems and intellectual difficulties. And this emphasis on means and methods naturally finds its most important expression in a method of evaluating ends and goals—in a method of bringing all available knowledge to bear on the questions of the course and direction of human action and conduct. It treats the American ideal of "democracy" as a means and instrumentality—as the institutionalized method of adjusting and compromising the differing and often conflicting desires of diverse groups and parties. Democratic methods are the methods of politics, of giving enough to each group so that its temper will remain below the boiling point, and it will go on bargaining and compromising with the rest.

It treats intelligence itself as a means—as a method of inquiring into problems, of discovering ends and values that will bring the utmost of satisfaction, and of finding, or constructing, the means that will most effectively lead to those ends. It finds such intelligence to be "social"—the effective knowledge and techniques of a society and its institutions for bringing that knowledge to bear on the problems of adjustment that have been generated.

And when American philosophy pushes its methods into a generalized method of intellectual criticism—of criticizing the abstractions which have served some particular interest, scientific, religious, or moral—when it pushes its methods, that is, into a genuine metaphysics, as it has done in its most distinguished representatives, in Peirce, James, Dewey, Woodbridge, Whitehead, or Cohen, it makes a significant contribution to the core of philosophy. It adds a new level to the long tradition of Western philosophical thought, because it brings the lessons learned from American experience to all the lessons men had learned before and left for us in the embodied philosophical wisdom of the past.

IX

THE SPIRIT OF AMERICAN LITERATURE

BY

ODELL SHEPARD, Ph.D.

Goodwin Professor of English, Trinity College, Hartford

This title, not of my choosing, suggests several questions. Has America in fact a literature of her own, mature enough now so that we can discern its main tendencies, prime characteristics, and essential spirit? Assuming that she has, in what degree is this literature really native, sprung of this soil and grown in the weather of the American mind and mood? What are the boundaries of the term "American Literature"? Ought it to include everything written within the present territory of the United States since the time of the first settlers—and, if not, just where and when should we say that it began? Finally, what is meant in this title, or what shall we agree to mean for the present purpose, by the words "Literature," "Spirit," and "American"?

Literature is primarily an art, and its main business therefore is with the creation of beauty for the sake of that delight which normal people find in the making and contemplating of beautiful things. In the art of literature beauty is created, and the delight that beauty gives is communicated, by the expression of significant human experience in words well chosen and arranged.

But literature is not, like music, a pure art, and the creation of beauty is seldom its only concern. By the nature of its materials and also of its medium of expression it is too entangled with human interests in their unimaginable complexity to remain unaffected—or should one say uncontaminated—thereby. And we are, of course, content that literature should remain impure, in the special sense I am now imposing upon that word. We expect from it, and we get, many kinds of value which no pure art can provide. Among other things, we expect that a large body of literature such as we Americans have produced will somehow reveal the essential nature or spirit of the race, the people, or the nation from which it came.

There is, to be sure, no obligation laid upon any artist, whatever his medium or his material may be, to characterize his epoch and country. Walt Whitman, we know, deliberately tried to do just that, but Edgar Allan Poe, Whitman's contemporary and fellow countryman, seems to have been just as deliberate in his effort to avoid every local and timely reference. One would not say that Poe's work was any the better or any the worse than Whitman's on this account. He did the work proper to a literary artist, as Whitman also did, in the creation of beauty.

And yet no man can write poetry or drama or fiction so purged of time and place that it reveals nothing about the land in which he lives and the people he addresses. Indeed, a writer's very refusal to characterize the world about him is inevitably, as with Poe, an implicit characterization. Thus all true literature, even when it approaches the purity of music, tells us something about the environment from which it sprang. Every civilized people does somehow describe itself, for the most part unconsciously, in its literature. From this it follows that when we can penetrate to the spirit animating the literature of a given people we begin to see and comprehend that people, so to speak, from the inside. We take that people off its guard, as though we overheard it talking to itself.

In its present context the word "spirit" means a dominant principle, an inherent quality, an essence, an indwelling genius of the sort that the Greeks called *ethos*. We may add that the spirit of a literature is not a temporary, intermittent thing but enduring, perennial, pervading, vitalizing the whole substance as breath does the body. Because it is a spirit, it cannot be defined, and it must be spiritually or imaginatively perceived. It is revealed only to those who can penetrate the letter that killeth to the spirit that giveth life. And when one believes that he has had his own revelation perhaps he can do no more for others than to quote a few highly characteristic sentences and then to say: "Here, in my judgment, is the very voice and accent and breath for which we have been listening. In these words I think I hear America speaking."

"America" one says, and says it glibly, easily, familiarly, as though one had thought out all that the word contains and implies! But how large a part, really, of that vast vague concept can we catch in the coarse net of language? To define a thing is to draw a line round it, to stake its boundaries. To define is to confine. Strictly speaking, we can define only that which is already finished. But America is still becoming. She stands even today in a dubious middle state between chaos and cosmos, and it doth not yet appear what she shall be. The effort to define her is like trying to paint a picture of a wind blown cloud. In order to suggest her protean nature we must speak in terms of movement, vicissitude, and change. Often we despair of finding any law that governs this incessant change, any perennial and innermost "spirit" that informs and guides and vitalizes our swiftly unfolding history. We are a badly bewildered people, neglectful of our own past, distracted in the present, and with no agreement about the future looming just ahead except that it is impenetrable to our straining eyes. Any clue that our literature might provide for us would, in our present situation, be welcome indeed.

In one of our characteristic proverbs we say that "we don't know where we're going but we guess we're on the way." Every nation and people in the world might say that, of course, with truth, but with us it has an added emphasis and a wider range of implications. It expresses our blind faith in activity for its own sake, our restless and random energizing, our willingness to "try anything once," and our ignorance of ourselves. Many critics of America have pointed out, but it will bear repeating, that we habitually spend our strength, unparalleled in amount, upon the improvement of means for the securing of unimproved ends. We are excellent at beginnings and fair at middles, but with the ultimate ends or goals of endeavor we are not much concerned. In methods, technics, ways and means, and in brave building for a future we seldom try even to imagine, we are the world's wonder. In the motives we assign for this building, when we pause to assign any at all, we are somewhat childish.

In extenuation of this fault and others of the same sort I think we may still plead that we are young—not, to be sure, with respect to the peoples or the ideas that make up the American mixture but as a political, social, and intellectual unit. It was less than a century ago that James Russell Lowell wrote to a friend: "I am the first poet who has endeavored to express the American idea," and then during the rest of his life he went on to show that he could not succeed in that endeavor.

It is partly because we as a people are so young, and because our literature is still younger, that we make such egregious blunders about ourselves and allow others to make them without refutation. For example, we regard ourselves as a materialistic people, hard-headed, this-worldly, and money-minded; but the fact appears to be that we care rather less about money for its own sake than any other modern people that one could name. Conversely, there is no modern country in which spiritual values have been given more attention and emphasis than they have been given, early and late, in our land. For half of our three hundred years the foremost minds of America brooded far more upon the soul's welfare than upon the body's comfort, and that long preoccupation has left its mark upon us. Not exclusively, but deeply, we are an idealistic people, and it is time for us to realize this fact of our nature.

True Americans have always lived on two levels, the practical and the spiritual. They have been obliged to struggle continually with the stubborn world of matter while subduing this continent to human uses, but while performing their titanic task of draining and bridging and building they have never quite forgotten the dream, the hope, the aspiration with which their forefathers came here. Consider, for example, the influence that the Bible has had in America. Instead of saying that we brought the Bible to these shores we ought to say that it brought us. The breath of ancient Hebrew prophets was in the sails that wafted the tiny Mayflower. The hope and faith of ancient poets, kings, and law givers was in the hearts of those who first sang the Lord's song in this new land. Our first dim outlines of a commonwealth in the Western world was drawn "as near as might be to that which was the glory of Israel." For three hundred years the solemn harmonies of David and Isaiah have sounded in the ears of American people, dignifying their speech, raising their thoughts above the level of the day's work, shaping their deeds, and filling their minds with images of grandeur human and divine. Most clearly of all, those harmonies have been echoed in our literature.

I have said that the spirit of America, as revealed in her literature, cannot be defined and will not yield to critical analysis. In some degree, however, it may be exemplified, and in such matters an ounce of example is often better than volumes of abstract generalization. Let us turn, then, to a few of our writers concerning whose intrinsic Americanism there can be no doubt. Let us look for them not in the eighteenth century because in that period we had not outgrown our colonialism, and not in the twentieth because the writing of our time is too close to us for full understanding. It is in the American literature that came of age at about the time of Emerson's address on *The American Scholar,* delivered at Harvard in 1837, that we shall find, I think, the clearest examples of the American spirit as it has been expressed in writing.

Upon entering the Public Library at Concord, Massachusetts, one sees the great seated statue, by Daniel French, of Ralph Waldo Emerson. The face of that statue expresses, as Emerson himself did in his life and work, two antithetical things. On the one side it is the face of a shrewd Yankee, hard to fool, worldly in every good sense, but on the other it is the face of a seer, a mystic, a man to whom only the things of the mind are real. It is a strange and arresting combination, this marriage of opposites, this paradoxical polarity, but it really did exist in Emerson as it does in us. That is one main reason why many of us feel sure, after allowing for his genius, that he was a typical, even a symbolic, American.

I choose from Emerson's writing one sentence in which this duplex nature of his and of ours, this conviction that man's life must be lived on two levels, is given a powerful and forever memorable utterance. The sentence is: "Hitch your wagon to a star!" There, I should say, in those six words, is the most compact expression that the American spirit has ever found for itself. Pausing upon that sentence, listening closely, thinking intently, weighing every word, I feel that I hear my country speaking.

The word "hitch" is a rustic and a barnyard word, suggesting daily chores. Some would say that no sentence beginning with that homely monosyllable could ever reach an idealistic, to say nothing of a spiritual, conclusion. Well then, they would be wrong—and seriously wrong because their opinion would be based upon the notion that the language of the spirit should be a special language, refined and elegant and remote from the actualities of life. Emerson holds, and he is here urging, just the opposite notion. He believes that the two levels of man's life interpenetrate, so that the language of the one may and should be applied to the other. He holds that the lowliest work may and should be done with the loftiest motives. And so he chooses the word "hitch" unerringly—a verb of action, one sees, in the imperative mood. He backs it up with the word "wagon," implying a journey of some sort, and a journey not in a chariot but in a vehicle completely utilitarian. But then comes the surprise, the paradox, the sudden vertically upward sweep to the word "star," with its idealistic implication that all work and all journeys have an eternal significance.

Consider the plainness, or what one may perhaps call the democracy, of that sentence, and then the infinite room it suggests for individual aspiration and freedom. See how it draws a thread of gold through a fabric of homespun. Observe that it is an oratorical sentence, shaped like so much of our American writing by the public art of the forum and pulpit and bar. It is a spoken writing or a written speech, addressed first of all to the ear and then to the nerves and muscles. It bristles with energy. Written in our own stinging style, it is not meant to soothe but to excite, even to startle. Its metaphor is bold to the point of extravagance, like our "tall tales" of the West. It shows that same vagueness about goals that I have already mentioned, for although a journey of some sort, and a lofty one, is implied, we are not told anything about that journey's direction. And I would point out, too, that this is the utterance of a mind essentially youthful addressing the young. In the writing of the Puritan Fathers of a hundred and fifty years before Emerson one feels the burden of the centuries, but this is the language of youth. Our literature has been growing younger for three centuries.

But perhaps this is enough to derive from one sentence, and that a brief one. Then let us consider a quiet remark made by Henry Thoreau, Emerson's neighbor and friend and in some sense his pupil: "If a man does not keep step with his companions perhaps it is because he hears a different drummer." The military metaphor, the symbol of marching or walking, is evident at once, and so is the dry under statement, the touch of sub-acid wit, so characteristic of the Yankee. Here, too, is the hint that we Americans live on two levels at once, and that we take our orders, or should take them, not solely from the captains of our human companies but also from within, or from above. Here, like the tone of a bugle, is that note of dauntless individualism, somehow to be reconciled with democracy, which has always been heard in our literature in so far as it has been really American. And here, finally, is another sentence which suggests that each of us is going a journey but that each should seek a goal of his own choosing, at his own pace, by his own route.

"If a man does not keep step with his companions perhaps it is because he hears a different drummer"—here is no hint of the goose step, no docile conformity, no fear of mass opinion. In this sentence one hears the authentic note of an individualism or personal independence which we have hitherto regarded, with some reason, as one of our major traits. Nowadays, however, the very word "individualism," recently soiled by all ignoble use, must be lifted out of the mire and cleansed before it can be applied to Thoreau without fear of misunderstanding. The rugged individualism he praised and practised was of course an attitude of the mind and the spirit, bearing no relation to what is now called "free enterprise" and the "profit motive." To be sure, Thoreau did value enterprise and freedom. He valued them so highly that he thought they should be the prerogative not merely of a few Americans at the top of the economic scramble but, in Jefferson's phrase, of "all men." And as for the profit motive, his writings echo with paraphrases of the everlasting question: "What shall it profit a man if he shall gain the whole world, and lose his own soul?"

To many of us, no doubt, Thoreau's individualism and Emerson's self-reliance now look somewhat antique, as though they had been the privilege only of an earlier and simpler America in which the problems of modernity had not brought their full weight to bear. However that may be, we are not now as a people living up to the declaration of personal independence which these men wrote and exemplified for us all. We have been called a herd-minded people, and have scarcely resented the charge. In our professional and business life, even in our schools and colleges, there is a shameful deal of pusillanimous "yesing the boss" and timorous conformity to low standards, which sometimes makes a thoughtful American afraid for the future. And yet of course we ought not to test the spirit of a people by their spiritless poltroons. Thoreau's sentence is true to the American tradition of upright and self-respectful manhood even though many of us are not. One's hope is that his words and example will do more to shape what is coming than any number of trucklers abasing themselves before "the bitch goddess, Success."

One hears it said that the inevitable trend of a democratic society is toward conformity, mediocrity, and the submergence of the individual. If that were true then we should at once declare democracy a failure and set up some other system, for no form of government or of society which does not steadily produce and maintain and defend individuals is even tolerable. But is it true that democracy and individualism are antagonistic? Walt Whitman did not think so when he wrote:

> One's Self I sing—a single, separate Person;
> Yet utter the word Democratic, the word *En Masse*.

And neither do the more considerate Americans of our time think so. That there is a real difficulty in maintaining personal independence in the midst of the crowd we do not deny, but neither do we yet believe that the task is impossible. This democracy has produced strong and self-reliant persons in the past. In the midst of the timid subserviency that we see about us, it is producing them still. And we cannot imagine the time when Americans, hearing or reading such words as I have quoted from Whitman, Thoreau, and Emerson, will no longer thrill at their expression of the essential American spirit as shown in American literature.

After admitting that I do not clearly understand what the word "American" means, I find that I have named several ingredients, so to speak, of the American spirit. Using as a guide two or three sentences from our literature, I have said or implied that the spirit of our country is youthful, aggressive, and kinetic, democratic and individualistic at the same time, idealistic, and determined to express itself on both the practical and the spiritual level. The literature this spirit has produced is aspiring, emotional and explosive, impatient of the restraints of literary form. It is weak in structure but mighty in pace and drive. Ours is not by any means the richest literature in the world, but year by year it is becoming more recognizably our own voice. With all its faults upon it, this literature is worthy of our close and affectionate attention, if only because it so clearly reveals to us our own faults.

X

THE SPIRIT OF AMERICAN EDUCATION

BY

JAMES MARSHALL, LL.B.

Member, Board of Education, City of New York

When I left for Europe last October (1945), I had thought of nothing to say about the spirit of American education, and, while I was on the other side, I completely forgot that I was supposed to talk here on that subject; then while I was trying to gather my thoughts a few days ago, I lost my voice, and I don't know how much of it there is today. So I suspect you are going to have a very unusual lecture. I think it will have to be a sort of travelogue with fading voice. It will end, I trust, by your sharing my time with me and using your voices, so that we can have a little conversation. Then I can rest my own voice.

I was very much interested in seeing what was happening in education in Western Europe. I had never studied education in Europe the other times when I had been over there, and what I saw was, I must admit, quite a surprise to me in spite of what I had read. I was impressed, of course, as every one must be impressed today, by the fact that in so many parts of Europe there is no actual education going on. Children go to school, teachers go to school; but there is and can be no education when youngsters and teachers have to sit in classrooms with their hats and coats on and see the breath issuing from their mouths, when the fuel is inadequate, when the windows are broken. The schooling facilities are short and time must be short in school for each child when there is—not starvation, I don't think there is now any starvation—but when there is hunger and inadequate diet. That is not a situation in which teachers can teach well and children can learn well. Yet it applies to a large part of continental Europe today.

Passing by those physical things, I think an American going to look at education in Europe is impressed by the selective character of European education. That is a polite way of saying it. Perhaps a more accurate way to say it would be the "class" nature of European education, and perhaps the most impolite way to say it would be the "undemocratic" nature of European education. For one is impressed constantly by the fact only a small proportion of the children of Europe can get into secondary education as we know it, or even as Europeans know it. Only a few children who are economically able to stand the expense of schooling can go on to secondary education. In England and on the Continent, only a small proportion of children are given a chance to get an academic education beyond the twelfth or fourteenth year of age.

One is also impressed by the fact that, at the age of eleven or twelve these children have to take an examination which determines their future intellectual and cultural life. At that time, they have to justify their going to a school which is either a grammar school in England or a lycée or gymnasium on the Continent. So young, they must show that they are the type of child which the school authorities think can be educated profitably.

This is no mere accident. I was interested in reading, in *Comparative Education* by Dr. Kandel, this statement which was so well borne out:

> Elementary education has everywhere, except in the United States, been considered as the education intended for the masses, which because of their social and economic status were regarded as unfit for secondary education provided for the training of the more favored classes for positions of leadership.[1]

You feel that very definitely in both England and on the Continent when it comes to public secondary education.

Now, that is justified in the eyes of many of these Continental people. I had a very interesting talk in France with one of the highest

[1] New York, Houghton, Mifflin, 1933.

school inspectors of the French Ministry of Education. We were discussing this question why more children couldn't get into lycées, why more children couldn't get secondary education in France. He said, "There is no question but that the parents of France are pressing for more education, for greater opportunity for secondary education for their children, but we are not so sure that is the right of all. Oughtn't we to maintain in the country a balance between those who go into the professional and intellectual life of the country and those who go into the working or laboring life of the country?"

It seemed to me that there we had, without any question, a great contrast between American education and European education. One very marked characteristic of the spirit of American education is that it tries to provide—though it hasn't always succeeded—education for the whole population through the secondary level at least. We believe that there must be no such thing as class education for our people. We don't want it. We believe that everyone should have an opportunity to go as far in education as his capacity will permit.

Now, I know we don't always succeed. There are situations, particularly in the rural sections and parts of the South, where children can't afford to go to school, where they haven't the shoes for bad weather, where the distances are too great, where the schools are not set up adequately for secondary education; but at least our principles, at least our aims, at least the spirit of American education, are against that kind of thing and favor a general education through the secondary level for all American children.

As I went on through the schools of Europe, I was impressed also by the classroom method, something we seem to be getting away from over here as much as possible. The method in the classroom is the old familiar one: the teacher asks a question, the child raises his hand to answer the question, the teacher looks around very learnedly—you can see that there are great processes of thought going on in the teacher's mind—to determine which lad is going to answer. "Bingo, you." The question-and-pounce method of education, I would like to call it.

Now that question-and-pounce method of education has many varieties as you go about. For example, it is very rude, in England, to snap your fingers. But when you come to France, and particularly Belgium, you may do that as fast as you can. In Germany you find a little different system—you wave your hand off your arm, just to show how passionately eager you are to answer the question.

That in itself seems to me to be illustrative in part of the spirit of European education—the competitive effort, the terrible competition in trying to get recognition, in trying to have your say, in trying to get what you have in you out, this terrific competition with your fellow students to be recognized.

So, you have there this learned statement by the teacher, the question and pounce, and in answer the great, excited competition for recognition. Another variety of this method is the choral answer. For example, the teacher will say, "Horses have four legs. How many legs has a horse?" Hands go up. "Yes?" "Horses have four legs. Horses have four legs." "Now, all together: horses have four legs."

This method of education is still found here and there in the United States, and was quite prevalent a generation ago; but it seems to have been largely abandoned here for what is perhaps a more flexible, less formal method of education, with less sense of finality in what the teacher says than in Europe, particularly on the Continent.

In giving this description of Continental European education, I do not mean to say that they have not many excellent teachers there. My estimation would be that the average teacher, particularly in the secondary school, knows a great deal more than the average teacher over here; and that if you accept their spirit of education, their frame of reference, perhaps they do a better job within it than we do within ours.

But now let us come back to this method of education which they use over there, and see what it shows with respect to the spirit of American education. I think we see that there is a much greater emphasis on inventiveness over here. We are interested in having the child not just repeat what the teacher or the book says, but think something through and work something out for himself.

We are interested, too, in developing adaptability. We must have adaptability in this country. That is the history of the American westward movement—adaptation of Americans and their institutions to a changing frontier, and then adaptation again from a rural agrarian life to an urban industrial life. We have the spirit of adaptation right in our Constitution—with various methods of amending the Constitution embedded in it. And we have made a great number of amendments.

We must, if we want to train ourselves to take our part in American life, encourage our children in adaptability. That seems to me to be in the spirit of American education, too, the idea, not of training youngsters to accept everything in its *status quo,* to accept the teacher or the authority as the final word, but of encouraging them to inventiveness, to thoughts of their own and self-expression, of developing the capacity to adjust to new situations. In more recent years we have come to the conviction that we must encourage children to work together in groups, not just as individuals competing with each other, trying to get the attention of the teacher or the authority. We want them to work together, to get group recognition and not merely individual attention.

I saw some interesting experimental schools in Europe, and what I am just saying to you was brought out very vividly by some of those experimental schools, particularly one at Sèvres just outside Paris, quite a remarkable school. I saw there an astounding thing—a class conducting itself with a teacher out of the room. That is something which just doesn't happen in Europe. Various projects were being worked out as they would be in a good school here—a little group working on a play, another group working on a machine. It was a perfectly remarkable example of cooperative effort, not competitive effort, and of serious study, where each child was trying to work with others and also to do his own thinking. That seemed to me to point out very vividly the difference between the spirit of the education on the Continent generally and education as we know it here, or as we are trying to develop it in this country.

For the same reason, I think that we have, as part of the spirit of American education, an intention to develop freedom, responsible freedom. One does not feel that about education where there is absolute domination of the classroom by the teacher, as he or she does dominate it in most of the world today, and unfortunately in many parts of the United States. In American education we aim to develop a sense of responsible freedom rather than subservience to those in authority. Such an aim is contrary to the idea of a class or selected group which goes on to higher education while the mass is limited to a lower level of education.

It seemed to me that the atmosphere with respect to the development of hand skills was quite different in Europe from what it is over here. I saw very little handwork in the schools. There was a little bit of knitting and crocheting and sewing by girls but very rarely a woodworking shop, except in a vocational school—or what passes for a vocational school. There I saw some shopwork. I was astounded to see in some of the industrial schools in Germany no shopwork at all; it was all a matter of lecture. One learned to be a butcher by having a man lecture to him about various cuts of meat, and then he might go out and get a job as a butcher's apprentice and learn the practical work; but there was no tie-up between the school and the practical work. It seems to me it is in the spirit of American education that handwork is not foreign to intellectual work and should not be. At the same time, intellectual pursuits, cultural interests, are not and must not be foreign to work of the hand. Each interest has something to share with the other. Whether they are primarily hand workers or intellectual workers, the technical skills and interests of each group have an important value for the other group.

Then I was very much interested—and this is particularly true in France—in the tremendous emphasis placed upon what is deemed to be intellectual. I would say somebody was an able person, and the answer would be, "Oh yes, very intellectual." I was interested in one school, a lycée for girls in Paris named after a French aviatrix. The faculty said, with great sorrow, "The name of this school must be changed. It should be named after some 'intellectual' person, not an aviatrix." I was interested, in Belgium, in how persistent is the study of Greek. One cannot go to a university and become a lawyer or a doctor without having Greek. The lycées and the universities there hammer at the classics. It is as though nobody could plead at the bar or treat a patient without a good knowledge of Latin and Greek.

I thought of our American scene. We are much criticized because

American education does not place emphasis on learning for the sake of scholarship alone. I am not saying that scholarship is not a valuable and important thing in the world; but when the emphasis of education is on scholarship, almost invariably there is left out much of the opportunity to develop personality, to develop character, and to develop individuality.

That is one of the difficulties, it seems to me, with secondary education for only the select few, as it occurs in Europe. It is so much on the level of intellect, so much on the level of scholarship, that these young people actually do not learn to adjust themselves to daily experiences, which must be given some kind of form and order if the problems of the world are to be solved and if the relationships between people in a nation, and between nation and nation, are properly to be solved.

Let me put it this way: For many generations, even centuries, the classics were the important thing as far as learning went. There was not as much else to learn, perhaps, as there is now. One must make choices today. I wonder whether in a world of atomic energy we ought not to pay a little less attention to the classics and a little more attention to atomic energy, social science, and human relations. There is a limit on time and effort for every person. We have to make choices. Do we want as large a proportion of people going into the classics as did formerly?

The matter of experience brings me to another illustration. I visited a little school in Le Havre. The original school just was no more. We had bombed it to smithereens. The student body of the school—or what remained of them—were attending classes in a sort of wooden barracks, constructed by students from Paris during their vacation time. The rooms were greatly overcrowded. I met there an alert little directress who spoke and read English fluently. She said that her ambition was to have in her school the kind of education found in England and America. I asked her what she meant by that, and she said,

Well, you know in our education here we recite in class about what we have heard or what we have read. I would like to have the children discuss what they have seen, and write about the things they have observed; and I would like to take them around the city and show them things, and then have them come back and use it in their classes.

I thought she had a pretty good idea about what American education was trying to do and we discussed that a little. She said,

Of course, I can't do it now. How can you do it with every inch of space in your classroom taken up by chairs? How can you do it when you have 76 children in your first-year class, and you only hold 48? I have to be glad when they are sick and can't all come. What can you do with older teachers? I have to let them go on as they always have while I work on the younger teachers.

It seemed to me that this little lady had caught what was really the basic thing in the spirit of American education. It was the importance of experience, the fact that education must be based, not just on words—whether they are spoken or written words—not just on papers, but on the experience which a youngster gets and with which he can interpret the learning, the scholarship, and the history of the race. It is through their own experience and the experiences of their families, teachers, and fellows that young people learn to reinterpret what is written and what is spoken.

This matter of the importance of experience was brought home to me by this little trip I had abroad. I thought I had read pretty well and had seen some pretty good pictures. There is no question about the excellence of American reporting, no question about the drama of the pictures we have seen in our magazines and newspapers and our moving pictures about Europe and its conditions. Yet, it was a shock to go over there and find that, in spite of all this good writing, in spite of the vivid pictures, one has to adjust oneself to something that is completely new. Then, strangely enough, when one comes home, he has to adjust himself all over again to his fellows who, with all the good will in the world, and all the good and careful reading in the world, have not had the experience that comes with a few weeks where there has been war and devastation.

I would like to see every congressman, every senator go to Europe and to Asia and go soon. I think it would be the saving of our country, our international relations, and the world, if we could have Congress adjourn and every congressman go and see the facts of life across the oceans. I say this to you with some feeling, because, as I said, it came to me as a shock that, in spite of intellectual experience and a strong belief that I had some sensitivity and some ability to feel for other people, I came upon things that seemed unheard of, unread, unpictured, entirely new. The importance of experience as compared with the word, was brought home to me with force then and impressed itself as the really important thing in the spirit of American education. The more we emphasize experience and the value of experience in translating the things of the spirit and of the mind, the more we shall have really educated ourselves, educated our young, and prepared ourselves to develop a world in which we can get on with one another and in which we, as a people, can get on with other peoples.

Of course, if we waited for experience alone to teach us, we should have to go through all the experiences of the cave men and the ancients, I suppose, and should never reach our own civilization. We have to have a combination. But what I am talking about particularly is the idea that you can learn everything through words, that classroom discussion can deal only with what is in the book and what the teacher says, minimizing the experiences in one's own life.

This matter was dramatized for me the other day. In a session of housecleaning my wife and I came upon a baby book of one of our children and discovered that the word or the phrase for naughty—being bad—was "down the lane." We worked out how that came about. We had read a book that all youngsters read, about Peter Rabbit who had gone down the lane to steal or nibble at some cabbages and was punished by his mother when he came back. So, "down the lane" meant something naughty and bad. I think that illustrates what I have in mind. Those words received their meaning from personal experience. Experience is the thing that makes words mean one thing to you, one thing to me, another thing to Dr. Johnson; and that is why it is important to have experience, and, if possible, to share experience.

Experience, from cradle to grave, is the basis of education, as I see it. I think this is so for all the better educators in America. Very slowly, and, like most folk art, were the degradation and popularization of an aristocratic art, which in this case was European.

Nevertheless, there were in colonial days modifications in styles and techniques imported from Europe, which were significant in foreshadowing later developments of distinctively American character. These are clearly marked in architecture. For example, in New England the abundance of wood led to its extensive use in building and the emergence of distinctive types of wall surface, such as clapboard and shingle. In contrast, the greater use of stone and brick in the central and southern colonies explains a closer adherence to English models. The use of wood, however, had a further influence, through putting in terms of wood architectural details carried out elsewhere in brick and stone. Not only did this produce distinctive variations, but because of the greater malleability of wood, it led to great precision and subtlety in the treatment of such features as mouldings and cornices. This precision and subtlety also appear in colonial furniture and silver, which are usually behind European work in originality and boldness of design, but reveal much feeling and skill in craftsmanship. Curiously, the reverse is generally true of painting. This was almost entirely limited to portraiture; and with a steady stream of painters coming from Europe, mainly from England, conceptions and methods were based on European example. But the standard of colonial demand was not too high; and colonial-born painters, such as Feke and Ralph Earl, tended towards a simplified, naïve form of current European work, with nevertheless, a direct and expressive quality of its own. There is, however, an exception to this. Copley, in his pursuit of technical perfection, brings painting into line with other arts.

Thus, despite his dependence on Europe, the colonial artist develops two distinctive characteristics. The first is skill in adapting a given style to local conditions, and refining upon it, even to the point of losing strength and vigor. This is not usually regarded as typically American; yet it is merely one aspect of the more generally recognized American manual skill and love of fine craftsmanship. Secondly, the colonial artist reveals much resource and ingenuity in the use of materials, to the point where imitation of forms in a new material develops into new and distinctive forms suited to local conditions.

These two characteristics, I suggest, lie at the root of America's distinctive contribution to the arts, and in a developed form shape much of her artistic activity today. They have not operated and do not operate equally in all fields, and other forces have joined them in shaping the history of the arts in America; but they give a continuity to that history and help to explain not only achievements but failures. Trace their working out when the United States comes to control her own destiny. In the period following the Revolution, up to the outbreak of the Civil War, American history is dominated by the great expansion westward, with the frontier the most vivid element in American life. By and large, the young Republic was mainly concerned with the practical needs of life. Even such an idealist and lover of the arts as Jefferson could say of painting and sculpture that they were "too expensive for the state of wealth among us. They are worth seeing but not studying."

The remarkable thing is, however, that so much was produced which was not purely utilitarian, but expressed a romantic vision of the new potentialities in American life. European standards and influence in the arts were still dominant. Training centers in the United States were very few, and many Americans went to study in England, France, and Italy; while the flow of artists from abroad into the United States increased rather than diminished. But what was learned, borrowed, and adapted began in many cases to take on a distinctively American air. In New England, the versions of the style of the Adams brothers associated with such names as Bulfinch and McIntyre of Salem, are a continuation of colonial practice, in their refinement and elaboration of borrowed themes. They represent the end of an older epoch rather than the beginning of a new one. More significant was the widespread influence of Roman architecture, since this was in part inspired and nurtured by the ideas behind the Revolution. Roman architecture became in American eyes, as it had previously been in those of Revolutionary France, a symbol of the grandeur and integrity of republican institutions; but it also stood for romantic aspirations, for the great realm which America hoped to build in the West. This double aspect of the Roman revival appears in the buildings designed by Jefferson himself. His house at Monticello, the Capitol at Richmond, and above all the University of Virginia, all represent a tribute to the past; but in their skilful adjustment to American needs they are equally an expression of hope for the future. Jefferson's buildings exercised powerful effect throughout the United States; but even more potent was the example set by the Capitol in Washington. This set a pattern for every king of public building, for those of great commercial undertakings such as banks and insurance companies, and even for private houses; and Roman influence has remained a constant and living element in American building.

Romantic sentiments nurtured by Rome found further sustenance in Greece. The Greek revival in America was inspired from Europe; but it found particularly fertile soil here, since the Greek struggle for independence against Turkey appeared to parallel that of the Colonies against England, while ancient Greece seemed a symbol of a golden age such as America herself was seeking. The Greek revival penetrated more deeply into American life than did Roman example. It traveled across the country with the advancing tide of settlement; and with more building to be done, and better manuals of instruction, it influenced building of every type, from the large public institution down to the modest farm house. Needless to say, in the course of its travels in space and in time, Greek motives underwent endless adaptations and variations, to the point of eccentricity. They were put in terms of wood and brick; structural elements became used as ornament; ornamental elements became structural. But the result was to yield a lively and sometimes delightful style of distinctively American flavor.

Overlapping in time the Greek revival, came another importation from Europe, the Gothic revival. This in Europe was a complete expression of the Romantic movement, and might have been expected to appeal very directly to America. But it found no answer in the republican sentiments and expansionist ideas of the times, and could not be so easily adapted to current needs, while the principles of Gothic building were less well understood. There was an efforescence of Gothic ornament in places, which reflected certain nostalgic yearnings of the period; but the true Gothic revival in the United States was to come later, after the Civil War, when the principles of Gothic buildings were to be fully integrated into American architecture.

It is easy to condemn much of the building of the period under discussion as pretentious and vulgar. Much of it was inspired not by romantic enthusiasm but by snobbish ignorance; and the results could be hideous. But a great deal from which the modern aesthete recoils with horror was a genuine attempt, however fumbling and illiterate, to express aspirations over and above those of the material world, whose claims at times threatened to engulf every activity. Moreover, this period of experiment in style, was also important for its exploration of technical possibilities in architecture. The iron age had arrived; and about the middle of the century the use of cast iron in the construction of buildings begins, examples of which still survive, notably the building fronts with large windows, once a feature of the river front in St. Louis. In this the United States was no pioneer, for in England and France the use of iron construction was well advanced. Also, much of the exploratory use of new materials was an attempt to imitate in one substance concepts born of the use of another, with at times horrifying results. Yet here again is evidence of American ingenuity in adapting materials to new purposes; an ingenuity which often passed beyond imitation into genuine invention.

Activity in other arts during this period paralleled that in architecture. One notable development was in shipbuilding, wherein a combination of daring design, efficient and ingenious use of material, and fine craftsmanship made the clipper ship famous the world over. The clipper ship, also, gave scope to another art, that revealed in the boldly carved figureheads adorning the vessels; an art which in the hands of William Rush of Philadelphia was a starting point for the creation of monumental sculpture of remarkable energy. Otherwise, American sculpture was uninteresting. The leading sculptors, such as Hiram Powers, Crawford, and Greenough, were expatriates, whose imagination worked within strict limits set by European academic example. Their work reveals American capacity for fine craftsmanship, and little more. Sculpture, in fact, was regarded mainly as a luxury, ministering to a somewhat snobbish taste, with no roots in the activities of daily life; and so it has largely remained, despite the skill and ingenuity of a long succession of carvers in wood and stone.

The case was very different with painting. Only a few years ago, the period between the War of 1812 and the Civil War was regarded as equivalent to the Dark Ages, relieved only by the activities of the Hudson River School, and a few mediocre portrait painters. Today, it is slowly being realized that the period was one of widespread and varied activity, and of considerable achievement. Mrs. Jameson, a sufficiently stern critic from England could with reason say, "While in America, I was struck by the manner in which the imaginative talent of the people had thrown itself forth into painting; the country seemed to swarm with painters."

One notable characteristic of the period was the extensive and generous patronage of contemporary painters both by private individuals and by organizations such as art unions. Another was the rapid widening of the restricted field of Colonial and Early Republican painting. American landscape painting developed vigorously, followed by American genre, both finding material and inspiration in American conquest of a continent. As the pioneers swept westward, painters moved with them; some recording the great plains, the mountains, and the rivers, others the farmers, the hunters, the lumbermen, the Indians, and all the varied aspects of frontier life. It is notable how many of these painters themselves came from the frontier, and how the passion to express themselves in paint triumphed over lack of training. So emerged a remarkable group of painters who were true primitives, of a type unknown in contemporary Europe, in whom sincerity of feeling and innocence of vision were joined with direct and simple technique, sometimes of high accomplishment.

The painting of the period has interesting literary parallels. In both, the arts were apt to part company with the realities of life, and to cast a romantic halo round them. While, for example, the advancing tide of settlement was driving out the American Indian, to the point of extermination, the arts glorified him as the type of noble savage conceived by Jean Jacques Rousseau. So he appears in Fenimore Cooper, and in the work of painters such as Seth Eastman and Miller. But both among painters and writers there were exceptions to this romantic optimism. Just as Poe and Hawthorne reveal beneath the surface of events a tragic disillusionment, so Martin J. Heade infuses into his work a nostalgic melancholy. Such writers and painters may perhaps be regarded as forerunners of those who, like Henry James and Whistler, found little inspiration in American life and in the American scene, and fled from it to Europe.

Pass now to the period following the Civil War. Territorial expansion had virtually ceased; the country was unified; industry and commerce developed amazingly; and wealth accumulated on a fantastic scale. Yet the situation for the arts was not altogether healthy. Comparatively stabilized communities and the increase of wealth gave increasing opportunities to patronize and to enjoy the arts. But some of the patronage was diverted from American to European artists, or to acquiring works of art of earlier periods. In fact, the great epoch of collecting in America opens, which in range and extent was to rival that of eighteenth century England. This brought both patrons and artists into closer contact with major European traditions; but it also bred imitation and artistic snobbery, both fatal to creative activity.

Nevertheless, that activity developed mightily, especially in architecture. Here there were two main trends. One consisted in restless experiment in adapting various styles to American uses on the part of architects who had been trained abroad, especially in France. Richard Morris Hunt brought into the field the influence of French Renaissance architecture; H. H. Richardson, that of Byzantine and Romanesque; McKim, Meade, and White, that of the Italian and French Renaissance, and of American Colonial; Ware, Upjohn, and, later, Cram and Goodhue, that of Gothic. But this process of adaptation was more intense than that of earlier periods. The styles utilized were more carefully studied, and the principles underlying them far more completely absorbed. At the same time, there was lavish experiment in materials, and in the use of varying textures and colors, which yielded very personal and distinctive results.

Out of this welter of experiment has emerged an eclectic, but integrated art, in which borrowings have ceased to be imitative and have been with great technical skill and resource fused to achieve fitness for purpose, variety and boldness of design, and beauty in color of texture, with all these qualities controlled and directed by romantic and dramatic feeling.

The second major trend in architecture had its roots in developments in constructional methods. In 1883-85, the first building in America with a completely iron skeleton was erected, the Home Insurance Company building in Chicago designed by William Le Baron Jenney. Thenceforward, during the eighties and nineties, Chicago was the center of great developments in building structure, associated with the names of Jenney himself, Burnham and Roote, Holabird and Roche, and perhaps most of all, Louis Sullivan. Technically, the work of this Chicago group was marked not only by the use of the iron skeleton, but by floating foundations (to cope with the mud on which Chicago is built), large horizontally elongated windows to give the maximum of light and, despite the great height of the buildings, a general emphasis to the horizontal elements in construction. But their work went far beyond skillful exploitation of technical resources to meet the needs of big business houses; and by feeling for proportion, sensitive handling of detail, and dramatic massing, they achieved the basic qualities of fine architecture.

The influence of technical developments was not confined to Chicago, though that city for a period led the way. Elsewhere, especially in New York, the most usual type of construction took the form of great towers, each with base, shaft, and terminal—the skyscraper, often regarded as the characteristic American contribution to architecture. Eventually, this conception displaced the earlier Chicago type of high building, even in Chicago itself, and, at the hands of Louis Sullivan, in other cities. Recently, however, the high building made possible by steel construction has undergone yet another development. Partly owing to zoning laws, partly to active architectural imagination, the simple tower type has been combined with supporting masses to yield the variety and drama of such buildings as Rockefeller Center.

The architectural possibilities of the skyscraper, also, have not been limited to commercial purposes, but have been used in other fields, notably in public buildings among which the Nebraska State Capitol by Goodhue is a magnificent example. In such a building as this, the varied aspects of the American genius meet. Ingenuity and resource in the use of material, a high level of craftsmanship, and romantic feeling combine to express a bold imaginative conception.

Similar character marks much modern domestic architecture. Local traditions in building shaped by inheritance, climate, ways of living, have held more firmly than is generally realized, and have saved and are still saving many cities in the United States from some of the offensive jerry-building which has ruined urban developments in many European cities. But at the same time the modern American architect has developed a vast technological apparatus for comfortable living—heating, plumbing, lighting, cold storage, and so on—which he groups freely, yet under the control of tradition, to produce the characteristically American house.

In fields closely related to architecture achievements have been equally exciting. Engineer and artist are being merged. Great projects such as the Tennessee Valley scheme, and vast planning schemes such as the great National Parks reveal a combination of technological skill, superb workmanship, and romantic imagination which I hold to be characteristically American.

The history of the arts other than architecture since the Civil War, is less inspiring. The work of such eminent sculptors as Augustus St. Gaudens and Daniel Chester French seems to have its roots in Europe rather than in the United States; and its fine craftsmanship, its delicacy and sensitiveness, to be mainly an embroidery on borrowed themes. Even so moving a work as Barnard's *Lincoln,* seems to draw its power more from association than from intrinsic quality.

So it is with much American painting. Successive waves of influence have come from Europe—from the Barbizon School, from Munich, from the Impressionists and, following the Armory Exhibition of 1913 in New York, from French and German Post-Impressionism. All such movements have found many skillful and faithful followers; but few of independence and distinction. Yet against this background of tasteful mediocrity, some painters of positive character and high achievement emerge. Leaving aside the expatriates, Whistler, Sargent, and Mary Cassatt, scarcely to be regarded as American save by birth, outstanding figures of an earlier generation are Albert Ryder, Winslow Homer and Thomas Eakins. Of these, Ryder is the pure romantic. At first sight, his choice of legendary and medieval subject matter seems to separate him from the main stream of American painting; but if his earlier work be studied, these subjects appear as primarily pegs on which to hang romantic interpretations of American landscape, akin in spirit to the paintings of the great plains and mountain ranges made by some of Ryder's predecessors. Homer and Eakins on the other hand, are basically realists in their use of American material derived from personal experience. Yet that material is seen in terms of a romantic vision. Behind Homer's paintings of seafaring men and the sea, of Maine and Canadian lakes and forests, lies the epic of American conquest of nature throughout a continent; while Eakins touches the hem of Rembrandt's cloak, in suggesting the potential grandeur of human beings behind a mask of homely features.

The same power of giving romantic savor to the stuff of daily life marks the work of a more recent generation, typified by the group known as The Eight, who found in New York the same kind of magic as was discovered by O. Henry. But in the period between the wars, American painting has hesitated, and has not wholeheartedly followed the lead thus given. The so-called Middle Western School of Grant Wood, Benton, and Curry, has sought so self-consciously to be American, as to become illustrative. On the other hand, abstraction does not seem congenial to the American genius, and seems to lead generally to simple pattern making. An outstanding exception is the work of John Marin, whose highly stylized interpretations of New York City and of Maine lack the intellectual quality and detachment of the French abstract painters, but have a romantic fire of their own.

Yet a solid core of men working in the tradition of romantic realism remains, in whom lies bright hope for the future. The importance of painting in daily life is being recognized; recent developments in the use of mural decoration are tying painting and architecture together; and the painters are following the architects in joining mastery of a craft to romantic interpretation of material to serve human needs.

XII

TECHNOLOGY AND FREEDOM

BY

LYMAN BRYSON, LL.D.

Professor of Education, Teachers College, Columbia University; Public Relations Counsellor, Columbia Broadcasting System

The great political problem of our time is to bring larger and larger groups of the world population under single governments without losing the creative values of freedom and diversity. Technology, the multiform pattern of gadgets that is made possible by scientific knowledge of the physical world, plays a great role in the process of enlarging states. It is also a challenge to liberty. Political problems are not made easier by "progress."

It is useful in the beginning to remind ourselves that problems are changed in character if they are changed in scale. This is one of the reasons why the wisdom of the ancients cannot be completely relied on in dealing with the British Empire or the Russian Union of Socialist Soviet Republics. The hackneyed remark of classical philosophy is still true. You can make a single nation out of as many men as can listen together to the sound of one man's voice. But a change from the Agora at Athens to a microphone in a broadcast network in America is just such a change of scale as makes a difference in character. The failure to take into account this kind of change often makes useless and empty the comments of modern wise men on modern conditions.

The ancient process, in fact the continuing process, is for states to tend toward greatness. Governmental units tend to enlarge themselves. As Boas has pointed out, the slow progress of civilization is marked by the gradual enlargement of what might be called the normal units of social and political organization. This was, Boas thought, beneficent. He evidently took it for granted that areas of peace and order could be enlarged without killing cultural difference. In the older days, before the invention of modern machines, the units of government tended to get larger, to proliferate into empires. Then they fell apart. The satrap on the edge of the empire was likely to get ambitious and think that no one in the center was paying much attention to him, caring much what he did. The emperor had always to stand ready to reconquer his distant dominions. The people in those peripheral states did not generally develop a strong feeling of unity with the central nation. In other words, great aggregations of population under single governments were at once loose and rebellious.

That might have been true in our own experience. It is hard to believe, but it is probably true, that great parts of the United States of America, possibly the Middle West, and almost certainly the West Coast in two or three different units, would have broken away from imperial headquarters at Washington if the European conquest of this continent had been in ancient times. It seems quite likely that we would have had a small republic with a great inland empire, in constant danger of disintegration, instead of a single unified nation, if we had not had modern means of communication.

Community and communication are not accidentally related terms. Community in any real sense depends on communication. It depends on communication not only as a possibility but as a reality and a purposeful activity. It is true, of course, that any human relation depends on communication and that hostility as well as friendly feeling can be generated only by the exchange of ideas. But without communication, used as a binding force, the great states of today would be the empires of yesterday with all their centrifugal dangers. The great states of today are possible because the great systems of communication are available. But a change in scale is a modification of a problem. What have we done to democracy in attempting it on such a scale as in the United States?

We might do well at the beginning to get rid of the idea, so comfortable in nineteenth century terms, that we are bound to succeed;

that our democracy is happily destined to inevitable and lasting glory. Empires have failed; so may democracies. Unless one believes that the rule of life and the management of business by which he was himself produced is the ultimate possibility in human devising, he cannot very well believe that democracy could not possibly fail when attempted as a large-scale operation. He must know that even his own vigilance and prayers may not save it. And we can get no good out of concluding that, since it is industrialism that makes our difficulty, we can have large-scale democracy without industrialism. Industrialism is the only economic condition in which democracy on a large scale is possible. Without our modern technologies our modern communication systems could not exist to hold the great experiment together.

The essential problem however is old, not new; it is a modern form of the never-ended conflict between unity and life. It is always possible to try for unity on a basis of lethal sameness and in some static societies it is almost achieved. But life will usually succeed in breaking out of a unity that is mere suppression, and life then means change and difference. How can we get unity without losing life and liveliness? The modern problem is only a specific form of that question. How can we get community on the scale of 150,000,000 persons and a span of continent 3,000 miles across, without losing creative difference?

There are two obstacles in the way of success in this venture. One lies in the nature of the communication by which technology can pull us together. The other is a result of industry also, but it lies in the change that industrialism makes in the nature of public business.

The communication that makes a unified nation possible is a two-way flow. It is necessary to get to the people what they need to know and to get back into the central organs of government what the people need to say about their own affairs. Right at the beginning, of course, there is some difference of opinion as to what the people ought to know. The oldest and most habitual of theories is that someone in the center should decide what is good for them and for the country and tell them. That this centrally conceived and distributed information is generally also what is good for those who happen to be in power is evident to observation but is never discussed in countries where the system is used. It is used now in Russia, for example, and the Russian people get from the central government the ideas and information that are "good" for them. There are many intelligent people outside of Russia who believe in this way of giving the people the materials for their choices, although it is obviously not really giving them any choice at all. A man rose in the parliament of Britain recently, in the parliament that is the mother of parliaments and of free speech, and said substantially this, "Everybody knows that free speech is a quite worn-out idea and I hope the British people will not cling any longer to anything so old-fashioned as free speech. What we need is the truth told to the people by the government."

The other idea of what ought to go out to the people is that the government should inform the people as men in power may see fit but that government information should be subjected to the sharpest and most searching examination and if need be to denial and argument. And also to surround all "official truths" with a flow of unofficial and private truths offered by anybody with a voice and a conviction. This method is believed more likely to arrive at a possibility of truth, workable and trustworthy truth, than the method of straight government dispensation. It does lead to confusion and noise; it does call on every man to listen patiently to doctrines and incitements that he thinks are vicious. But it is the method that is called for by the way of thinking we have always called democratic. Other things have been called democratic in other places and are being called better forms of democracy than ours in many places now. But the free and open battle of ideas is what we have always believed in.

Whichever way a nation chooses, freedom or official truth, there remains the problem of getting the flow of ideas out to the people. They should have a chance to listen together to the sound of one man's voice. And they must have ways of talking back. How does modern technology solve this practical problem and what moral and philosophical problems are raised by the effect of the technological solution?

We can get a good perspective on this by thinking of mass production and distribution of merchandise, a typical achievement of modern technology. How is it possible for us to have, for example, so many motor cars? They are the result, we say, of mass production.

But mass production is not merely a matter of having a great many factories of different kinds, it is not only a matter of having a large production plant. It requires also a very large production of a small range of products. Motor cars provide an excellent example because some countries are industrially capable of producing large quantities of cheap motor cars but produce comparatively few. What they do produce is a good many different models. When the buyer pays for his choice he pays much more than an American would pay for an equally good car. Why? Because you cannot make cars at rock bottom cheapness unless you can count on a very large market, a very large volume of sales. This is mass production. You count on a large sale because there are only a few competitors to challenge you. So the customer has very few choices. He gets cheapness instead of choice. This is probably a good way to merchandise motor cars.

Is it a good way to merchandise ideas and information? Are mass production and mass distribution good methods to use in getting ideas to the people? In the merchandising of motor cars, mass production methods, offering a few models at bargain prices, are not only good for the consumer, they are also democratic. By these methods it is possible for a very large proportion of the buying public to have motor cars. Does it work democratically in spreading ideas? Mass production means huge quantities of things that are all alike and owned by nearly everybody. Do we want mass production of ideas?

Let me hasten to say that there are many cultural goods that can be and should be produced in this fashion. Good music, for example, and simple factual news, and humorous entertainment and many other things that all men should have plenty of, without sacrifice of time or money. I see no great loss in creative force when millions listen together to a great orchestra or when they laugh together at a great clown.

But this is perhaps not true of all cultural goods. There may be areas in which it is more important to have choice than cheapness. Suppose, for example, that mass production should come to be the only way in which books could be produced for American readers. It is useful and important for us to have cheap books for everybody because the reading of books is a form of self-education for which nothing seems to be a satisfactory substitute. And books are costly. Why cannot we have them cheap? We can, of course, as present developments in the publishing business are demonstrating. But these same developments are showing also the dangers of mass production in the tools of mental life.

Ten years ago, we made some experiments at Teachers College in producing books for everybody. A number of educators and publishers and writers and scientific investigators had been working for a long time, trying to find out why so few Americans read books. The American Association for Adult Education undertook to go further. All the elements of cost and distribution were studied and all the accessible elements in the books themselves such as their readability and appeal. It was evident enough that books were not produced in large enough quantities nor offered for sale in enough shops for most possible book readers to have any chance or temptation to buy. The public libraries did all that was possible with their meager means. But the limited power of able and devoted librarians to meet any great problems of public reading is shown by the fact that there are states in the union where the public expenditure for public library purposes—all library purposes including salaries, buildings, and books—is only enough to buy one ten cent weekly per person once a year. Those of us who were engaged in that study thought it quite clear that we needed books in mass production.

Most of us still think so. But we know more now than we did then about the mass production and distribution of ideas because great achievements have been made in the meantime and we can now see some of the concomitant results that we should have been wise enough, perhaps, to anticipate. We can now see that, although the mass production of motor cars may be a great social and material advantage, when you substitute cheapness for choice in books you shut out not only the strange, the original, the peripheral, the challenging books. You also shut out new writers.

The number of bookshops in this country has never been more than two or three thousand. In most places where people live, farms, country towns, small cities, there have been no bookstores of any kind. There were plenty of places where reading matter could be purchased, magazines and possibly a few cheap reprints, but no new titles. The book clubs, huge as some of them are, do very little to meet the need. But all this, we must remember, is a result of the fact that book publishing, the actual manufacture of books, is confined to one or two cities for the whole country. We do not have cultural centers for regional populations, even populations of greatly developed diversity like the South, for example, or the Spanish Southwest. Books not published in New York might almost as well not be published at all. And the books published in New York had until recently almost no way of getting sold in any but the very largest cities because there were no bookstores.

There are two possible remedies. The situation is unsatisfactory because not enough people are in touch with the new and the surviving ideas that are current in the culturally alive centers, such as the college towns and the larger cities. Too many citizens of the country get their ideas from newspapers, magazines, the cinema, and broadcasts. These are suitable and effective channels of distribution, of course. They are not, I think, completely satisfactory substitutes for books. To provide that a larger proportion of our people may read books, then, would require either that books be published in many centers and locally sold, or that books published in New York should be more widely available to consumers. Both these remedies are being tried. The first, to publish in many places, does not take advantage of modern technologies nor provide any communal sharing of ideas. If books are to be published in many places, they will have still less national circulation than they have now. And they will continue to be very costly.

The other remedy is more in harmony with our modern way of working and thinking. We have developed technological solutions for the problems of book manufacture and distribution. First we began to spread reprints in great numbers. Reprints are inexpensive. The titles are established and do not need expensive promotion. They are not experimental; customers can be counted on. But if only books that have already had a moderate success can be sold in reprint form, not much that is new or original can be put on the lists. And it has, in fact, been discovered by reprint publishers that only books of quite obvious merit as entertainment will do well in reproduction.

However, they found ways of selling these wares in many places where there were no bookshops. We have now, as we did not have ten years ago, manufacturers of very inexpensive books, mostly reprints, that have as many as 100,000 instead of 5,000 possible places of sale in the United States. They sell books by the millions and millions. This is wonderful, and we can be grateful because it does enormously increase the reading of books. It increases pride in the ownership of books and brings other real cultural gains. It is mass production in ideas in one form, and it means that any book chosen will be read by 150,000 or more instead of, perhaps, by a few thousand.

The slow dismay that follows so often on the realization that we have made a great achievement comes now, however, when we think of what kinds of books can be confidently put into the hopper of the great printing mills for editions of 150,000. The new writings of the new writers? The strange, the peripheral, the original, the challenging books? The new writer, in this system, has the same chance that an odd-looking motor car would have in the low price, mass market. That is, no chance at all. The original writer, as well as the beginner, must still be a serious risk, and publishers do not take risks in editions of 150,000. We need, then, to keep the old system of publishing books, the shy uncommercial guesswork of venture publishing, as well as the mass publishing of the new ways. The mass production of accepted ideas is a great contribution to cultural growth and to national unity. It cannot be permitted to bring us to a pass in which the only ideas that would have any chance at all will be those already accepted by a mass audience.

This business of books is a good example of the way in which technology can solve some of our problems without completely supplying our spiritual needs. Broadcasting shows another danger of technologically acquired community, another phase of the danger of monopoly in thought.

Any mass production and distribution, being essentially the process of making and offering large quantities of the same thing, is dependent on a widespread commonness of taste. I do not mean vulgarity of taste; that can be something different. But there must be common or widely shared taste for the same values, if mass methods are to work. In books we are arriving at a temporary compromise by producing accepted values, many of which are minor values, in mass form and mass quantity, while we continue to support at greater cost the rare and the new. But broadcasting, a still further step in technological methods of making national unity, is a mass medium or it is nothing. What further technological inventions may do to change this fact is not now entirely clear. We can at least say, I think, that when frequency modulation broadcasting makes it possible to have many more broadcasting stations than are possible now, we shall have less of a natural monopoly. But it will still be true that in broadcasting, a potentially universal form of communication, you always compete with the best and you cannot remove all the elements that make it a natural monopoly.

No change in the management or the ultimate responsibility for broadcasting can make it anything but a natural monopoly if it is to fulfil its function as a device by which to make a community out of our scattered people. In this matter, as in so much of popular thinking, the critics of broadcasting refuse to accept the necessary alternatives. If you are to have one man's voice reach millions, for the sake of making those millions into a community and a nation, then few voices can be heard. Take a concrete instance. Think of any respected and successful radio commentator. He may speak once a week to four or five million listeners. In the most successful lecture trip he could not speak face-to-face to more than a small fraction of that number; it would take him years to address, even once, all the members of his regular audience. But if he were doing his work that way, other voices, that now have no hearers, would be heard by those listeners in other face-to-face meetings. If millions are to hear one voice, many voices will never be heard. And here again, we solve a problem that is a natural result of trying to be democratic on a big scale by a technological device, and the device creates new problems in the essential working of democratic life.

We believe in the diversity that is in our kind of a democracy because we believe that the conflict of ideas and cultural forms is in itself creative. We believe that the differences between me and my neighbor may honor both of us and that we may both be offering values to our democratic community because we bring choice and variety into its cultural forms by our differences of choice in personal ideals. Democracy does not merely tolerate difference. Democracy, as we understand the word in America—although our practice is often impatient and shortsighted—still means that differences are valued and nurtured for their creative power.

With such an ideal we may well question how much we may be paying for the unity of multitudes that the gadgets make possible, payments made by giving up our rights to be our different selves.

In the beginning, I said there were two obstacles in the way of our making a success out of democracy on a great scale. I did not promise to offer any satisfactory plan of action to get by either of them. What is needed now is diagnosis. The first obstacle is the set of problems brought up by the technological devices which are our only possible way of getting nationwide communication in ideas. The second is the change in the nature of national business made by the scale of our operation. We have achieved our industrial greatness by mass methods, and mass methods depend not only on masses of likeminded consumers but also on concentrations of industrial facilities. So we get, in the familiar chain, great combines of capital and equipment that have to be balanced by great combines of labor. As these two masses struggle against each other for power and material advantage, the general public is crushed unless the political system is changed to give governmental agencies enough power to act as umpire between them. How much of the good life will be achieved for all of us by the uneasy balancing of monsters is still to be discovered.

Our immediate concern is with democracy as a way of individual life that is dependent on the possibility of real choice. What choice has the individual in his political and work life in the present situation? He can, of course, be a tiny drop in the ocean of public opinion. The ocean is made up of drops and public opinion is made up of small personal voices. But how much experience of real choice, and of taking the consequences for personal choice, is now available in these areas?

We are not enough frightened by this threat to our democracy because we so easily forget that the democratic way of life exists to give people the experience of freedom, not to get the "best" solutions for great problems. At this point we find it most difficult to explain our ideas of democracy to some of the totalitarians who are conscious of being friends of man and anxious to find the "best" answers to life's problems. They cannot see that we are committed by our system to the belief that the end of governmental and economic activity is not only, perhaps not principally, to solve political and economic problems in any best way. Our system has the growth and development of human personality as its goal and we believe that choice is a way of learning and of growth and that it is better for men to choose for themselves even if they make the wrong decisions than it is to have those decisions made for them. We choose freedom and freedom is not a solution of problems. It is a way of action that is in itself more important than the results.

If it is true, then, that choices in political and work life are no longer very real to the individual, we need to face that fact as a threat to democracy and not be fooled by the assertion of what may be true but is not conclusive, that the choices being made in our behalf are better than we could make for ourselves. At the same time, we know that we probably cannot change this trend. To preserve our democratic ways of life we need to open up the new areas in which choice is still ours and is still important.

What those ways are going to be cannot be confidently prophesied. This is, I said, diagnosis. But it is clear that we shall be compelled, as technology simplifies our lives in some areas, to find other areas where the human spirit can find free play. It may be that we can successfully recapture some political areas, especially community management. We may find it possible to give to creating comfort and beauty and safety and happiness the energies we used to give to politics of a more brutally material kind. It may be that in our provision for lifelong learning we can bring new ways of creative living to ordinary lives. It is clear enough that we have to try. The meaning will go out of our democracy unless we succeed. The next democracy is going to be a democracy of culture built upon the achievements of the democracy of political choice, which we have systematized by change in scale, and upon the achievements of economic democracy which is still in the making.

Perhaps the most important thing to say is that technologies, machines, can be used but never trusted. They not only solve problems; they make new problems Even more than that—and this is in the long run painful but wholly beneficent—they compel us to find new goals and new ways of reaching toward the goals that we hope will last forever.

XIII

WOMAN'S BATTLE FOR STATUS

BY

ELINORE M. HERRICK, A.B.

Personnel Director, New York Herald Tribune

Women have a unique opportunity today to contribute to the social progress of the world. Tremendous changes in the status of women everywhere impend. Increasing industrialization is bound to affect profoundly the status of women in every country. In Asia and in the Orient generally these changes are apt to come swiftly. Even in those countries now highly industrialized—or in those partly so—women are at a crossroads. They can press forward or turn away from the challenge offered. How women in other lands determine their destiny is going to affect us in America. Will they sell their labor cheaply? That will affect our own industrial future. Will they from the outset organize to secure equal opportunities of education and work, equal status as citizens? The progress of American women toward these goals may be slowed by the action of women in other lands.

It is to be hoped that the women in those countries in which economic and political change will probably come most suddenly will not have to repeat the one hundred and fifty years of struggle of American women. What are the landmarks here of our struggle for status?

First, it seems to me, comes the price set upon the labor of women. They have always held their labor too cheaply. The result of that failure to assert their worth has been to hold back their progress in every field of activity and at every level of opportunity. It has had an effect on the potentiality of women as citizens, on their social and legal status.

Beginning with the early pioneer woman no cash value was placed upon her services even when she did all the cooking, spinning, weaving, even education of children, as well as helping with the farm chores. The "butter and egg" money of farm women was the first feeble expression of rebellion. With this background it was perhaps inevitable that with women's emergence into industrial employment their wages should have been low as compared with those of men.

Our working women have from the outset had a tendency to be satisfied with substitutes for the cash valuation which men have long past put upon their own labor. Harriet Martineau of England, visiting the earliest textile mills of our own New England, paid lavish tribute to the dormitories and libraries supplied the farm girls and women who flocked to the mills to work from sunrise to sunset for a mere pittance. Low wages, child labor, and poor living conditions have long characterized the industries in which large numbers of women have been employed. As women proved their usefulness to industry, their employment has increased and more opportunities have opened to them but always characterized by a wage lower than that of men in similar occupations.

Going back only as far as World War I what do we find? In factory, office, and school, women have received less pay for similar work, although the long time trend in earnings has been upward. In 1914 women workers in manufacturing industries averaged only $7.25 a week while male labor received $13.65; or nearly twice as much. World War I brought higher wages to both, however, and in 1920 the money earnings of women workers had mounted to $17.71 a week, as against $31.69 for men. The depression of the 1930's brought a precipitous drop in wages but reduced the differential, so that women were earning in 1932 about two thirds the weekly wage of men. By the close of 1943 male labor received an average weekly wage of $53.26 while women workers in the same industries earned only $29.96. Some part of this difference is accounted for by the fact that women—as so often happens—tended to be held down to the less skilled jobs at the lower rates of pay.

By December, 1943, the hourly earnings of women equaled those of unskilled males in only two of twenty-four industries. Increasing shortages of men and government and union policy of equal pay for equal work began to have their effect, and in February, 1944, in five of these industries the earnings of women equaled those of unskilled men. Before V-J Day weekly earnings of women workers increased, hovering around $50 in automotive factories, while paychecks in rubber, electrical, machine shop, aircraft, agricultural implement, lumber and millwork establishments ranged between $35 and $40. But the men still earned more.

The lower wages paid to women through the years have had a vital influence upon women's legal and social status—as in industry. Men came to regard them as undercutters of union pay scales won by men. Even so the unions have not been anxious to organize women though it would have helped to stabilize their own wage rates. But women have always formed a shifting part of the national labor force. They marry and leave, or else home demands require them to quit. Even during World War II women were often admitted to membership—particularly in the old A. F. of L. craft unions—only on an auxiliary basis without the right to vote. At the end of World War I there were 250,000 women in unions. At the peak of World War II there were three and a half million women trade unionists.

Nevertheless, the experience following World War I has modified the attitude of unions. They saw many women retained in wartime occupations simply because they were cheaper in terms of pay rates. During World War II the unions generally followed the course of demanding that the women get equal pay for equal work in order to protect their own pay scales and also to counteract the tendency to retain women in peacetime solely because of the lower pay they would accept. But with adoption of the equal pay principle the unions resisted attempts of women to win promotion to the highly paid jobs.

The government took a hand in the pay problem. The War Labor Board adopted the equal pay principle in decision after decision. In instances of various electrical companies the Board even went so far as to order higher pay for women on certain jobs to bring their earnings up to that of men, although men had never been employed on the work involved. Several states enacted equal pay laws, New York taking the lead. Now a federal equal pay bill is pending in Congress.

Thus substantial progress is being made in removing the discrimination against women in the matter of wages.

Women's legal status constitutes a second problem. For the past fifty years many laws applying only to women's work have been passed based on the principle that government had the right and duty to protect the health and wellbeing of women and minors. Actually, most of the conditions harmful to women were bad for men, too, but the courts refused to sanction similar safeguards for men until very recently when the federal Fair Labor Standards Act was passed, to a limited extent regulating the hours and fixing minimum wages of both men and women.

There is no doubt that most of these laws were beneficial to women and that indirectly they improved the working conditions of men, for example, in the voluntary reduction of men's work hours to conform to those permitted for women when both were employed in the same plant or on the same operations. But some of the laws passed for the welfare of women have limited their opportunities and, now, with universally shorter work weeks and days, with better transportation facilities, street lighting, and police protection, the old prohibitions against women's work after ten o'clock at night are outmoded. Laws have a curious way of becoming "sacred cows" which no one dares change long after the original justification has ceased to exist. For example, because of the women's night work laws in state after state, employing industries which are continuing to operate on the multiple eight hour shift basis are being compelled now to dismiss women whom as a war emergency measure they were allowed to employ until midnight.

There are other legal discriminations against women, on which the battle for status in this and other countries is still to be won. In many states married women are still literally under the absolute rule of their husbands. In some states wives must turn their property and their earnings over to their husbands. Often a wife cannot make legal contracts without her husband's consent. In others, fathers have the sole right to the control of the earnings of minor children. The Nineteenth Amendment of 1920 settled the matter of suffrage only. Although women may now vote, some states bar them from public office or jury service. There is no easy catch-all cure for these situations. Women in state after state must battle to erase legal barriers to their full status as citizens on a par with men. The so-called "Equal Rights Amendment" pending in Congress is not a sound remedy for this situation, for it would jeopardize desirable legislation while correcting specific faults such as those outlined above.

The opportunities for women in gainful employment in industry or the professions is a third phase of the battle for status. Today American women face again their age-old problem of limited opportunities. As of February 1945, there were approximately 53,000,000 females 14 years of age or over in the population; 17,777,000 were women, 390,000 of whom were unemployed, were in the civilian labor force. After Pearl Harbor the number of women actually employed increased by 6,140,000. Married women at work outside the home were 4,180,000 in 1940 and by March, 1944, this number had increased to 7,300,000.

Many married women employed outside the home would prefer to make their contributions to society by working in the home and would not enter the labor force if there were some alternative plan. The Women's Advisory Committee of the War Manpower Commission recommended shortly before the close of the war the adoption of the following program:

1. Extension of the present child-aid program so that allowances are not restricted to fatherless children or those similarly handicapped.
2. A sixteen-year school-leaving age.
3. A Secretary of Education in the Cabinet.
4. More low-cost housing.
5. General school nutrition plans.
6. Nursery schools as part of the public school system available to any mother, and after-school programs.

Wars always throw an increased burden of family support upon women. There will be more women unmarried, widowed, or divorced, and more women with children and old people depending on them for support. It follows, on the emotional side, that more women than ever before will have to depend on their work not only for a livelihood but for a satisfying life. And we must never forget that in the main most women work outside the home because of sheer economic necessity. More employment opportunities will have to be offered women in the postwar years. There must be increased social facilities provided to enable women to work and at the same time meet the responsibilities of the home which so often devolve upon the working woman.

Certainly we have no right to say to American women, "You gave us fine help during the war, thank you, and good-bye." Neither can we separate the problems of women from those of men. Both deserve the opportunity for full employment and utilization of their abilities.

Thus far we have been speaking chiefly of the industrial woman. What are the opportunities for the professionally trained woman? During this past war we have seen an exceptional demand for the services of women, not only in industry but in the professions. Women doctors had fine hospital appointments and patients galore. Women lawyers were snapped up by the best law firms. Women found it easy to get jobs on newspapers, in colleges, to do many interesting things that had been reserved before for men. And women—industrial and professional—were praised extravagantly by men in desperate need of their help.

But the women doctors, lawyers, chemists, physicists have long fought an uphill battle for the opportunity to get a training as good as that given men. Women doctors had to open their own hospitals, found their own medical schools. The history of their effort to win the chance at adequate training has been the same in all fields.

How much have women really advanced? Some changes have come about. Harvard is opening its medical school to women but its law school remains closed to them. There has been a spotty advance in training opportunities but true equality is still awaited.

Some distinct gains have been made in the work relationships of men and women. Men have become used to women working alongside and this will count in the long run, but not enough. Already industrial women are being replaced by men. Employment offices are more and more saying, "men preferred" or "male only." In the professional field editors are awfully glad to see their men return from war. Health organizations are replacing women doctors. Law firms don't want to bother with women now.

Shortly before the end of the war the Women's Advisory Committee of the War Manpower Commission said: "Government and industry must not assume that women can be treated as a reserve group during the war only. . . . The American people must demand consideration of the status of women in all postwar plans." Yet the first draft of the federal Full Employment Bill calmly excluded women with domestic responsibilities from the planning. Women's organizations rallied to the battle and the clause was deleted in subsequent drafts. Ultimately, however, the decision as to who is employed rests with the individual or organization that pays the wages or salaries or professional fees.

What is the attitude of employers? When women were needed for war work, honeyed appeals to patriotism lured them. But now dissatisfactions begin to be expressed. Men say "there is too much quarreling among women workers, too much weeping on the supervisor's shoulder." Businessmen say that women foment feuds in offices, that they resent the authority of the woman in charge who, they add, often gives orders disagreeably and whose attitude sours with age.

Labor leaders are again charging that women unionists pay their dues reluctantly and lack the firm purpose and loyalty that is essential to build a union organization. There is a lack of professional attitude toward their work on the part of some women, no doubt, but the criticism that springs forth when women are no longer needed for vital war work suggests that the basis is, at least in part, economic rivalry.

To the extent that these limitations upon women's advancement are based on the attitude and behavior of women in their employment, the women themselves must overcome these handicaps. They can, by developing a more professional attitude, by self-discipline, by learning to work pleasantly with their associates. Women have proved their courage and intelligence time and again. These criticisms can be made a passing phase of the woman problem.

Returning to the larger aspects of our question of women's status, we see clearly the difficulties that lie ahead—the extent to which women here in America must continue to struggle toward a greater freedom and equality and better training opportunities. How can progress be accelerated? What can the women of other countries do to avoid at least some of the hardships that have beset the footsteps of American women on their uphill road?

I am convinced that the greatest aid to women comes from organization—not just women's pressure groups, though they are helpful in some situations—but women in political and economic organizations banded together to remove barriers both legal and social. American women have had the franchise for twenty-six years, yet Frenchwomen to whom suffrage has only just been given elected more women to their national government than we have today in our Congress—and we have no woman in the Senate. Nor are women frequently found or conspicuous in state governments. The extent to which women are elected to public office is at least one measurement of their effectiveness in political organization. American men have been smart. Too often they have given women the illusion of importance by appointments to subordinate political positions as a sop rather than in response to the strength of organized women.

It is in the exacting sphere of public life that I am convinced that American women must make the greatest effort. Women must not shy away from politics. They must work for advancement of all women through the political system. We need more women in public office, not just on the school boards and institutional boards. We need more women in our legislative bodies, too. Women in every field must cultivate the determination to overcome prejudice and indifference and must learn to accept responsibility in their work relationships and to exercise leadership at every level.

To the women of other lands I would say, "Start now to organize as both economic and political groups and never relax your efforts. With sufficiently strong organizations it may be possible for you to emerge into industrial and professional life unfettered by the handicaps we still experience in America."

In our own self-interest American women should take steps to help the women of other lands enter their industrial revolution on an equal pay basis, with minimum wage and hours regulations for both men and women, without restriction on the property rights of women and with an equal legal status. It is only when women everywhere enjoy and exercise the privileges of full citizenship, bear the responsibilities that it entails, and have an effective voice in determining governmental and social policies affecting us all, that we can say the victory in the women's battle for status is in sight.

XIV

THE STRUGGLE FOR CULTURAL UNITY

BY

CHANNING H. TOBIAS, D.D.

Senior Secretary for Colored Work of the National Council of the YMCA

The struggle for cultural unity in America at the present time involves three principal problems of relationships—anti-Semitism, anti-Japanese sentiment, and prejudice against Negro Americans. The first two, while admittedly serious in their immediate effect and their far-reaching implications, are nothing like as baffling, and at times as apparently hopeless, as that of Negro-white relationships. I shall, therefore, say a few words about anti-Semitism and prejudice against the Japanese, and then devote most of my talk to the question that I am a part of, that I know most about, and that you are most interested in hearing me discuss, namely, Negro-white relationships.

I. ANTI-SEMITISM

Prejudice against Jews in America, akin to the type practiced by Hitler's Germany, is alive and growing today and must be faced and dealt with frankly, in spite of the advocates of "Hush! Hush!" within the Jewish community and the Gentile apostles of "Leave well enough alone." There are whispering campaigns against Jews as vicious as they are untrue, and they are proving so effective that even children are accepting the charges at their face value and giving expression to their hatred and contempt by desecrating synagogues and cemeteries and doing violence to unoffending Jewish children. "Silver Shirters" and "Christian Fronters," who a short time ago worked under cover, are now operating openly and brazenly, and prejudiced individuals having no organization medium through which to express their hatred and contempt, are becoming more and more bold in public expressions of anti-Semitism. Some time ago I entered a dining car of the New York Central Railroad, between New York and Poughkeepsie, just as it was filling up for lunch. I was given a seat at a table for four. After I was seated there was one vacancy left. In the rush for that seat there was some jostling of passengers in the aisle, and above the noise I heard a man, in the uniform of a naval lieutenant, say in a rather loud voice to the man back of him, "You dare do that to a Gentile!" I was stunned to realize that such a thing would be said openly in a crowded car. On a second look I realized that the words were addressed to a Jewish lad, who said nothing in reply as the naval lieutenant took his seat beside me. That this is not an isolated instance is borne out by the frequency with which smoking room conversation on Pullman and parlor cars is directed toward expressions or innuendoes discrediting the personalities of Jewish people.

II. PREJUDICE AGAINST THE JAPANESE

There is one chapter in the history of the war just closed that all loyal Americans would like to erase, namely, our handling of Japanese-Americans first in herding them into concentration camps regardless of whether they were aliens or citizens, and afterwards in establishing them in so-called relocation centers, while at the same time taking care not to accord similar treatment to enemy aliens of the white race. The summer before last, during a visit to the Pacific Coast, I went over large, desolate, blighted areas of San Francisco and Los Angeles that had once been occupied by the Japanese and from which they were driven overnight without consideration of the illegality of confiscation of property and humiliation of person. It is to the credit of the American people as a whole that these conditions have been partly remedied, although I am told on good authority that the attitude of many of the people of California and other Pacific Coast cities toward the Japanese who have been slowly returning to their homes, is anything but friendly and hospitable.

III. NEGRO-WHITE RELATIONSHIPS

I can think of no better way of introducing this, the principal part of my subject, than by quoting from the last published statement of the late Wendell Willkie. It is from an article published in *Collier's, The National Weekly* of October 7, 1944, and, in quoting it, I think I should say that the author, in my judgment, had the keenest appreciation of the factors involved in Negro-white relationships in America of any person of the white race that it has been my privilege to know. And I think I should say further that his sincere interest was as keen as his appreciation. As a matter of fact, even after he went into the hospital in his last illness, he was so concerned about this question that he dictated a note to me from his sickbed calling attention to the article and requesting that I be sure to read it and pass on to him my comments upon it. The article was entitled, "Citizens of Negro Blood," and in it is to be found the following paragraph:

The war has given new opportunities to the Negro and at the same time has emphasized the injustices in our attitude toward him. More than that, it has made us conscious of the contradictions between our treatment of our Negro minority and the ideals for which we are fighting. The equitable treatment of racial minorities in America is basic to our chances for a just and lasting peace. For it cannot be too much emphasized that in the world today whatever we do *at home* affects our foreign policy, and whatever we do *abroad* affects our domestic policy. The two are necessarily interrelated. On no single question is this truth so inescapable as in the repercussions all around the world that result from our treatment at home of our colored citizens.

One of the widespread consequences of this war is the growing determination among colonials, subject, and minority peoples everywhere to want for themselves a share of the freedom for which the allied nations are fighting. This is the great quest of our time. To future historians it may well overshadow all other aspects of the present conflict. We, as Americans, cannot be on one side abroad and the other at home. We cannot expect small nations and men of other races and colors to credit the good faith of our professed purposes and to join us in international collaboration for future peace if we continue to practice an ugly discrimination at home against our own minorities, the largest of which is our thirteen million Negro citizens.

Before attempting an analysis of the problem itself, it may help us at the outset to ask the question, "Who is this Negro American who is looked upon by his fellow Americans as a problem?"

In the first place, as a slave, his labors helped to lay the foundations of the original colonies. Through his toil on the plantations of the South, where he lived in greatest numbers, he helped to create the very wealth that subsequently was used in the war more securely to bind the shackles of slavery about him. In spite of the hardships of servitude, he produced or was the inspiration of most of the things that were unique in the literature and art of the South. Whatever may be the attitude of other sections of the country, the South should never look upon the Negro as a problem; rather should it recognize the fact that most of its distinctive, creative contributions have been seen through the Negro's eyes, spoken in his dialect, or have breathed his spirit. The folk tales of Joel Chandler Harris, especially the "Uncle Remus" stories, have had wider circulation throughout the world than any other American folk stories. If you remove from a Southern songbook the songs written in Negro dialect or about Negro life, there would be little left worth mentioning.

The Negro has also made distinguished contributions along scientific lines, as is borne out by the work of the late George Washington Carver, who helped to make possible the quantities and diversities of food and useful byproducts that enabled America to keep its armies and those of its allies in all parts of the world well fed and strong.

The Negro has participated in every war in which America has engaged, beginning with the Revolution. Let it be recalled that Crispus Attucks, a Negro, was among the small band of martyrs that fell in the Boston Massacre. The Negro distinguished himself also in the Battle of Rhode Island, in the Battle of New Orleans, and in the Civil War. It is interesting to recall that his entrance as a soldier in combat units marked the beginning of the turn of the tide of fortune for the Union armies. The achievements of the Ninth and the Tenth Cavalry in the Spanish-American War were recounted with deep gratitude by Theodore Roosevelt as he remembered how, with reckless abandon, they came to the rescue of the "Rough Riders" on San Juan Hill. In World War I the Old Fifteenth, New York, covered itself with glory, as it was in the thickest of the fight, coming out without having a single man taken prisoner, with more than one hundred members of the regiment decorated with the Croix de Guerre, and the whole regiment cited for bravery.

In the war just closed, in spite of every effort to humiliate the Negro in the armed forces by keeping him separate from his American fellow citizens of other racial groups, and in spite of false reflections upon his loyalty and bravery, the Negro soldier came out with a highly creditable record of deportment and achievement.

It would seem, then, that a race that has proved such a constructive factor in the development of a nation would be accorded ungrudgingly a right to the enjoyment of all the privileges of citizenship granted to other racial groups that make up the population of America. That such is not the case, however, all of us know full well. As a matter of fact, there are present indications of a rising tide of racial antipathy toward Negroes that is assuming dangerously serious proportions. And this at a time when it is absolutely essential that there be greater unity than ever between the races in America.

During the past national election, the campaign for the reelection of Senator Hill of Alabama was fought out on the issue of "white supremacy," an issue that was wholly extraneous. The real issue was whether or not a man of intelligence and comparative liberality, who achieved national distinction by joining with three other senators in a nonpartisan demand for the adoption of a truly international foreign policy by the United States, should be replaced by a man of narrow vision, subservient to the great absentee-owned industrial interests that so largely dominate the politics of the state. In the course of the campaign one of the newspapers carried once a week a picture of Mrs. Roosevelt shaking hands with a Negro serviceman, or a Negro Red Cross or USO worker. I saw a copy of this newspaper that carried a screaming headline, entitled, "Eleanor Greets a 'Nigger' Friend." The one encouraging thing about this campaign was that the wicked misrepresentations and vilifications were carried so far that they proved a boomerang, and Senator Hill was reelected, which was a reflection of the innate sense of decency of the masses of the people of Alabama.

Another illustration of how false issues are raised to the detriment of Negroes, is shown in the character of the debates that have been carried on in the Congress of the United States from time to time, when bills have been offered to abolish the poll tax, or to abolish lynching, or to establish a Fair Employment Practice Commission. Let me quote a *New York Times* report of an incident in connection with one of these debates:

> Senator Theodore G. Bilbo of Mississippi charged that the FEPC was "married" to the view that any type of segregation between the white and Negro races was discrimination, that the agency was created "in a political mind" and that "its hope and dream is to build up a greater race by intermarriage of the two races." He spoke of his plan to send Negroes to West Africa and noted that it had been criticized by Mrs. Roosevelt. "Of course," Mr. Bilbo said, "She did not understand my ultimate plan. If I succeed eventually in resettling the great majority of Negroes in West Africa, I might entertain the proposition of making her queen of that Greater Liberia."

Such flagrant outbursts of racial animosity and contemptible reflection upon the advocates of justice and fair play are serious, but I am not half as much troubled by them as I am by an apparently naïve conformity to a double standard of personality and citizenship on the part of the average, decent, law-abiding American citizen. Mr. Willkie sensed what I have in mind when, in another article, he used this sentence: "The Constitution does not provide for first- and second-class citizens."

The crux of the so-called Negro problem in America today is in the fact that most Americans have a mental and spiritual reservation on the application to Negroes of the guarantees and safeguards of our federal Constitution. Thoughtful Negroes are greatly appreciative of all that is being done by sincere individuals and organizations along welfare lines to help improve the condition of the Negro in this country, but they must continue respectfully to insist that such approaches to the problem are superficial, and that no lasting solution will be found until the double standard pattern itself has been destroyed, until segregation on account of color, in all its forms and expressions, has been done away with. Let me illustrate.

A year or two ago, a lynching of a Negro took place in a small town in Maryland. The victim had been charged with a vile crime, found guilty, and sentenced to death by the court. Immediately after he was sentenced and was on his way out of the courthouse in the custody of the police, he was seized by a mob, bound with a rope, attached to an automobile and dragged through the streets to the public square where he was placed on a pile of wood, saturated with oil, and burned to death. The decent citizens of that town were shocked at the horror of such a demonstration of savagery and expressed their regret through public utterances and in the columns of their local paper. Under no circumstances would these citizens have engaged in the actual deed of burning a man to death, but the cold fact is that this man became a victim of the mob because he had first been a victim of a double standard of personality and citizenship. His personality and citizenship were not up to par. He had lived all his life across the railroad tracks, in a ghetto where there were few or no electric lights, where the streets were unpaved, where there was little or no collection of garbage, where the house in which he lived was substandard, where his children went to school in an antiquated, tumbledown building with a teacher poorly paid and poorly prepared for her work. He lived in this ghetto because the double standard of citizenship compelled that he be segregated. The crime that he committed was the result more largely of his living environment and lack of opportunity than of innate depravity, while the persons who actually dragged this man through the streets and applied the torch that burned him to a crisp were guilty of murder and should have answered for their crime before society and before God, I insist with emphasis that the respectable citizens of the community were even more guilty, because it was they who were responsible for the double standard that made the victim the type of person that he was, and that led ultimately to the terrible crime that he committed.

I know that there are sincere and honest white people who not only have an idea that segregation is desirable as a means of keeping peace between the races, but are laboring under the mistaken impression that Negroes themselves do not object to segregation. At this point I think I should classify Negroes, as they are related to this particular issue, into four groups:

First, there is the Negro who bends and bows obsequiously in the presence of white people; who lies about conditions under which he lives, and about what is in his own heart because the white man has something that he wants and he thinks that that is the way to get it. He represents a comparatively small group, and cannot be relied upon, of course, because he is dishonest.

Second, there is the Negro who is not intentionally dishonest, but who gets weary in the struggle for his rights as a citizen and is willing to compromise, taking an inferior status if only he and his be permitted to live peacefully among themselves without participating in the affairs of their community, their state, or their nation. This type is commonly known among Negroes as the "Uncle Tom" type, and is rapidly disappearing.

Third, there is the ultraradical, wholly irresponsible type that is never satisfied with any situation, never sees any signs of improvement as worthy of commendation, and, in fact, would be disappointed if the things that he clamors for were granted, for then he would be deprived of the one thing for which he lives, and moves, and has his being, namely, eternal agitation for the sake of agitation. This is a comparatively small group.

Fourth, there is the Negro who does not bend and bow, with hat under his arm, in the presence of those who consider themselves his superiors; who does not weary in the fight for a single standard of personality and citizenship; who is willing to cooperate with his white fellow citizens, but only on the basis of mutual respect. This is the Negro who is dominant in the life of his racial group today, and is popularly called the "new Negro." It is he who must be reckoned with by the people of America who sincerely desire to find a solution of the problem that we are discussing this morning. Deep down in his heart he does not believe in segregation because he knows that the enforced setting apart of any group carries with it the implication of unfitness for contact on the part of that group with people of other groups throughout the nation, and no man with self-respect can ever look upon himself as essentially unfit for contact with other people.

Fortunately, there are white people who are beginning to realize how serious it is to permit segregation to go unchallenged. The most eloquent protest against segregation that I have read comes from the pen of the well known author of *Strange Fruit,* Lillian Smith. I quote at length from a recent article of hers ("Addressed to White Liberals," *The New Republic,* vol. III, September 18, 1944, pp. 331-333):

> Segregation is not merely a Southern tradition, a result of poverty, of certain economic patterns, etc., etc. Segregation is an ancient, psychological mechanism, used by men the world over whenever they want to shut themselves away from problems which they fear and do not feel they have the strength to solve. When men get into trouble they try to put barriers between themselves and their difficulties. We white people got into deep trouble long ago when we attempted to enslave other human beings, a trouble we have never faced truly and never tried with all our strength to solve. Instead, we have tried to push it away from us, and in trying we have used a mechanism so destructive that it, in itself, has become a menace to the health of our culture and our individual souls. Segregation is a way of life that is actually a form of cultural schizophrenia, bearing a curious resemblance to the schizophrenia of individual personality. It is a little chilling to note the paranoid symptoms of those among us who defend segregation, their violence, their sensitiveness to criticism, their overesteem of themselves, their stereotyped replies to criticism, their desire to withdraw from everything hard to face. Racial segregation, political and economic isolationism, cannot be considered apart from man's whole personality, his culture, his needs. Neither can man's needs be considered apart from the destroying effects of segregation. Nor can the South's major problems be solved by trying to put a loaf of bread, a book, and the ballot in every one's hand. For man is not an economic or political unit. To believe that he is, by ignoring personality, it to oversimplify a complex, subtle, tragically profound problem.
>
> It helps us sometimes to see this if we look into the restricting frame of segregation in terms of the needs of children. A child's personality cannot grow and mature without self-esteem, without a feeling of security, without faith in his world's willingness to make room for him to live as a human being. Self-esteem and security are to character what vitamins are to the body. No colored child in our South is being given today what his personality needs in order to grow and mature richly and fully. No white child, under the segregation pattern, can be free of arrogance and hardness of heart, and blindness to human needs—and hence no white child can grow freely and creatively under the crippling frame of segregation. I per-

sonally would prefer that my own child do without shoes than do without the esteem of his fellows, and I would prefer that he never look into a book than that he look down upon another human being. We simply cannot turn away and refuse to look at what segregation is doing to the personality and character of every child, every grown-up, white and colored, today. Segregation is spiritual lynching.

Now I think I should say that I am dwelling at considerable length on the question of segregation because, as I have said, I think it is the core of this problem. This does not mean that there is any lack of appreciation on my part of the importance of facing the practical problems of jobs, housing, eduaction, health, etc., but I have the strongest kind of conviction that, in the first place, these problems cannot be worked out successfully within the framework of complete racial segregation, and, in the second place, even if they could be worked out, there would still be this violence to personality that enforced segregation imposes upon the group affected by it. Fortunately, there are growing evidences of awareness of the seriousness of this problem, and indications of the desire and the will to attack it. For instance, toward the close of the war, in response to widespread protests on the part of Negroes and liberal whites, some experimentation was made in integrating Negro soldiers in the regular fighting units in the European theater of war, while the Navy, through forthright orders from Secretary Forrestal, announced that there should be no segregation of men in that service according to racial lines.

Possibly most significant of recent indications that I have observed, showing the desire and the will to face up to all the implications of segregation, is an expression that came out of the Conference of Protestant Church Leaders of America To Study Ways and Means of Bringing About a Just and Durable Peace. Never have I known Protestant church leaders, representing approximately twenty million communicants in this country, to be more explicit on this issue that was this Cleveland conference in the following paragraph of its message to the country:

We face likewise the necessity of establishing justice. Justice demands the unsegregated opportunity for a free man to earn his own living, serve his fellow man and achieve the good life. A man's opportunities must be based upon his character and capacity, not his color or creed. Justice moves from the domestic to the international sphere and demands the goal of autonomy for all subject peoples. For those now ready, freedom must be given at once. For those not ready, an international trusteeship must provide the means for the development and eventual freedom of the World. "Subject peoples" must become a term no longer applicable to contemporary society.

Now let me say, as I come to the close of this talk, that I would like to anticipate and reply to the question that I know is in the minds of all of you, namely, what can be done about these intercultural problems?

The time will not permit me to present a blueprint of plans and procedures of interracial cooperation. After all, there are several brief outline publications that you may secure with little difficulty, such as Lillian Smith's *There Are Things To Do* and Kendall Weisiger's *Background for Brotherhood*. Both publications have special reference to the South, but they contain suggestions that would be helpful in any part of the country. Also, there is *The Story of the Springfield Plan,* published by Barnes & Noble, New York, for which Professor Clyde R. Miller of Teachers College wrote the introduction. The National Conference of Christians and Jews, the Department of Race Relations of the Federal Council of Chruches, the American Council on Race Relations, the Southern Regional Council and the Southern Conference for Human Welfare, all are prepared to furnish valuable suggestive material that may be helpful to those who are desirous of either working individually or organizing for action on intercultural relationships.

What I would like to do in my closing words is to suggest a few important reasons why America must do something about intercultural and interracial relationships now:

First, the tendency to view racial problems in the light of the harmful effect of prejudice upon the victimized groups is a superficial approach. For instance, when the Fair Employment Practice Bill was filibustered to death in the United States Senate in the most disgraceful attack upon innocent and unoffending racial and religious minorities ever uttered in the chief legislative hall of any nation in the world, those newspapers and persons who referred to it called attention to the injustices done to these minority groups. I cannot say too emphatically that such papers and such persons missed the point entirely. The thing for us to keep in mind, in the case of the vicious insults to Negroes and Jews voiced by the Eastlands, the Bilbos, and the Russels, and supported by other senators, is that while specifically their attacks were directed at minority groups, the real attack was upon American democracy at its very root; for their whole procedure was in the interest of preventing an expression of majority opinion on a bill that they felt they could defeat in no other way. To repeat what Wendell Willkie said so eloquently, "The Constitution makes no provision for first- and second-class citizens." If the rights of any minority are permitted to be trampled under foot, our whole democratic structure is placed in peril.

Second, we must realize that any discrimination against an individual based solely on race, color, or national origin, places the individual or group concerned in an impossible position. If a man is discriminated against because he is ignorant, he can study, acquire knowledge, and overcome the handicap. If he is discriminated against because of poverty, he can work, acquire wealth, and overcome the handicap. If he is discriminated against because he is unclean, he can wash, acquire habits of cleanliness, and overcome the handicap. But if the discrimination is based upon color or race, he cannot change that. The responsibility for his being nonwhite is not his but God's. Therefore, it is not merely an injustice to the man to exclude him from fellowship on account of color; it is an affront to the God Who made him as he is.

Third, insistence upon racial discrimination in America is making it difficult for our country to exercise the leadership among the nations of the world for which it is otherwise qualified. All of us recall that after the decision was made by the United Nations to establish headquarters in America, delegates from countries with preponderant colored populations insisted that the UN headquarters should be established in that section of America where people of color would not be subjected to discrimination and humiliating insults. It was my personal observation, in a trip around the world some eight years ago, that the people of China and India, and the islands of the Pacific held America in high esteem on account of its position of preeminence in science, particularly engineering. Also from reading our history they had been impressed by our refusal to encourage imperialism in our foreign policy. But in all the conferences I held with religious and political leaders of the Far East there was disappointment over the stories of the lynching and burning of human beings, and the observance of rigid color lines in some parts of our country.

We are today trying earnestly to avoid future wars, but it is important that we realize that this cannot be accomplished simply by having the representatives of our State Department join with diplomats of other nations in drawing up blueprints for international peace. We must furnish the example of brotherhood and true democracy among our own people, if we are to exercise the influence for the peace of the world that our hearts so much desire. Personally I believe that America has the capacity and the spirit to meet this challenge. I like the way that Russell Davenport expresses it in his great poem entitled, *My Country*,[1] and I can think of no better way of closing my remarks than by quoting at length from that poem:

> America lives in her simple homes:
> The weathered door, the old wisteria vine,
> The dusty barnyard where the rooster roams,
> The common trees like elm and oak and pine:
> In furniture for comfort, not for looks,
> In names like Jack and Pete and Caroline,
> In neighbors you can trust, and honest books,
> And peace, and hope, and opportunity.
> She lives like destiny in Mom, who cooks
> On gleaming stoves her special fricassee,
> And jams and cakes and endless apple pies.
> She lives in Pop, the family referee,
> Absorbing Sunday news with heavy eyes,
> And in the dog, and in the shouting kids
> Returning home from school, to memorize

[1] Reprinted from *My Country* by permission of Simon and Schuster, Inc. Copyright, 1944, by Russell W. Davenport.

The history of the ancient pyramids.
And still she lives in them when darkness wakes
The distant smells and infinite katydids,
And valleys seem like black and fearsome lakes
Guarded by windows of American light,
While in the wind the family maple rakes
The lucent stars westward across the night.
And still, however far her sons may go,
To venture or to die beyond her sight,
These little windows shine incognito
Across incredulous humanity;
That all the peoples of the earth may know
The embattled destination of the free—
Not peace, not rest, not pleasure—but to dare
To face the axiom of democracy:
Freedom is not to limit, but to share;
And freedom here is freedom everywhere.

XV

LABOR'S COMING OF AGE

BY

MARK STARR

Educational Director, International Ladies' Garment Workers' Union

"Labor's Coming of Age," like other metaphors, has its weaknesses, because labor, viewed from contrasting viewpoints, is simultaneously in its adolescence and its senescence. Nevertheless, the unprecedented size, power, rights, and responsibilities of organized labor in the United States at the present time do suggest a maturity meriting current consideration.

Most certainly, the approach to labor in religious circles has changed remarkably in the past forty years. During the month of August, 1902, President George M. Baer of the Philadelphia and Reading Railroad Company, then in a bitter fight to break the United Mine Workers, received a letter from a photographer of Wilkes Barre appealing to him as a Christian to settle the mining strike. Mr. Baer replied:

I see you are evidently biased in your religious views in favor of the right of the workingman to control a business in which he has no other interest than to secure fair wages for the work he does. I beg of you not to be discouraged. The rights and interests of the laboring man will be protected and cared for, not by the labor agitators, but by the Christian men to whom God in His infinite wisdom has given control of the property interests of the country.

And for many years, before and after the Social Encyclicals of Pope Leo XIII and Pope Pius XI had endorsed workmen's associations, the unions in their early days were opposed by organized religion in its role as a pillar of the *status quo*.

Please do not think that Mr. Baer's naïve assertions of divine assistance are yet outmoded. Joseph Pew, chairman of the Sun Shipbuilding Company, in a speech to 33,000 employees was reported by the *Pathfinder* in 1934 as saying:

> Let us not waste our time talking of peace or conditions of a postwar world. These problems will clarify themselves automatically in God's own way as the years go by.

Most recently in February, 1946, Congressman Dudley G. Roe of Maryland, supporting a move to cripple the Office of Price Administration in its fight against the black market, declared:

> The law of supply and demand is a divine, God-given law. The sooner we let God's laws operate without human interference, the sooner we will have prosperity.

It is too bad that social intelligence tests are not compulsory for Congressmen and heads of corporations before they are entrusted with responsibilities.

But to return from this detour, may I suggest that the promoters and participants of this Institute share in the credit for creating that welcome current change in the relations between organized religion and organized labor. And let me quote a personal experience to show that organized education has also shared in that change. At the end of this month it will be my privilege to give the Inglis Lecture at the School of Education at Harvard. Forty-one years ago, Charles W. Eliot, then president of Harvard University, in *Harper's Magazine* (March, 1905) glorified the scab strike breaker as an "American hero." If Harvard so changes, can other institutions be far behind? Other days bring other ways and higher education is no longer hired by vested interests opposed to trade unions.

Labor won out in its early struggle for existence. Labor is now an important recognized part of American society. The United States Department of Commerce, reporting on January 24, 1946, estimated the civilian employed labor force at 51,360,000 of which over seven million are in agriculture.

Figures on wages and employment given by the Bureau of Labor Statistics, excluding marine workers, farmers, government employees and domestic servants, covered a total of 27,037,000 employed in November, 1945. Average wages ranged in November, 1945, from $68.46 per week for brokerage workers down to $28.88 for retail workers. At that time the Heller Committee budget estimated that the average wage earner's family required at least $58.00 weekly to maintain standards of decency and health.

The most recent Bureau of Labor Statistics figures available cover a total of 30,947,000 employed in December, 1946. Of these, slightly over twelve million are in manufacturing; 819,000 are employed in mining; nearly four million in public utilities; over eight and one half million in trade; and over five million in finance, services and miscellaneous. The average weekly earnings in manufacturing, listed in the same official table, are $46.86. The bituminous coal miner's weekly average was $69.56. The electric light and power employee received $54.58. The brokerage worker's average had fallen to $64.48. The retail worker had gone up to $33.73.

In view of the increase in the cost of living, the record shows that the worker's real wages have not been increased adequately.

Out of the total population of nearly 132,000,000, over 38,000,000 were working for wages in March, 1945 (Labor Information Bulletin, U.S. Department of Labor, May, 1945). This total does not include self-employed persons, proprietors of unincorporated businesses, unpaid family workers, farm laborers, domestic workers, and personnel in public service and armed forces.

It is this laboring section of our population (particularly the fourteen million or so wage workers in various kinds of trade unions that make up organized labor) whose maturity we now consider.

But these wage earners, organized and unorganized, do not form a regular pattern. Their names in the payrolls and time-sheets are Abruzino, Anderson, and Aumiller; Bendick, Boisvert, Brown, and Bronikowski; Cohen, Cooper, and Cudahy; Dziuk, Dzingielewski, and David; Ellis and Evjue; Garfield, Green, and Gonzales; Hanson and Howell; Levy, LaBarba, Llewellyn, and Loduca; Murphy,

McGwier, and Mineo; Olson, Panzeca, and Perlstein; Robinson and Rome; Schiller, Sturdevant, and Smith; Tobias, Totten and Tuma; Van Steele, Walker, Ward, Weinberg, and Zimmerman.

They make things, large and small. They build skyscrapers, ships, sewers. They dig coal and climb telegraph poles. They drive locomotives and adjust watchsprings. They build planes and man power stations. They weave cloth and make dresses. They turn out trucks and tiny sewing needles; autos, armatures, boilers, and buttons. They bake bread and make bridges. All the mining, shaping, melting, forging, building, printing, canning, cooking, spinning, and sewing that are necessary to feed, clothe, shelter, amuse, and educate the whole population are done by individual members of that forty million army.

They live in Chattanooga and Chicago, Sauk Center and Seattle, New York and New Orleans, Milwaukee and Macon, Peoria and Pittsburgh, Boston and Baltimore, San Francisco and Savannah. They are the basic America that Whitman saw:

The Negro that drives the long dray of the stone-yard, steady and tall he stands pois'd on one leg on the string-piece.

. . .

The carpenter dresses his plank, the tongue of his foreplane whistles its wild ascending lisp.

. . .

The jour printer with gray head and gaunt jaws works at his case, he turns his quid of tobacco while his eyes blur with the manuscript.

And what is the range in the reward of labor in dollars and cents? Well, current wages range from the St. Louis bricklayer who earns $2.00 an hour to the southern mill girl who must work a whole day for that sum. Before the spread of unionism in the New Deal decade, 1933–43 and before the Fair Labor Standards Act fixed a minimum of $11.00 weekly for a week of forty-four hours, a wage of $5.00 a week for unskilled workers was not uncommon. With many plants working overtime on war production, the official figures in February, 1943, showed an average weekly wage of $47.17 for the durable goods group and $32.17 for the nondurable. The most recent official figure given in November, 1945, shows that the average weekly earnings in durable goods were $43.97 and in nondurable $37.88.

Tragic indeed it is that the majority of us as citizens never give a thought to the soldiers of this great labor army and the conditions of its service until that army threatens to stop work.

But, to appreciate labor's maturity and the toughness of its growing-up, we must look back upon its role and history in America. And the story of early industrial life in America during the colonial period is largely a threnody of suffering. Generations of workers bent beneath the slave driver's lash. They suffered the cold of winter and the heat of summer. The first chattel slaves were raided from their native Africa and shipped under unimaginably horrible conditions to the plantations of the southern states. The indentured worker from Europe had mortgaged his future in order to get passage money to the New World and perforce remained in virtual slavery until he had redeemed himself. Criminals in prison were promised their liberty if they would undergo the dangers of work in the American colonies. Thousands of people were kidnapped and compelled to become part of the early working force of the United States. What the early pioneers did to the native American Indians does not furnish matter for the white man's pride. But soon it was clear that the United States was not going to be another Europe, for there was no room for caste privileges when the early settlers battled nature on the frontiers.

Thus, by free and forced labor, the first forests were cleared and the fields tilled; the roads made; the cities built and the foundations of the vast industrial system of the modern United States created. Even when physical compulsion was abandoned, economic pressure, racial and political persecution drove men and women to the United States and thus presented to the young country a ready-made trained labor force. As sources of mental virility and strength, came the victimized trade unionists and the Chartists from Britain; the disappointed revolutionists of 1848 from Germay; courageous opponents of Tsarist tyranny escaping from Polish ghettoes and Siberian exile in Russia; and the radical pioneers from Italy bringing the ideals of Mazzini and Garibaldi. Significantly enough, the key of the destroyed Bastille hangs in George Washington's home at Mt. Vernon; Lafayette sent it to the Father of his country by Tom Paine because Lafayette thought that the American example of 1776 had inspired the French Revolution. Freedom in the United States indeed has international roots and many races have enriched our ideals.

The labor movement championed freedom from want long before the Atlantic Charter; but freedom is difficult to define. We use it here in no absolute sense but as an understanding of necessity, changed by our controls over nature and our increasing powers of production. Usually it is best appreciated, like good health, when it has been lost. The poet Shelley made it clear by describing its opposite:

> What is freedom?—Ye can tell
> That which slavery is too well,
> For its very name has grown
> To an echo of your own.
>
> 'Tis to work and have such pay
> As just keeps life from day to day
> In your limbs, as in a cell,
> For the tyrants' use to dwell,
>
> 'Tis to be a slave in soul,
> And to hold no strong control
> Over your own will, but be
> All that others make of ye.

And to generations of workers the constitutional equal rights of "life, liberty and the pursuit of happiness" must have seemed a mirage; their dreams about "the land of the free and the home of the brave" were shattered by the reality expressed in the poet's lines.

The indentured workers, however, could not be kept in permanent submission. The demand for labor was so great that they were encouraged to attain their independence and indeed many soon became self-employed master workmen. The earlier attempt to transplant European serfdom into Virginia had proved vain for the imported serf could easily escape to till land of his own instead of cultivating the manor of his feudal lord. Often the imported criminal was only a rebel against unjust institutions in the Old World and made good in the New. Truly, some of the immigrants may have left their native country for their country's good, but even these were able to make a new start.

Chattel slavery in the United States, as we know, was not eliminated until a bitter civil war (1861-65) rent the country and gave leadership to the industrialist over the plantation owner. (Even now, the continuing racial discrimination against the Negro is one of the darkest stains upon our claims to progress.) Despite pioneering hardships, conditions soon became better for the workers in the United States than in Europe. Yet, compared to our modern standards, they were astonishingly low. At the time of the successful rebellion of the Thirteen Colonies, two shillings (50¢) was a day's pay for the unskilled worker; it increased to about 90¢ in 1800 and a dollar in 1825. The drab existence of the workers is pictured thus by the historian MacMaster (as quoted in *Labor in America,* Faulkner and Starr, New York, Harper & Brothers, 1944, p. 31):

> Sand sprinkled on the floor did duty as a carpet. There was no glass on his table, there was no china in his cupboard, there were no prints on his wall. What a stove was he did not know, coal he had never seen, matches he had never heard of. . . . He rarely tasted fresh meat as often as once a week, and paid for it a much higher price than his posterity . . .
>
> If the food of an artisan would now be thought coarse, his clothes would be thought abominable. A pair of yellow buckskin or leathern breeches, a checked shirt, a red flannel jacket, a rusty felt hat cocked up at the corners, shoes of neat's-skin set off with huge buckles of brass, and a leathern apron, comprised his scanty wardrobe.

The high school textbook, *Labor in America,* adds the following details:

> Farm hands received from seven to fifteen dollars a month, depending on demand, season, and locality, with the general average tending from the lower to the higher figure as time went on. Compensation of agricultural labor without board rose from 50 cents a day at the opening of the century to $1.50 and even $2 by 1860. The average of skilled labor, both agricultural and industrial, ran from $1 to $2 a day. An average about 1825 for skilled mechanics and factory operatives was around $9 a week. Judged by standards of today this income seems low indeed, but reckoned in the stan-

dards and prices of the period it was not intolerable. Skilled workers until the late 1830's were able to maintain a fair standard of living.

When the factory system was set up in Waltham, Massachusetts, girls worked seventy hours weekly. Harriet Martineau described the ideal paternalistic factory which she admired during her visit to the United States. But most of the American factories exploited child labor as ruthlessly as they did in the worst days of the early factory system in Britain.

When we think about the struggle for civil liberty and political rights in the United States, the warning summons made by the Liberty Bell at Philadelphia comes into mind. No one can overestimate the appeal which that bell made to the minds of men rightly struggling to be free.

But the struggle for political liberty is only half the battle. There is another bell, the Mechanics Bell, now a museum piece in the Bronx, New York, which shipwrights hung a hundred years ago in Lower Manhattan. It pealed out at Stanton and Goerck Streets, near the shipyards of the East River, with its great nine-hundred-pound throat of bronze, to signal the end of each ten-hour day. That clang was necessary to break down the oldtime custom of the 1830's which had forced artisans to work "from dark to dark."

The Mechanics Bell signaled the dawn of a new day for the workers. For what good was political liberty unless workers had leisure to read and think about their welfare and not be mere work beasts from sunup to sundown?

All down through the decades of the nineteenth century, labor's lot was far from ideal. Later on there were company towns which were really work barracks for the miners and the steel workers, who were forced to buy at the company stores. Even the church was under the domination of the steel mill. For many decades the courts were used to hamstring all forms of union activity. Injunctions were taken out to prevent the workers from informing the general public about their plight. Injunctions were obtained from compliant judges to prevent any proposed strikes. Trade union leaders were not only victimized and hunted from pillar to post because of their allegiance to the trade unions, but they suffered also from legal persecution. When the workers finally resorted to strikes, then the strong-arm men of the company, the local police, the state militia, and even on occasion Federal troops, were used to suppress the riots of the desperate workers. The robber barons later became respectable and united in great trusts but that brought no lessening in their antagonism to unions.

Not until 1842 did the unions secure from the courts legal recognition of their existence, although this meant recognition, in many instances, for the purpose of legal prosecution. Faulkner thus pictures the situation of the workers in the years following the Civil War:

Despite the long agitation for the ten hour day, the average work day in 1865 was eleven hours. Many worked much longer; the steel industry, for example, did not end the twelve hour day until 1923. Until prices broke after the end of the war and particularly after the Panic of 1873 wages lagged behind. In any case wages were low enough. Agricultural laborers in 1880 received on an average $1.31 per day, cotton mill operatives $1.24, shoemakers $1.76, printers $2.18, carpenters $2.42, and masons $2.79. Prices were, of course, much lower than today, but these wages by no means afforded a decent standard of living. The increasing use of women and children in industry kept wages down as did the large immigration throughout these years. Not only were hours long and wages low, but discipline was rigid and arbitrary. Working conditions were often unhealthy, unsafe, and the rules humiliating. In many communities workers were forced to trade at company owned stores and purchase at high prices. Laws on the statute books favored the employer rather than the worker. The courts, generally speaking, seemed more sympathetic toward the employer than the worker. Efforts at unionization were often prevented by forcing workers to sign a pledge that they would not join a union ("ironclad oath"). Union members were discharged and then blacklisted to prevent their subsequent reemployment.

However, no matter how intense oppression or severe the setbacks, there are always some gallant spirits to rise again and challenge tyranny. Back in 1790, an indictment against some Philadelphia shoemakers for forming a combination to "conspire" against their employers showed that workers even then dared to unite and protest against bad conditions. One of the earliest large scale attempts to fight for economic freedom in the United States was the Knights of Labor set up in 1869. Every new member, when initiated into the Noble Order of the Knights of Labor, was given the following instruction:

Labor is noble and holy. To defend it from degradation; to divest it of the evils to body, mind, and estate which ignorance and greed have imposed; to rescue the toiler from the grip of the selfish—is a work worthy of the noblest and best of our race. . . . We mean no conflict with legitimate enterprise, no antagonism to necessary capital, but men, in their haste and greed, blinded by self interests, overlook the interests of others, and sometimes violate the rights of those they deem helpless. We mean to uphold the dignity of labor, to affirm the nobility of all who earn their bread by the sweat of their brows. We mean to create a healthy public opinion on the subject of labor (the only creator of values) and the justice of its receiving a full, just share of the values or capital it has created. We shall, with all our strength, support laws made to harmonize the interests of labor and capital, and also those laws which tend to lighten the exhaustiveness of toil.

In the mining areas there were secret organizations which tried to meet intimidation by violence and accomplish their ends by assassination and terror. In the mining valleys of Pennsylvania, old men still talk about the Mollie Maguires who were finally exposed by a Pinkerton stool pigeon in 1876.

In the years 1830 to 1840, the workers had tried to reduce the twelve hour day to the ten hour day. They fought against the property qualification for voters and also objected to the one time right of a rich man to buy the services of a substitute for military service. The workers abolished imprisonment for debt and tried to save the tools of the mechanic from confiscation by garnishee proceedings. They tried to prohibit the sale of the products of convict labor.

When the shortcomings of the modern industrial system of the United States were revealed, there were, in the years 1840 to 1850, prominent advocates of fundamental social changes. Robert Owen not only fought against child labor but introduced cooperative experiments in the United States, as he did in Britain. There were attempts to set up Utopian colonies according to the plans of Fourier. Many notable Americans agitated for the right of the worker to escape industrial exploitation by securing a free homestead. Later on, many of these reformers became active in the abolitionist movement. Both Marx and Engels were keen students of American affairs and wrote about them. Their followers organized study groups and in New York City the First International found refuge in its closing years.

As we have seen, the Civil War accelerated the development of American social problems. The Knights of Labor attempted to stop Jay Gould and other prominent industrialists from carrying through their boast that they could buy one half of the workers to shoot down the other half. The Knights of Labor, however, suffered from aims which were too mixed and general. There was no clear stratification of economic groups in their membership. The Knights included the self-employed worker and, indeed, all other classes with the exception of publicans and lawyers.

Out of the failings of the Knights of Labor, there grew the American Federation of Labor, founded in 1881 and taking its present name in 1886. Here was an effort, not in general unionism but in craft unionism; the federation of nationwide autonomous unions concerned with practical trade matters.

Forsaking vague and general aims, the A. F. of L. concentrated upon immediate betterment. "More and more, here and now" was its slogan. In the main, the members were skilled workers who were in a relatively more powerful bargaining position than the unskilled workers. The A. F. of L. continued the fight for the shorter workday, aiming now for the eight hour day and indeed starting the custom of making May Day a labor celebration and a demonstration for that reduction in work hours. The unions shared in the protests made by the Populists of the agrarian states against the trusts and Wall Street.

Greatly influenced by Samuel Gompers, the A. F. of L. resorted to political action and lobbying only for self-defense. Gompers believed in "voluntarism" and thought that the workers' unions should be independent of the state in the struggle for the workers' economic betterment.

While the American Federation of Labor brought stability and permanence to organized labor, it did not succeed in organizing the mass production industries. During World War I, its strength rapidly increased; but when that war came to an end, the A. F. of L. lost many hundreds of thousands of members. Under the euphemistic title of the "American Plan," there was a definite attack made by employers against trade unionism. Company unions were started to prevent the setting up of genuine organizations. Company unions in the United States, with two million members, attained a greater strength than such organizations had ever achieved in any other country.

In the twenties of this century, despite the great development of industry, trade unions showed little increase in strength. There had been a rebel movement, of course, challenging the control of Gompers. The Wobblies, as the Industrial Workers of the World were nicknamed, starting in 1906 had attempted to set up revolutionary mass organization for the unskilled workers. However, the strength of the IWW was confined largely to migratory workers. It conducted spectacular protests but did not set up permanent organizations with contracts recognized by the employers. During the war, while the American Federation of Labor sacrificed its right to strike and cooperated fully with the government in the war effort, the Wobblies were accused of sabotage. Wartime hysteria was made the occasion for suppression of the Wobblies by legal and illegal means.

The various socialist parties had tried to influence the A. F. of L. but with little result. Eugene V. Debs, starting as an organizer for the railroad workers, had thrown in his lot with the Socialist Party and had won fame as their presidential candidate. Later he suffered imprisonment as an opponent of the First World War. During the years of alleged prosperity, the carpings of the critics of the American Federation of Labor fell upon deaf ears. The only serious attempt made to start a third party representing the town and country workers subsided quickly after the failure to elect LaFollette as President in 1924.

Then came the great crash of 1929. The unions lost membership and mass unemployment shook American optimism to its foundations. The New Deal decade, 1933-43, arrested the depression and gave a new status to the trade unions. Company unions, which had been fostered in the previous decade, were outlawed by the National Labor Relations Act. The new wine of increased opportunities for organization burst the old A. F. of L. bottles, and in 1935 there began the Committee for Industrial Organization which two years later became the Congress of Industrial Organizations.

The CIO was able to spread organization into steel, autos, rubber, glass, and other mass production industries which had previously resisted all attempts of trade union organizers. The trade unions in wartime achieved the unprecedented strength of over fourteen millions of organized workers. They are making endeavors to train and educate their members in new constructive roles. They are determined that, now the war is over, no tidal wave of reaction shall sweep away their gains. And for my own part I am still convinced that the A. F. of L. and CIO can and should cooperate both in the industrial and in the political field and that, despite all previous friction, the membership of the two organizations should aim to reunite the family of organized labor.

The unions in wartime participated in a significant movement toward union-management cooperation. A new pattern was developed in industrial relationships. Farsighted employers have recognized that unions are here to stay and that union leaders are responsible and reasonable men with whom they can and should discuss the problems of industry. We have a good chance of leaving behind us the old industrial conflicts which were literally civil wars, and passing on to the civilized procedures of collective bargaining. The pages of future history must no longer be stained with bloody incidents such as the Memorial Day Massacre in Chicago.

In the New Deal period labor learned how to use legislation to improve its lot. The Fair Labor Standards Act has put a ceiling on the work week and a floor below which wages cannot go. Attempts have already been made to provide for the dangers of unemployment, sickness, and old age.

The growth of unionism has, of course, increased labor's responsibilities. In many instances, it has asked for a greater say and for participation in the control of industry. It aims at partnership in the affairs of industry and state. Because the triumph of Fascism meant death to all that labor held dear, it threw itself wholeheartedly into the fight against Fascism at home and abroad.

A tremendous peacetime job in the adjustment of men, materials, and machines gives the unions a great opportunity for constructive statesmanship. The unions, too, will need the help of all thinking men and women in the community to improve our plans for social security so that the third great freedom, Freedom from Want, can be really enjoyed. Even before the harnessing of atomic energy, the war had greatly increased industrial productivity. (See the January and February, 1946, issues of *Fortune* for details of this current industrial revolution.)

From slavery to freedom; from conflict to cooperation; from bloody rebellion to orderly progress by consent—that is the story of organized labor in the United States as in other modern countries. And labor is now the largest organized element in the community and as such must be even more aware than ever of its role as an all important agency for community welfare.

But you will say, What about the postwar strikes, the clashes between Big Unionism and Big Business? What about Quill and Petrillo—Sewell Avery, Tom Girdler, and Ernest Weir? And we agree that such industrial strife indicates how we fall short of intelligent and mature behavior in our industrial relations. In 1945 there were 4,600 strikes and lockouts involving 3,325,000 workers and creating thirty-five million man-days of idleness. In 1946 the totals will be greater.

Recently in New York City one A. F. of L. and one CIO union caused considerable trepidation to our fellow citizens. In the first instance, on Lincoln's Birthday, Mayor O'Dwyer shut down the city instead of either forcing the employers to arbitrate or alternatively taking over the tugboats and running them as a public service until such time as the employers agreed to arbitrate. The reason why the tug workers were so recalcitrant before they agreed to arbitration was that they had long been denied any wage advance. Their union was not responsive to the pressure of the rank and file and finally the indignation of the members blew the top off.

The remedies are obvious—unions with a greater amount of

rank and file participation, internal democratic procedures in the union, and the settlement of disputes as they occur would have served as a safety valve, preventing a later explosion.

In the case of the subway workers of the Transport Workers' Union (CIO), the situation was more complicated. One of the outstanding failures of the LaGuardia régime had been his inability to set up a transit labor management committee. He and Mr. Michael Quill, president of the Transport Workers' Union, had indulged in mutual defiance, but there was no meeting of minds because LaGuardia took refuge in the dubious argument that a government could not recognize a union for collective bargaining without infringing upon civil service regulations. He did this despite the fact that in Detroit, in Philadelphia, and in several Connecticut cities—to mention only a few places—A. F. of L. unions have made collective bargaining contracts with the local councils.

The tragic thing in both the subway and the tugboat strikes is that people did not recognize the importance of the work done by these people until its withdrawal was threatened. For years the subway workers suffered from relatively low wages in carrying through their job, which is essential to the industrial life of New York City. The Transport Workers' Union cannot have a closed shop under civil service and hence its job should be to make the union so attractive that the members would want to belong in order to secure social, recreational, and sick and death benefits, etc.

At the last moment a Transit Committee was set up to consider wage advances and the TWU dropped its request for exclusive bargaining rights. This latter was both discreet and wise because a large number of employees are organized in rival unions and would have contested the exclusive claim. However, the Transit Committee should become a part of the industrial relations of New York City. It is nonsense to think that subways can be run under conditions of military discipline and nonsense to think that a city government can avoid discussing wages, hours, and conditions with the legitimate representatives of its workers.

All the abuse against Quill and his methods avail nothing. The majority of the people, of course, want to see the subway workers decently paid; they also want to see a pattern of cooperation between management and labor set up so that there will be a recognized medium for dealing with all disputes.

We badly need an examination of that employer trouble created by the fact that heads of business corporations get more in a week than a worker does in a year and yet, when it comes to representing their corporations before a government inquiry, they have to engage high priced lawyers to advise them. We want to avoid the trouble created by employers who, from false assumptions about their superiority relative to community welfare, proceed to foregone conclusions about their rights to escape social responsibilities both to their shareholders and to the general body of citizens.

The workers gave up the right to strike during war when their labor power could have secured boom prices. When the war ceased, they suffered big cutbacks in take-home pay by the cessation of overtime. They saw managerial salaries greatly increased during the war and maintained at the same level after the war. They knew that profits had risen to an unprecedented peak despite the increase in depreciation allowances and in the liquid assets of the corporations. They had also noticed that Congress had given the corporations a cushion to fall down upon by way of recapturing some of their taxes if the postwar years were lean. Meanwhile the worker's wife experienced a constant increase in prices.

The wonder is that strikes are so few under such circumstances. And all the union baiting hysteria of Congress will only make the matter worse. You will recall that the Smith-Connally Bill, passed over the late President's veto, made a strike ballot compulsory. Instead of stopping strikes, this made strikes more probable because the members immediately at the beginning of wage negotiations had to place themselves on record to be willing to strike and this perforce destroys the atmosphere in which conciliation and arbitration could operate successfully. Now, of course, even our Congressmen are prepared to abandon the Smith-Connally Bill which they rushed through in such indecorous haste.

Some opposition has been aroused by the NLRB decision that foremen may now join unions but foremen surely cannot be denied the right to organize. As Lewis Corey has shown in a recent pamphlet, technicians and professional workers are increasing at a much quicker rate proportionately than any other section of workers. With the demonstrated power of organization to raise standards and win respect, surely these technicians are going to unite to safeguard and improve their standards. If the big corporation heads are prepared to exploit both the technicians and the absentee shareholders for the sake of their own personal aggrandizement and huge salaries, then obviously they must expect organized protests.

Punitive laws against the unions are no solution. The current Case Bill, for example, is like throwing gasoline on a fire to put it out. Secretary of Labor Schwellenbach has rightly denounced this attempt to revive the injunction and impose compulsory arbitration. It is Congress which needs a cooling off period. Union members as individual citizens have not the slightest immunity under the law. Unions, however, cannot be made responsible for the acts of members over whom they have no legal control. As statistics show, there are large areas of industry in which trade unions are only weakly represented if at all. Hence no person is compelled to suffer under the alleged tyranny of paying union dues to enjoy union protection and conditions.

Legal suppression failed in Britain where the Scabs Charter, passed in 1937, was finally repealed in 1946 by the Labor Government. The swing to the Labor Party was in part a revenge against the Tories' attempt to limit the sympathetic strike and the political activity of the unions.

Industrial peace is like health, to be secured by forethought and appropriate exercise and nutrition. It will be nourished by the recognition that: (1) Collective bargaining is the law of the land; (2) unions, as partners in industry, should have access to all relevant facts; (3) workers should have a higher standard of life, based upon their greatly increased labor productivity and the unprecedented wartime profits business reaped; (4) this improved standard will be the best preventive against the return of the depression years.

Senator Robert M. LaFollette explained the causes of the present strike wave in *The Progressive,* February 11, 1946:

First, industry was treated very generously during the war and faces the prospect of exceptionally good business at least until the backlog of demand is satisfied.

Second, labor felt it was held down during the war, and now was the opportunity, if ever, to demand more.

Third, Government reports and surveys tended to substantiate labor's position that general wage increases could be made without commensurate price increases, due to greater productivity of labor and the prospects of near-capacity production levels.

Fourth, wage increases fitted in with the sound economic theory that in the long run mass purchasing power must remain high in order to buy the products of industry.

His conclusions were:

A clear-cut victory for labor may finally establish genuine collective bargaining in corporations which have never accepted it wholeheartedly. It will mean that recalcitrants and rugged individualists in management will hereafter have to follow the lead already established by farsighted employers, in giving labor a larger share of industrial income.

A victory for management will smash the upsurge of unionism, but it will be a short-lived victory. In the long run, the public will never permit the arbitrary exercise of managerial power to deprive the workers of fundamental rights.

The labor movement recognizes that it has a tremendous job in educating its members and its officers to their current responsibilities. It is the role of workers' education to help in this important work. Already some outstanding unions, such as the International Brotherhood of Electrical Workers, have agreed to labor-saving devices and the Building Trades Workers in New York City have waived many of their previous restrictive regulations to help overcome the current shortage of houses.

Only education of the right sort can prevent the unions from abusing their great power and help them to recover from the mental hangovers of the industrial civil war period. Racketeering and jurisdictional disputes should be quickly tackled. Social security would remove any justification of made work and "feather bedding" practices. However, such education will not make labor tame and servile. It will rightly push to organize foremen, technicians, and professional workers as they become a more important section of industry. Labor will point out the gross disparity between the $8,827.00 received weekly by Charles E. Wilson of General Motors in 1943 as compared to the $44.80 received by the G.M. worker who now is asking for $58.40 through a thirty per cent increase. Workers' education will help the workers to understand the income tax returns which, for example, show that profits after taxes in 1944 were twice as big as in 1939 and that liquid assets of the corporations were increased by fifty billion dollars compared to prewar.

Labor, by understanding the economic system better, will press its case for an increase in wages with prices unchanged. It will ask President Truman to attempt no further bulges in the price line by way of the Big Steel Formula, but ask him to return to his policy of August 18, 1945, and to the declaration made by W. H. Davis in September.

Additionally to this self-education, labor is undertaking more activity in public relations. Thus far misguided people who thought that labor would suffer a disastrous and divided retreat in the postwar years have been disappointed. With few exceptions, the big mass strikes have not been accompanied by violence, and black and white workers have marched the picket lines in solidarity together. The steel strike of 1946 was not broken as was the steel strike of 1919. Union membership is holding up.

Another related problem, now that labor is come of age, is the preservation of internal democracy in the unions. Those interested might well read the paper presented by Dr. Philip Taft of Brown University to the January, 1946, meeting of the American Economic Association. The problem is to reconcile efficiency with democratic control; to give to the rank and file rights over policy making and over their officers without atomizing the union's strength. Dr. Taft concludes his paper with a plea for the setting up of an impartial body to which individual trade unions and trade unionists could appeal. He prefers that the labor movement itself should set up such an impartial tribunal which would give quick and inexpensive review of protested decisions.

How to meet this difficulty of members' control in large unions is a complex question. Workers' education, producing a mentally alert rank and file with a grasp of labor history and philosophy would be of tremendous assistance. Educational activities in a union must steer between the two perils of creating an antiadministration opposition clique and of creating a yes man chorus, and thus avoid both constant carping and blind acceptance. Obviously union education supports the *status quo* in union administration, just as does education maintained by any institution. Yet that should not rule out the duty of constructive criticism and the discussion of dissenting opinion in union classes. Indeed wise union leaders would encourage this.

What one can be sure about is that in the union journal and in union meetings channels for discussion and criticism ought to be forever kept open; that union officers should welcome and encourage ideas and criticisms from the younger members; that those younger members, instead of being driven into permanent opposition (and being built up and flattered by the Communists and outside agencies to be used as their tools, which has happened in the case of some right wing unions) should be given posts of responsibility so that they can sober the fanaticism of youth with administrative experience.

Union leaders and business agents should see that the economic power which they hold through the closed shop and the union shop is never used to penalize individuals who disagree with them. (A staff member of a union, Will Herberg, in *Antioch Review,* Fall, 1943, made an excellent critical and thought provoking analysis of this danger.)

Presumably, bureaucracy exists when means become more important than the end sought and when rules and procedures are continued because persons have vested interests in their continuance. An awareness of the necessity of constantly examining both means and ends and a recognition that they can and must be changed to meet unavoidable changes of growth—this would be the best antidote for bureaucracy in the unions as elsewhere. Unions should, in line with Professor Taft's suggestion, set up a court of appeal to which any member might go in case of suspected blacklisting by his union, just as he would go to the union if the employer tried to blacklist him. In some instances the unions should set up such a court of appeal composed of officers in other unions and of trusted friends of labor from educational and legal circles. Fundamentally, the development of general civic intelligence and a keen desire to apply democracy to industry and to trade union practices, would be the real and lasting safeguards.

In the light of our historical survey of labor's achievements in its progress from birth to maturity, it is fair to claim that what has been good for labor has been good for the community. Labor has made considerable contributions to community welfare. It has enriched and completed our ideas of democratic living by applying them to industry. In its future, as in its past, labor needs the support of every healthy and progressive element in the community to achieve the ideals of industrial democracy. Grow old along with Labor; the best is yet to be.

XVI

THE SPIRITUAL ROLE OF AMERICA

BY

F. ERNEST JOHNSON, D.D.

Professor of Education, Teachers College, Columbia University; Executive Secretary, Department of Research and Education, Federal Council of the Churches of Christ in America

In assuming the task of bringing to a close this series of addresses on "Wellsprings of the American Spirit," I have a troubled mind. The topic on this final day is logical enough. It is natural that after examining the sources of the American spirit and reviewing the struggles through which it has found expression we should ask, What is the spiritual role of America? Yet as I formulate that question today there comes ominously to my mind the ancient admonition, "To whom much has been given, from him shall much be required." I am weighed down by the accumulating burden of evidence that my country is not ready to be cast in a role corresponding to its heritage.

Rich in material resources, incredibly superior in scientific and technological achievements, without the hampering tradition of empire, and now completely victorious over her late enemies, surely America should be ready, if any nation ever was, to keep her appointment with destiny. But how different is the actual situation! Though "conceived in liberty" America is today uncertain as to what freedom really means and how widely it is to be shared. Scarcely touched by the material ravages of war, we have, it seems, to be begged and cajoled into accepting the most moderate curtailment of consumption in order that millions may not starve. Proud in the earlier years of our history of being an asylum for the distressed and afflicted of the earth, we now watch so jealously our ports of entry that we become agitated over the plight of European victims of unparalleled persecution only to the extent of urging that they go somewhere else, rather than inviting them to come to our shores. Having won a war to overthrow the dogma of the supremacy of naked power, we are counting heavily on the unilateral possession of the most hideous of all destructive weapons, our use of which has not been above a suspicion of wantonness.

Not only do our moral sensibilities seem to be blunted, but we are strangely blind to the consequences of what we do. We fail to see that an awful preponderance of power and a dazzling wealth of possessions can only breed fear and hatred of a nation thus distinguished unless offset by an overwhelming, disarming generosity. Our very advantages of position spell our national peril. There is an element of deep tragedy in this situation, which is pointed up by the present controversy over the proposed British loan. Two completely irreconcilable views appear, each supported by a convincing logic once the respective premises are granted. From a traditional nationalistic standpoint the American government is being extremely generous. Did we not cancel the greater part of the loan resulting from World War I? Are not the terms of the proposed loan unprecedentedly easy—so easy that it can hardly be called a business transaction in the ordinary sense? What shall be said of a government that complains of such treatment? Surely, an English classic has given us the answer: "Oliver Twist has asked for more!" But there is Oliver's point of view, which is something else again. If the recipient of aid is not a client, but a partner in peril and in sacrifice, then the norm of treatment is not furnished by the marketplace but by the family. There is all the difference in the world between a transaction and a shared ordeal. And surely it looks as if, for better or for worse, we are in this thing together.

Even family affairs are not always simple to negotiate. One member may seem to the others to be spendthrift and a bad budgeter. Does not many a man have to advertise that he is fed up with paying his wife's bills? This is about what many Americans have been saying about their British cousins. And the accession of a Labor government has not exactly helped that situation. But the hot question is, Where do we go from here? If we cannot get on together just how do we propose to get on separately? All signs point to the end of hostility and rivalry as a successful pattern of international relationships. More specifically, the key question in such a controversial situation is, How can this be managed so as to leave a working deposit of good will?

And this is true no matter which of our world neighbors is involved. Mr. Walter Lippmann's column this morning contains these solemn words:

> During this past week we have come to the point where it is no longer a theoretical possibility that we may fail to make peace. We are at the dividing line where it is easier to fail than it will be to succeed, where the chances of war are in sober truth greater than the chances of peace. We are at that line in our relations with the Soviet Union where, though there is as yet no formal diplomatic rupture, the process of diplomatic negotiation is believed in less and less seriously.
>
> Among great powers that is a most critical point. For if once it is passed, if once the conviction becomes fixed that no vital issue can be settled by negotiation, diplomacy after that consists in preparing for war. Diplomacy no longer expects to settle issues but only to postpone them, to gain time, to gain a more advantageous position, to mobilize opinion, to mobilize the wavering and uncertain nations, to mobilize the more powerful coalition.[1]

This is not to suggest that good will is to be purchased at any price, or that principle is to be sacrificed to expediency for the sake of smooth sailing. But we should know that national prosperity no longer means anything if it incites to envy; that national "rights" are not worth the paper they are written on if they are in the eyes of the rest of the world claims to permanently superior advantage; that business transactions between nations can henceforth not be considered advantageous if they do not engender commensurate reciprocal good will. Every dollar we spend today to alleviate world suffering, every *bona fide* effort to insure to other peoples the same kind of security we want for ourselves is worth infinitely more to us than the sharpest bargain our temporary advantage may enable us to drive. Expenditures for international education through exchange of students, and for worldwide intellectual and scientific cooperation,

[1] *New York Herald Tribune,* March 12, 1946.

will yield returns far beyond those of the conventional export of capital and of goods.

Such an approach to foreign policy involves a sharp break with the American tradition in its latter phase. Our national history during the past two generations contains strange paradoxes, but none stranger than the contradictory elements in the conception of America's role in international affairs. We were spared by a combination of historical and geographic factors during the period of our territorial expansion from falling into the typical imperialistic pattern of great powers. Yet we developed toward the end of the past century a kind of assertive benevolence—a "white man's burden" complex, American style. Professor Ralph Henry Gabriel has documented this development in disquieting fashion.[2] The religious contribution to it is not pleasant reading today. In my student days one of the most influential writers on religious and social questions was Josiah Strong. His book *Our Country,* written in 1885, seems to have cast quite a spell over a whole generation of Americans. He was a Christian social prophet but, if *Our Country* had been published today, you and I would have called it a dangerous book. Here are some of the things the eminent divine wrote:

> It is manifest that the Anglo-Saxon holds in his hands the destinies of mankind, and it is evident that the United States is to become the home of his race, the principal seat of his power, the great center of his influence.

Again,

> Long before the thousand millions are here, the mighty centrifugal tendency, inherent in this [Anglo-Saxon] stock and strengthened in the United States, will assert itself. Then this race of unequaled energy, with all the majesty of numbers and the might of wealth behind it—the representative, let us hope, of the largest liberty, the purest Christianity, the highest civilization—having developed peculiarly aggressive traits calculated to impress its institutions upon mankind, will spread itself over the earth. If I read not amiss, this powerful race will move down upon Mexico,

---

[2] *The Course of American Democratic Thought,* New York, The Ronald Press Company, 1940.

down upon Central and South America, out upon the islands of the sea, over upon Africa and beyond.

And,

> It would seem as if these inferior tribes were only precursors of a superior race, voices in the wilderness crying: "Prepare ye the way of the Lord!" [3]

The book had an enthusiastic reception and a wide circulation both in this country and abroad. Did it, I wonder, contribute to a certain fear of American intentions that we are surprised to discover in various parts of the world? It fitted into the mood fostered by the outcome of the Spanish-American War and the acquisition of the Panama Canal, and furnished a sort of benevolent ideological framework for the concept of "manifest destiny," which Dr. Gabriel calls the "mission of America" idea. How much it influenced the Christian missionary movement no one can say. But the important thing to note for our present purpose is the fact that social idealism even of a religious type could become so fused with an aggressive nationalism as to deceive even the elect about the real nature of the combination. The "mission of America" mood was not only broadly humanitarian; it was actually pacifist in its intention. Why should there be war, when our "manifest destiny" was so clear and convincing to all reasonable men?

The First World War brought disillusionment, and a cleavage in the American mind. The pacifist movement, stripped of its nationalist aura, gained the proportions of a great social force, while the nationalist fever subsided into a cool and sullen isolationism. The Second World War liquidated both these forces and the nation has had to make up its mind all over again concerning its role in world affairs.

Where do we stand today? Is there not growing among us a new phase of "manifest destiny," the substance of which is a sense of omnipotence symbolized by the atomic bomb (which, according to all accounts, we continue complacently to stockpile) coupled with a sublime self-assurance that we are preeminently the people to whom

---

[3] Josiah Strong, *Our Country*, quoted by Gabriel, *op. cit.*, pp. 341-2.

power can be safely entrusted? The most insidious thing about national "destiny" is, paradoxically, its moral ingredient—the spurious guarantee inherent in our high purposes that we will use our power for the benefit of mankind.

This is certainly too naïve to "fool all the people all the time." A few weeks after Hiroshima, in a Pullman car on a transcontinental train, I heard a conversation that has dwelt in my memory. A young officer was talking with a civilian about the atom bomb. He was all for it as a weapon against the Japanese—thought we should have dropped more—but he added cynically, "A hundred years from now there'll be no world!" The civilian wanted to know who the aggressor nation would be. "*We* may be it, ourselves," said the officer. There was no glamour about it, no heroics, just cynicism.

But if that dire surmise of American aggression should ever be actualized, I venture to say it will be all wrapped up in humanitarian ribbon. It will be the "white man's burden" over again—a benevolent purpose made to sanctify a nationalistic exploit. There is nothing more terrible than an exploit that has got itself baptized as a crusade. The universal degenerates into the unilateral, and is buried. We, too, like England at the height of her imperial power, need to listen to Kipling's warning—

> Far-called, our navies melt away;
> On dune and headland sinks the fire;
> Lo, all our pomp of yesterday
> Is one with Nineveh and Tyre!
> Judge of the Nations, spare us yet,
> Lest we forget—lest we forget!

A valid conception of national destiny, as the prophets of Israel well knew, implies a great sacrificial dedication. Power may be a constituent of destiny, but it is not of its essence. America can play a great role among the nations only as her national ends are convincingly subordinated to the realization of One World. With nations as with individuals there is no lasting good that is essentially private.

To my mind the conception of national destiny finds its best exemplification in the history of Israel. Here was a people trained to feel the imprint of the finger of destiny, but this selection and designation for a great role was understood, at least by the prophets, to be an *election* to discipline and sacrifice. This conception of destiny entrusted to a people is immortalized for us by the Deutero-Isaiah:

> Behold my servant, whom I uphold; my chosen, in whom my soul delighteth: I have put my Spirit upon him; he will bring forth justice to the Gentiles. He will not cry, nor lift up his voice, nor cause it to be heard in the street. A bruised reed will he not break, and a dimly burning wick will he not quench: he will bring forth justice in truth. He will not fail nor be discouraged, till he have set justice in the earth; and the isles shall wait for his law. (Isaiah 42: 1-4)

This, of course, is the antithesis of secular nationhood and of national destiny in the historic sense. I know well that to erect it into a norm in our day seems like a counsel of perfection—and despair. Nations do not live and act on so high a level. But I am really saying that nationality as we have known it must pass into eclipse if the One World is to be realized; that to visualize a spiritual role for America is to project a new era. Here is the new frontier to be crossed, the moral equivalent of the old frontier. Is it not for this that the American spirit was born and has struggled toward maturity? What else can give meaning to our historic political struggles; our religious pioneering; our indigenous art, literature, and philosophy; our crusades for cultural unity, equality of the sexes, and the emancipation of labor; our quest for freedom in a technological age? The things that make America great are universals, not particulars; their significance appears only when projected on a world screen.

This is not mere utopianism. It is not romanticism. It is historical realism. I would be among the last to discredit the slow, faltering steps by which progress toward the goal of One World is effected. Impatience with inevitable slowness becomes the handmaid of reaction. The important thing is the direction, not the tempo. I can hear someone protest, "But there is no longer time for slow steps. Destruction is at our doors." That may be. But destruction will not be averted by feverish efforts to bring about what only a regenerated human spirit can create. Panic is not a valid reaction to crisis. What the world needs from us today is convincing evidence of intention to build unity among the nations, to cast in our lot with our neighbors. We must believe that our power has come to us not to be wielded as an instrument of national policy but to be pooled in the society of nations. We must accept, as a principle of our own policy, that the unilateral is to give way to the universal. Stubbornness and suspicion we undoubtedly shall encounter. In large part they will be the results of our past words and deeds. What is now imperative is a convincing demonstration to other peoples that we are prepared to use our power only to implement aims that originate in concert—not those that are separately evolved.

We in America are peculiarly advantaged for carrying out within our own borders a major task, which is commonly defined as the realization of unity in diversity. We pride ourselves on our cultural pluralism, which affirms the intrinsic worth of cultural differences. This is the collective counterpart of the worth of the individual. Yet we have been driven by force of circumstances, as well as by desire, to seek passionately for national unity. There is always and inescapably a high tension between these polar values. That tension can be supported and made constructive only if there exists what Felix Adler was fond of calling an "overarching end." There can be no fruitful relationship between pluralities, merely *as* pluralities. Differences that are total differences at best neutralize each other. It is meaningless to talk glowingly of the value of cultural differences as good in themselves. Just as unity without an aspect of diversity is simple sterility, so diversity without an aspect of unity is simple disorder. And disorder is a prelude to a spurious, enforced, totalitarian unity.

It is a fair question whether we have not spent too much time and effort in glorifying our cultural differences—sometimes perhaps romanticizing about them—while giving all too little attention to their functional relationships in a dynamic democratic society. Even genuine appreciation of the different as an esthetic achievement, quickly dissolves in time of strain if it is not geared to a sense of mutual dependence. Cultural status depends on functional indispensability. What is not indispensable easily becomes incompatible. This means that there must be something going on in which all have a stake and for the consummation of which all are necessary. Cultural differences are worth cherishing only as they become interrelated in a common enterprise. We in America have all the essentials of a genuine cultural orchestration; yet the world often hears from us a Babel of discordant notes.

Again, our composite ethnic structure as a nation gives us a capacity for a direct contribution to a world culture. Nationalism in large measure reverses a normal process, for it makes adoption of a country by peoples coming to its shores equivalent to a repudiation of their past. This is cultural deracination. We have encouraged it in our country through the too indiscriminate concept of Americanization. Within our national life we have made place for concentric loyalties—to family, community, innumerable voluntary associations, and the nation as a whole. But a multiple loyalty as between countries we have frowned upon, and reluctantly tolerated when it could not be eradicated. This is, of course, the historic pattern. Its defect is not evident in a country that is virtually homogeneous, where immigration has been incidental. But America has been built largely out of divers portions of the world. Why should loyalty be monolithic? I am not suggesting a substitute for that formal allegiance of new citizens which national security requires, but a spiritual loyalty and reverence for one's cultural origins. May it not be that America has a "mission" to demonstrate the compatibility of multiple spiritual loyalties among people who have a variety of cultural backgrounds? America should never have been thought of as just one more nation. She is unique among the nations. Potentially we have in America the strongest bond, a personal bond, of unity among—and with—virtually all the peoples of the world.

Finally—and here I come back to an idea that I have stressed on many occasions—the necessity of recovering some unifying spiritual principle of life, a synthesis of thought and of ideals, which the Western world has conspicuously lacked since the medieval synthesis ceased to be controlling in the culture of the West. In Professor

Randall's address much is made of the pluralistic temper of American thought. As a counterpoise for the binding tradition of the Old World it has profound significance. My contention has been, not for an eradication of that temper, but for a framework of values and ends which can give unity to the common life. The title of this series contains the words "the American Spirit"—singular, not plural. To actualize that concept a truly spiritual achievement is required. I believe that the persistent dualism which exists in America between the religious and the so-called secular contributes to our unreadiness to meet the world's need for organic spiritual unity. Lacking any over-all moral framework within which to resolve our cultural and economic tensions, we are catapulted into the international scene equipped with an outworn diplomacy which has two ultimate points of reference—sovereign claims and naked power. It is infinitely pathetic that with the peoples of the world, including our own, yearning for the successful implementation of the United Nations, there is no adequate juridical framework, no recognized universal moral law, no accepted principle governing the composition of competing national forces, that would make possible a transition from an age that is dying to one struggling to be born.

I am aware that much of what I have said has a somber sound. It would perhaps seem more fitting at the conclusion of this series of addresses on the American spirit to speak in eulogistic vein of the promise of American life. But it is not pessimism to eschew a lighthearted optimism. A true prophetic vision is never a rosy one. The prophets of Israel had much to say of doom as well as of blessing. If Isaiah, or Amos, or Hosea were in our midst today, they would say many things the newspapers would not choose to print. Their diagnosis of our Western culture would not be flattering. But if we hearkened diligently to their forebodings we should then hear their reassuring words: "This is the way; walk ye in it."

INDEX

Acosta, Uriel, 94
Adams, John, 49, 53-55, 56, 67
Adler, Felix, 232
Age of Jackson, The (Schlesinger), 19
"America," meaning of, 137-38, 143
American Association for Adult Education, 172
American Council on Race Relations, 199
American Economic Association, 221
American Federation of Labor, 213-14, 215, 217
American Revolution, 43
Anabaptists, 2, 26
Anglicans, 17-18, 28, 29, 30, 31-32, 35
Antioch Review, 222
Antiochus, III, 87
Anti-Semitism, 189-90
Architecture, 157-59, 161-63, 165
Arnold, Benedict, 53
Art(s), 104, 105; American, spirit of, 155-65; literature as, 135-36
Articles of Confederation, 43-44
Athanasius, St., 61
Atom bomb, 229-30
Attucks, Crispus, 192

Babylonia, 93
Background for Brotherhood (Weisiger), 199
Backus, Isaac, 27
Baer, George M., 203
Bain, Alexander, 103
Balaam, 88
Baldwin, A. M., 36
Baldwin, J. M., 105
Baltimore, Lord (Sir George Calvert), 38
Baptists, 3, 10, 18, 26, 27-28, 33, 34, 35
Beard, Charles A., 63n, 120, 126
Becker, Carl, 31

Beginnings of the American Peoples (Becker), 31
Benton, Thomas, 164
Berkeley, George, 103
Bible, the, 4, 10, 21, 138-39
Big Steel Formula, 221
Bilbo, Theodore G., 194
Boas, Franz, 105, 120, 125, 167-68
Books. *See* Literature.
Boston Museum of Fine Arts, contributor from, 155
Brief Retrospect of the Eighteenth Century (Miller), 40
Broadcasting, 174-75
Bryson, Lyman, paper by, 167
Building Trades Workers, 220
Burke, Edmund, 17, 18
Busher, Leonard, 18

Calvert, Sir George (Lord Baltimore), 38
Calvin, John; Calvinism, 2, 9, 10, 12, 40, 42
Cannon, Walter B., 107
Capitalism, 1
Carolina, Constitution of, 15
Carroll, Charles, 67
Carroll, Daniel, 67
Carver, George Washington, 192
Case Bill, 219
Cassatt, Mary, 155, 164
Catholics, 18, 25, 27
Charles II, king of England, 26
Chicago, architecture in, 162
Christianity, Protestant. *See* Protestantism.
Church, and the State, 15-21, 25, 84-85. *See also* Religion.
Clarke, John, 26
Classics, study of, 150-51
Cohen, Morris R., 121, 133
Collective bargaining, 219, 220

235

Colliers, The National Weekly, quoted, 191-92
Columbia University, contributor from, 1, 97, 117, 167, 225
Commerce, U.S. Department of, 204
Communication, modern, 168-76
Community, and communication, relationship, 168-70
Comparative Education (Kandel), 146
Congregationalists, 3, 27, 53
Congress of Industrial Organizations, 215
Connecticut, 17
Constable, William G., paper by, 155-65
Cooley, Charles H., 105, 120
Cooper, Fenimore, 161
Corey, Lewis, 219
Cornbury, Lord, 31
Cotton, John, 25
Cromwell, Oliver, 18
Cultural pluralism, 232-34
Cultural unity, 189-202

Darwinian concept, 107
Davenport, Russell, 201
David, Rabbi Abraham ben, 94
Davidson, Philip, 35-36
Davies, Samuel, 32-33
Davis, W. H., 221
Debs, Eugene V., 214
Declaration of Independence, 49
Deism, 50, 68
Democracy, 129-30, 132, 142, 168-69, 170, 175-78; the individual in, 110-11; in labor unions, 221-23; and racial discrimination, 200-01; and religious liberty, 70
Dewey, John, 104, 105, 106, 110, 120, 121, 124, 127, 129, 130-31, 133
Dickinson, John, 30
Dinwiddie, Governor, 33
Discrimination, racial, 200-01
Dissent: influence of, 37-38; use of term, 17-18
Doddridge, Philip, 32
Duffield, George, 35, 36

Eakins, Thomas, 164
Earl, Ralph, 156

Eastman, Seth, 161
Eddy, Mary Baker, 22
Education: foundations of, 114-15; and labor, 204, 221-22; spirit of, 145-54
Edwards, Jonathan, 4, 7-8, 9, 10, 12, 119
Egalitarianism, 124, 128-30
Einstein, Albert, 109
Eliot, Charles W., 204
Emerson, Ralph Waldo, 2-3, 9, 12, 121, 139-41, 142
Employment, statistics of, 204-05
Engels, Friedrich, 213
Enlightenment, the, 1, 9-10; tradition of, 39-47
Environment, influence of, 72
Episcopalians, 57-58
Europe: and American art, influence on, 155-56, 157; education in, 145-54
Experience: as basis of education, 152-54; philosophy of, 102
Experimentalism, 124, 127-28
Ezra, 87

Factory system, 210
Fair Employment Practice Bill, 199-200
Fair Labor Standards Act, 182, 206, 215
Faraday, Michael, 40, 109
Fascism, 215-16
Fauguier, Francis, 33
Federal Council of the Churches of Christ in America, 85-86, 199
Federalism, 119, 124-25
Federalists, 55-56, 67-68
Finkelstein, Louis, paper by, 87-95
Fitzsimons, Thomas, 67
Foreign Missions Conference of North America, 85-86
Forrestal, James, 198
France: education in, 146-47, 150; Revolution, 54, 55-56, 208
Frank, Waldo, 114
Franklin, Benjamin, 8-9, 40-41, 49
Franz, S. I., 107
Freedom: meaning of, 208; religious, 15-38 *passim,* 69-86, 87-95; and technology, 167-78
French, Daniel C., 139, 163
Freneau, Philip, 42, 46

Index

Freud, Sigmund, 1, 46
Frontier, the, 160; spirit of, 97-115; the "true," 123
Frontier Spirit in American Christianity, The (Mode), 19
Function, concept of, 109-10

Gabriel, Ralph Henry, 228, 229; paper by, 39-47
Georgia, 17, 31
Gershom, Rabbi Levi ben, 93-94
Gompers, Samuel, 213, 214
Gooch, Governor, 32
Goodhue, 161, 163
Goodwin, John, 18
Gordon, William, 35
Gothic architecture, 158-59
Gould, Jay, 213
Government, and religious liberty, 82-86
Great Britain, 226
Greek architecture, 158
Greek philosophy, 90
Groups, rights of, 75, 78-82, 85

Hall, Thomas Cuming, 21-23
Hamilton, Alexander, 49, 56-57, 66, 67, 119
Hamilton, Allan, 57
Hamilton, Walton, 120, 125, 127, 130
Hamilton, Sir William, 103
Harkness, R. E. E., 25-26
Harper's Magazine, 204
Harris, Joel Chandler, 192
Harvard University, 204
Hawthorne, Nathaniel, 11-12
Heade, Martin J., 161
Hegel, Georg W. F., 126, 130
Heller Committee, 205
Herbart, Johann F., 103
Herberg, Will, 222
Heredity, influence of, 72
Herrick, Elinore M., paper by, 179-87
Hershberger, G. H., 29
Hertz, H. R., 109
Hewes, Joseph, 35
Hicksite Quakers, 2
Hill, L., 193-94

Hillel, school of, 91-93
Hobbes, Thomas, 103
Holmes, Obadiah, 26
Homer, Winslow, 164
Hours, working, 182, 210, 211, 212
Huguenots, 2
Human Nature and Conduct (Dewey), 131
Hume, David, 68, 103
Humphrey, E. F., 36
Hunt, Richard Morris, 161
Hutchinson, Anne, 3
Hyrcanus, Rabbi Eliezer ben, 92

Indian, American, 207
Individual, the, 41-43, 71-77, 86; versus culture, 110-14
Individualism, 141-43
Industrial Workers of the World, 214
Industrialism, 169-71; and labor movement, 210-12, 215; and women, 179
Infeld, 109
Information, access to, 73-74, 78-79, 83
Institutionalism, 124, 130-33
International Brotherhood of Electrical Workers, 220
International Ladies' Garment Workers' Union, contributor from, 203
International relations, 226-34
Ireland, Church of, 30
Israel, history of, 231

Jackson, Andrew, 19
James, Henry, 161
James, Henry, Sr., 12-13
James, William, 13, 104, 105, 106, 120, 121, 124, 127, 128, 131, 133
Japanese, prejudice against, 189, 190
Jay, John, 49, 56, 67
Jefferson, Thomas, 28, 34, 38, 39-41, 46, 49, 58n, 119, 157, 158; religion of, 61-63, 67, 68
Jenney, William Le Baron, 162
Jewish Theological Seminary of America, contributor from, 87
Jews: prejudice against, 189-90; and religious liberty, 87-95

Index

Johnson, F. Ernest, paper by, 225-34
Johnson, Samuel, 10, 119
Jubilees, Book of, 88
Judaism. *See* Jews.

Kandel, I. L., 146
Kant, Immanuel, 43, 103
Kierkegaard, 128
King, Rufus, 67
Kipling, Rudyard, quoted, 230
Knappen, M. M., 22
Knights of Labor, 212, 213
Knox, John, 19

Labor, labor unions, 181; historical survey of, 203-23; and women, 179-82
Labor, U.S. Department of, 205
Labor Government (England), 219, 226
Labor in America (Faulkner and Starr), quoted, 209-10
Labor Statistics, U.S. Bureau of, 205
Lafayette, M. de, 207-08
LaFollette, Robert M., 219-20
LaGuardia, F., 217
Laissez-faire, 101
Lashley, Karl S., 107
Last Puritan, The (Santayana), 3
Leo XIII, Pope, 203
Liberty. *See* Freedom.
Lippmann, Walter, 227
Literature, American: and mass production, 171-74; and painting parallel, 160-61; spirit of, 135-43
Locke, John, 15, 18, 28, 35, 40-41, 61, 68, 103
Lollardism, 21, 22
Longfellow, Henry Wadsworth, 11
Lowell, James Russell, 138
Lutheran Theological Seminary, contributor from, 69

McNeill, John T., paper by, 15-38
Madison, James, 15, 28, 49, 57-59, 67, 119
Maimonides, 93-94
Makemie, Francis, 31, 32
Man: the individual, 41-43, 71-77, 86; new psychology of, 106

Manifest Destiny, 98-102, 107, 229-31
Marin, John, 164
Marshall, James, paper by, 145-54
Marshall, John, 49
Martineau, Harriet, 180, 210
Marx, Karl, 1, 213
Maryland, 17, 31
Mason, John Mitchell, 56
Mass production, 170-76
Massachusetts, 17, 24-25, 26-27
Massachusetts Bay colony, 21, 22
Mather, Cotton, 10
Maxwell, James Clerk, 109
Mead, George Herbert, 105, 110, 120
Mechanics Bell, 210
Mecklin, John M., 23-24, 27, 29, 33
Meir, Rabbi, 92
Methodists, 3-4, 10
Mill, James, 103
Mill, John Stuart, 103
Miller, Clyde R., 199
Miller, Perry, 3, 118
Miller, Samuel, 40, 41
Milton, John, 18
Minorities, racial, 189-202
Mitchell, Wesley C., 120
Mode, P. G., 19-20, 34
Moehlman, C. H., 25, 27
Moody, Dwight L., 22
Moore, Bishop, 56
Morris, Gouverneur, 49, 59, 67-68
Moses, law of, 87-88, 92
Münsterberg, Hugo, 20
Murton, John, 18
My Country (Davenport), quoted, 201-02

National Conference of Christians and Jews, 199
National Labor Relations Act, 215
Nationalism, 229-34
Natural rights, 41-43, 45, 70, 85-86
Needham, Joseph, 107-08
Negro, the, 189, 191-200, 209
New Deal, 214-15
New England, Puritans in, 2-13, 17-18, 21
New Hampshire, 17
New Jersey, College of, 33
New Light Presbyterians, 3

Index

New Testament, 60, 61, 63
New York (City): architecture in, 162; Board of Education, contributor from, 145; labor in, 216-17
New York (State), 17
New York *Herald Tribune:* contributor from, 179; quoted, 227
New York *Times,* quoted, 194
Newton, Isaac, 40-41, 43
Nichols, R. H., 15n, 37
Niebuhr, Reinhold, 128
Noah, 88, 92
Nolde, O. Frederick, paper by, 69-86
North Carolina, 17, 31

O'Dwyer, William, 216
Oersted, 109
Old Testament, 4
"One World," 230-32
Our Country (Strong), quoted, 228-29
Owen, Robert, 212

Paine, Thomas, 38, 67, 208
Painting, 160-61, 163-65
Pareto, Vilfredo, 46
Passover service, 90
Pavlov, Ivan S., 107
Peirce, Charles Sanders, 104, 105, 106, 120, 121, 124, 133
Penn, William, 28, 36
Pennsylvania, 28-30; Quakers in, 2
Perry, Ralph Barton, 2, 3
Pew, Joseph, 204
Pharisees, 90-91
Philadelphia and Reading Railroad Company, 203
Philosophy, American, spirit of, 117-33
Physics, 109
Pietism, effect of, 10-11
Pius XI, Pope, 203
Platonism, 10
Pluralism: in American philosophy, 124-27; cultural, 232-34
Plymouth colony, 21, 22
Poe, Edgar Allan, 136
Politics, women in, 186
Power, struggle for, 45-46
Powers, Hiram, 159

Presbyterians, 2, 3, 10, 19, 30, 31-37, 54
Priestley, Joseph, 68
Progressive, The, quoted, 219-20
Prosperity, effect of, 9
Protestantism, 1-2, 21, 23-24; and religious liberty, 69-86
Psalms, Book of, 89
Psychology, 103-08, 110
Pumbedita, Academy of, 93
Puritanism, 1-13, 17-18, 21, 22, 118
Puritanism and Democracy (Perry), 2

Quakers, 2, 3, 26, 27, 28-31
Quill, Michael, 217

Race, problems of, 189-202
Radio, 174-75
Ramus, Peter; Ramism, 118
Randall, John Herman, Jr., 233-34; paper by, 117-33
Randolph, Edward, 27
Regionalism, 126
Religion: and dissent, 15-38; of the Founding Fathers, 49-68; and institutionalism, 132; and labor, attitude toward, 203-04; liberty, 15-38 *passim,* 69-86, 87-95; meaning of, 50-51; of nature, 42-43
Religious Background of American Culture (Hall), 21
Religious Liberty, Bill for (1886), 28
Rhode Island, 25-26
Richardson, H. H., 161
Roe, Dudley G., 204
Roman Catholics, 18, 25, 27
Rome, ancient, 92; influence on architecture, 157-58
Roosevelt, Eleanor, 193, 194
Roosevelt, Franklin D., 102, 130
Roosevelt, Theodore, 193
Rousseau, J. J., 43, 161
Royce, Josiah, 117, 121, 124
Rugg, Harold, paper by, 97-115
Rush, William, 159
Ryder, Albert, 164

Sadducees, 90-91
St. Gaudens, Augustus, 163

Saints and Strangers (Willison), 22
Salvation Army, 22
Sandwich, Mass., 5
Sandy Creek, N.C., 28
Sandys, Sir Edwin, 38
Santayana, George, 3, 121
Sargent, John, 155, 164
Scabs Charter, 219
Schlesinger, A. M., Jr., 19
Schneider, Herbert W., paper by, 1-13
Schwellenbach, Lewis B., 219
Scotch-Irish, settlers, 29-31, 37
Sculpture, 159-60, 163
Segregation, racial, 195-99
Separatism, 22
Separatists, 3
Sevier, John, 38
Shammai, school of, 91-93
Shelley, Percy Bysshe, quoted, 208
Shepard, Odell, paper by, 135-43
Sherrington, C. S., 107
Shipbuilding, 159
Skyscraper, the, 162-63
Slavery, Negro, 192, 207, 209
Smith, Lillian, 197, 199
Smith-Connally Bill, 218
Socialization, trend of, 112-14
Sociology, 105
South Carolina, 17
Southern Conference for Human Welfare, 199
Southern Regional Council, 199
Speech, freedom of, 76-77, 79-80, 83, 86
Spencer, Herbert, 103
Spinoza, Benedict, 94
Spirit, meaning of, 121-22, 136-37, 143
Spiritual role, American, 225-34
Standish, Miles, 5
Starr, Mark, paper by, 203-23
State, and Church, 15-21, 25, 84-85
Stearns, Shubal, 28
Stockton, Mrs. Annis Boudinot, 53
Story of American Dissent (Mecklin), 23
Story of the Springfield Plan, The, 199
Strange Fruit (Smith), 197
Strikes, labor, 210-11, 216-18, 221
Strong, Josiah, 228
Sullivan, Louis, 162

Sun Shipbuilding Company, 204
Sura, academy of, 93
Sweet, W. W., 22, 26, 34, 36

Taft, Philip, 221, 222
Talmud, the, 93, 94
Tarphon, Rabbi, 92-93
Taylor, Jeremy, 30
Taylor, John, 67
Technology, and freedom, 167-78
Tennent, William, 35-36
There Are Things To Do (Smith), 199
Thomas, 105, 110
Thoreau, Henry, 141-42
Tobias, Channing H., paper by, 189-202
Tocqueville, Alexis de, 20
Toleration, Act of (1689), 31, 32, 33
Transport Workers' Union (CIO), 217
Trinity College, contributor from, 135
Troup, Robert, 56
Truman, Harry, 221
Turner, F. J., 19, 97, 98, 123, 126

Ulster Scots, 30
Union Theological Seminary, contributor from, 15
Unions. *See* Labor.
United Mine Workers, 203
United Nations, 200, 234; Charter of, 85
United States Congress, 194
United States Constitution, 16, 36, 49, 68
United States Navy, 198

Veblen, Thorstein, 101, 105, 110, 120, 126
Virginia, 17, 21, 25, 28, 31-34, 58; Bill of Rights, 15-16; University of, 39, 158

Wages: statistics of, 205, 206-07, 209, 211; women, 180-82
Waltham, Mass., 210
War: Negro in, 192-93; and women, effect on, 183-84
Washington, George, 39, 43-45, 49, 50-53, 56, 57, 67
Washington, D.C., 39
Weber, Max, 2
Weisiger, Kendall, 199

Wesleyans, 2
Westminster Confession of Faith, 36
Whistler, James, 155, 161, 164
Whitefield, George, 33
Whitehead, A. N., 108, 121, 133
Whitman, Walt, 136, 142
Willard, Samuel, 5-6
Williams, Roger, 3, 25-26
Willison, S. F., 22
Willkie, Wendell, 191, 194, 200
Wilson, Charles E., 221
Wilson, James, 49, 60-61, 67
Winstanley, Gerrard, 18

Witherspoon, John, 35, 36, 67
Women, status of, 179-87
Wood, Grant, 164
Woodbridge, F. J., 121, 133
Workers. *See* Labor.
World War I, 229
World War II, 229-30
Wyclif, John, 21-22

Yale University, contributor from, 39
Yankees, 7-8
YMCA, contributor from, 189